Introduction to
HUMAN INFORMATION PROCESSING

Introduction to

HUMAN INFORMATION PROCESSING

DAVID E. RUMELHART
University of California at San Diego

JOHN WILEY & SONS
New York • Santa Barbara • London • Sydney • Toronto

Library of Congress Cataloging in Publication Data:

Rumelhart, David E.
   Introduction to human information processing.
   Bibliography: p.
   Includes indexes.
   1. Human information processing.   I. Title.
BF455.R85   153   76-54653
ISBN 0-471-74500-6

Printed in the United States of America

10 9 8 7 6 5 4 3 2 1

PREFACE

This book is the outgrowth of a course in human experimental psychology that I have been teaching for nearly a decade. At first I taught the course as a series of topics—psychophysics, perception, memory, concept formation, language, and the like. Through the years, however, my objective has been to build a coherent conceptual framework that provides my students with a way of integrating the various subareas of the course. This book is the result of my latest effort to construct a view of the human information processing system that is a coherent whole.

I have organized the book from the outside in: that is, I have traced the flow of information through the system—beginning with disturbances in the environment that affect our sense organs and following through to percepts, memories, and thoughts. This book is a blend of theoretical concepts and empirical findings. In general, a theory is woven and empirical results are described in the context of the theoretical models on which they bear. No attempt is made to be exhaustive either in the coverage of empirical findings or in the cataloguing of proposed theories. Instead my purpose is to be selective and to pick out for special treatment the theoretical concepts that are most promising and the empirical findings that are most germaine to these concepts. Some experiments are described in great detail, but many others are only mentioned in passing. The experiments that best illustrate the points I am making are thoroughly explained. I believe it is important that students be given a clear idea of the experimental situations in which data are collected. Thus, I often concentrate on examples at the expense of more exhaustive coverage. I also explain at length particular models of the human information processing system. In my opinion, it is more important to have a deeper more sophisticated understanding of the key theoretical concepts than a shallower understanding of a broader range of theoretical proposals.

Understanding of the human information processing system is continuing to grow and change. This book is, a current "best-guess" as to how the system is organized. The material in the book is to be read in that light. Nowhere in the book's discussion is a theoretical position described that does not have its critics. Perhaps all of the data presented will be given alternate interpretations at some future date. Still, we are making progress. Our understanding of the way humans interact with their environment continues to evolve. I have given only an outline of its current stage of development.

I owe a special debt of gratitude to the numerous colleagues and students who contributed importantly to the existence of this book. I especially thank Donald A. Norman, who first introduced me to the human information processing perspective of human behavior, George Mandler, without whose encouragement this book surely would not have been written, and Marilyn Rumelhart, my wife, whose help at every stage of the preparation of the manuscript was essential.

David E. Rumelhart

La Jolla, California

CONTENTS

INTRODUCTION

The means whereby information about the environment is transformed into complex patterns of thought and those patterns changed into behavior has long been the primary target of psychological theories. The development of information theory in the late 1940s and later the advent of modern computer systems has strongly affected many new developments in theoretical psychology. It is becoming increasingly popular to view the human as functioning like the computer, as a complex information processing device. In the case of the computer information enters the system from keypresses on a teletypewriter or from holes punched in a card. Depending on how the computer is programmed, the information is then transformed through a series of stages and finally results in an output which can be read or interpreted by the computer programmer. To understand the operation of the computer is to be able to chart the flow of information through the computer (i.e., to know the sequence of transformations the computer performed on the input and the conditions under which these transformations are applied). In the case of the human, information enters the system in the form of light particles absorbed by the retina, as molecular vibrations push-

1

ing against the tympanic membrane (eardrum), as pressure against receptors in the skin, or as chemical agents contacting taste buds on the tongue or reaching olfactory receptors in the nose. This information then undergoes a series of transformations. Certain information is lost. Certain other information is carefully preserved by the system. Eventually, when the system is properly queried, the effects of the light particles, the molecular vibrations, the mechanical pressure on the skin, or whatever become apparent in the behavior output by the organism. The problem for the theorist is to chart this flow of information—from input to output. The problem for the experimentalist is to develop appropriate techniques whereby he can measure the information flow at various points along its course.

This book is divided into five substantive chapters: sensing, recognizing patterns, understanding language, remembering, and reasoning. These five labels correspond roughly to five points along the continuum at which the process can be tapped. The form of the experimental query differs, but the same underlying set of systems is being examined at all five points.

In the study of sensing, the emphasis is on the interface between the environment and the sense organs. The primary questions concern the fidelity of transmission by the sense organs themselves. To study these processes, carefully controlled experiments are used to expose the nature of the physical stimulus and the physiology of the translation process.

The study of pattern recognition emphasizes the coding of complex sensory inputs. This really involves two separate problems. One concerns the initial coding of the stimulus inputs. What information is preserved and what information is discarded? The second concerns the sensory-memory interface. How are newly arriving patterns matched with stored patterns? How do our prior knowledge and current expectations interact with the incoming information to determine our perceptions?

The study of the process of language understanding is really an extension of the pattern recognition process—but here recognition constitutes discovering the *meaning* rather than simply the name or category of the input. The major problem now involves the discovery of how our knowledge of the world, our knowledge of grammar, the current context, and the characteristics of the current input all combine to allow us to comprehend linguistic inputs.

The study of remembering also has two important parts. The first is the problem of information decay and loss with time. What are the temporal characteristics of the memory storage system? What is the nature of forgetting? The second is the investigation of the nature of the organization of the memory structures designed to store information for long periods of time. How can information be retrieved from memory storage systems as large as those of humans? What is the nature of the memory search? How are memories structured to facilitate retrieval?

In the study of reasoning the emphasis is on those processes which operate on our structured memories to allow us to make inferences. What is the nature of our processing systems which allow us to derive new information from our memories and thereby allow us to solve novel problems? What sorts of strategies do we have available when we encounter new problems? Where do these strategies lead to difficulties?

All of this begins when changes in the world cause disturbances in our local environment and affect our sensory receptors. Thus, we begin our discussion of the human information processing system with an analysis of our sensing mechanisms, those devices that allow our environment to affect our mental life.

1
SENSING

The points at which fluctuations in patterns of energy in the environment are translated into fluctuations of neural activity are of special importance to the information processing theorist. It is through these points that information enters the system and from these points that the information flow begins. The theoretical problem is to characterize the form of the information as it enters the system and then to observe the changes which occur with time after its entrance.

In studying this initial translation process it is necessary to use only very simple experiments so that later stages of processing (for example, pattern recognition, remembering, and reasoning) influence the subjects' responses as little as possible. This is accomplished by using simple homogeneous stimuli whose physical characteristics are well understood and then by asking subjects to detect small changes in the stimuli.

The simplest such experiment is for intensity discrimination. In one form of this experiment, two stimuli are chosen which differ only slightly on the intensity dimension. On some trials, one of the stimuli is presented; on other trials the other is presented. The subject indicates on each trial whether he thought the more or less intense signal had been presented. The experimenter manipulates the intensity difference between the signals until the subject can detect the difference 75% of the time. This level of intensity difference is referred to as the "just noticeable difference" or j.n.d.

It is assumed that pattern recognition and memory play only small roles in the determination of responses in this situation. The characteristics of the sensory system are assumed to play the determining role in such experiments. The task for the theorist is to account for the form of the relationship between the observed j.n.d.'s and other parameters of the stimulus energy distribution (duration, overall intensity, etc.). In accomplishing this task, known characteristics of the sense organs and the nervous system are used and the restrictions implicit in these characteristics play significant roles in the theory development. In order to make these comments more concrete, we will discuss the visual and auditory transduction[1] process in some detail.

THE VISUAL TRANSDUCTION PROCESS

The basic model we will discuss is derived from classical quantum theory in vision (cf. Hecht, Schlaer, and Pirenne, 1942 or Pirenne, 1967). This theory is unique in the precision with which it characterizes the information flow from the environment and in the elegance of the rule describing the translation of physical energy to neural code. Fundamental to the theory is the concept of a light source as emitting streams of photons, or light quanta.

Figure 1, shows, in schematic form, from right to left the assumed sequence of sensory events. A stream of light quanta (photons) is emitted from a point source of light. (Table 1.1 illustrates the number of quanta expected in a brief time over a small region from a variety of light sources.) Many of these quanta are lost by reflection when they strike the cornea; still others are absorbed as they pass through the inner eye. Only between 2 and 10% of the photons initially striking the cornea are absorbed by light-sensitive substances of the eye. The image is blurred passing through the eye so that even though we begin with a point source of light, absorption occurs over a considerable area on the retina. *Each time a photon is absorbed within a receptor, a neural response is generated by that receptor.* These responses (along with those generated spontaneously by the retina) are passed through the *bipolar cells* to the *retinal ganglion cells* which in turn relay responses to the brain. *If and when*

---

[1]A transducer is a device that receives energy from one system and retransmits it, often in another form, to another system.

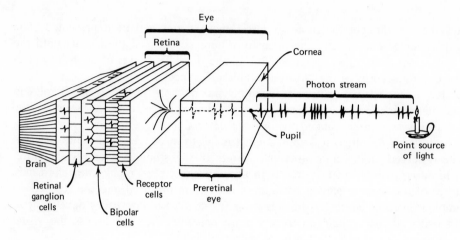

Figure 1.1
Schematic diagram of the visual information processing system. Light is emitted from a light source in the form of a stream of light quanta or photons. Some of these. photons pass through the pupil into the eye. After passing through the pre-retinal eye, about 10% of the emitted light quanta are absorbed by the receptor unit of the retina at the back of the eye. There, through a chemical reaction, the photon energy is converted into neural responses. This response is relayed through and refined by the bipolar cells and then the retinal ganglion cells at the very back of the eye. From there, the neural response is relayed to the brain for further processing.

enough impulses are counted, over a brief period of time and over a small retinal area, a visual experience is reported.

In what follows, we proceed by first examining the nature of the photon stream entering the eye. Then we look at our ability to detect a dim flash of light as a function of the number of photons emitted by the flash. From this and our knowledge of the physiology of the eye we can create a rather detailed and elegant picture of this all important transduction process which converts energy in the world to neural events in the brain and thereby initiates the processing of seeing.

THE NATURE OF THE PHOTON STREAM

The first problem for the theorist is to characterize the nature of the photon stream which initiates our visual experiences. Photons are discrete packets of energy which, when emitted from a light source, travel in a straight line at the

Table 1.1

Condition of Illumination	Average Number of of Quanta at Cornea per 100 msec
Absolute threshold	100
	1,000
White paper in starlight	10,000
	100,000
White paper in moonlight	1,000,000
	10,000,000
	100,000,000
Normal reading level	1,000,000,000
	10,000,000,000
	100,000,000,000
White paper in sunlight	1,000,000,000,000
	10,000,000,000,000
	100,000,000,000,000
Tungsten filament	1,000,000,000,000,000

speed of light until they strike something and are either absorbed or deflected. It is the absorption of a quantum of light by the visual pigment in the receptors that starts the chain of events that leads us to say we have "seen" a light.

The emission of light quanta is a random process. Even constant sources of light do not emit quanta at regular intervals. Thus, if we were to measure the number of quanta striking the cornea during brief periods of time we would not always get the same number. Fortunately, the distribution of the number of light quanta emitted from a light source is known (it follows the Poisson distribution). Thus, although we do not know on any particular trial exactly how many quanta will strike the cornea we do know the probability that any given number will strike the cornea.

In order to make this a little more concrete, consider the following example. Suppose we have a very dim light which delivers an average of 5 quanta on the cornea every millisecond. If we could count the number of quanta during each millisecond (msec) flash, we would find that we do not always have 5. Sometimes we would observe more and sometimes we would observe less. Figure 1.2a gives the expected number of times, out of 100 flashes, we would count a particular number of quanta. Figure 2b gives this distribution for a source generating 10 quanta per msec. Notice that a source which generates an *average* of 5 quanta per msec (Figure 1.2a) yields 5 quanta per msec less than 18 times

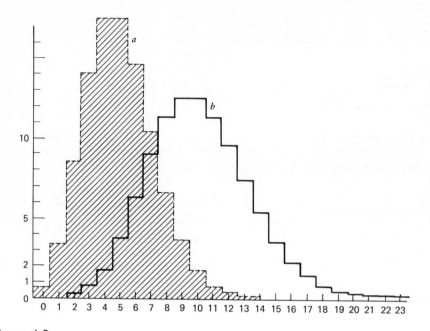

Figure 1.2
(a) The number of times, out of 100, that a light source emitting an average of 5 quanta per millisecond would be expected to emit exactly 0, 1, 2, etc. quanta per millisecond. *(b)* The number of times out of 100 that a light source emitting an average of 10 quanta per millisecond would be expected to emit exactly 0, 1, 2, etc. quanta. Note especially that even if our eye was able to *exactly* measure the number of quanta emitted from a light source, we could not always tell which light source had emitted the light—even though one emits quanta twice as rapidly as the other.

out of 100. Moreover, a source that averages 10 quanta per msec actually generates 10 per msec less than 13 times in 100. There is thus considerable variability in the number of light quanta actually striking the cornea. Notice also that even if the eye were a *perfect* optical instrument it could not always tell these two light sources apart although one is twice as bright as the other. Suppose, for example, on some particular flash the eye observed 7 quanta of light—which light source was presented? We would observe 7 quanta from the dimmer source about 10 times in 100 and from the brighter source about 9 times in 100. The best guess would be that the dimmer light was flashed (odds 10:9); however we would be wrong 47% of the time. But, of course, the eye is not a perfect instrument (about 90% of the incident light is lost before it even reaches a receptor).

One might suppose that tthe sensitivity of the visual system is such that fluctuations in the photon rate are much too small to have any observable effect. Even if the eye were capable of observing such small effects, other "psychological" variables would surely render such variations wholly unobservable. It is a remarkable fact that the human visual system is so sensitive that simple experimental procedures allow us to observe the effects of a single quantum of light and to infer accurately the characteristics of the underlying physiology of the retina.

THE ROLE OF INDIVIDUAL LIGHT QUANTUM IN SEEING

In a now classic experiment, Hecht, Schlaer, and Pirenne (1942) demonstrated (1) that the eye is so sensitive that the absorption of a single quantum of light by a receptor can lead to a neural response, and (2) that the fluctuation in the number of quanta delivered to the eye plays a critical role in the determination of the threshold of vision.

In their experiment, very dim flashes (delivering to the cornea an average of from 20 to 400 quanta) were presented to the subjects. The subjects responded "yes" if they saw the flash and "no" otherwise. Figure 1.3 gives the percentage of "yes" responses as a function of the average number of quanta delivered to the cornea, for these subjects. They all say "yes" to a flash delivering an average of about 100 quanta to the eye roughly 50% of the time. Moreover, since no more than 10% of the quanta delivered are absorbed by the receptors, fewer than 10 quanta absorbed lead subjects to say they saw the flash. Furthermore, since these 10 quanta are spread over from 300 to 500 receptors, the probability that any given receptor is hit by more than 1 quantum is very small. Thus, we can conclude that a single quantum of light falling on a single receptor is enough to generate a neural response.

Now, suppose we are presented with a flash from a light source that delivers an average of 100 quanta per msec to the cornea. Since over 90% of these quanta are randomly deleted, we find that the distribution of *the number of quanta absorbed* has a mean of about 10 quanta per flash. In fact, the distribution given in Figure 1.2b illustrates the variability in the number of quanta absorbed at threshold level. In that figure, notice that when the mean number of quanta absorbed is 10 we nearly always have at least 1 absorbed. Nevertheless, we only responded "Yes" about 50% of the time. It is thus clear that even though 1 quantum is enough to generate a signal from a receptor, it is not enough to generate a response of "Yes, I saw the flash." How many quanta

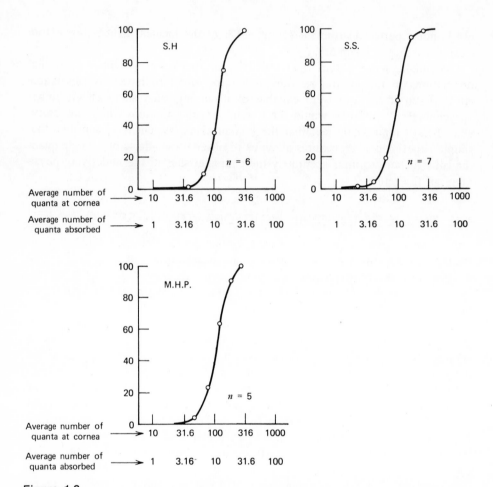

Figure 1.3

The percentage of time each of three subjects responded that they saw the flash as a function of the average number of quanta delivered to the cornea. The solid lines are derived from the assumption that a subject says "yes" just in case *n* quanta have been absored. The three subjects show values of *n* of 6, 7, and 5, respectively.

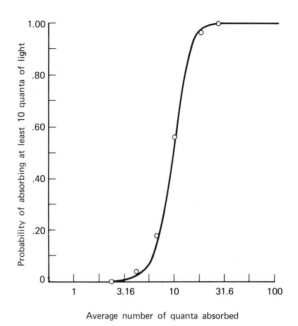

Figure 1.4
The probability of actually absorbing 10 or more quanta of light as a function of the average number of quanta absorbed. The open circles are the data for subject S. S.

does it take to say "Yes"? Suppose that the single imperfection in the visual system was that only 10% of the incident quanta were absorbed. Then we would have an accurate account of the exact number of quanta absorbed. Suppose further that whenever 10 or more quanta are in fact absorbed we have the experience of "seeing" a flash. What data would we expect? Figure 1.4 illustrates the probability of *actually absorbing* 10 or more quanta of light as a function of the *average number of quanta absorbed*. The open circles are the data for subject S.S. The close fit would seem to prove that much of the behavior we observe subjects make at threshold level is directly attributable to the fluctuations in the number of quanta absorbed by the visual pigment in the receptors.

If the eye is so sensitive that it can respond to a single quantum of light, why do we need 10 quanta to see? The most frequently given answer is that sometimes a receptor will generate a response even when no light quanta have been absorbed. Presumably the "spontaneous activity" (called "dark light") in

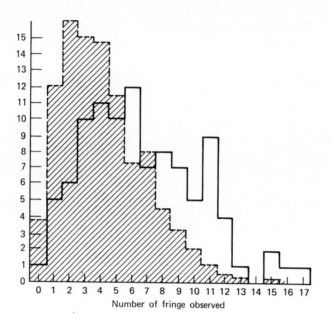

Figure 1.5

The response of a single ganglion cell to a 10-msec flash containing an average of 5 quanta. The open bars give the distribution of the number of responses observed over a 200-msec period following the presentation of the stimulus. The shaded bars give the distribution of counts observed over a comparable period of time when no stimulus was present. The shaded bars thus represent the amount of "dark light" the system must deal with. When no stimulus was present there was an average of 4.14 firings during the 200-msec period. When the stimulus was present the average number of firings increased to 6.62. (Data from Barlow, Levick and Yoon, 1971.)

the receptors is primarily due to thermal sources (i.e., body heat) and activity in the blood vessels near the receptors. The system must somehow avoid responding to this "dark light." Thus, only when there is enough concentrated activity over a brief time and small area do we get the perception of light.

A recent experiment by Barlow, Levick and Yoon (1971) nicely illustrates the nature of the problem for the visual system. Barlow and Levick attempted to measure the effect of a single quantum of light on the retinal ganglion cell of the cat. (Note from Figure 1.1 that the retinal ganglion cell is the major relay system from the eye to the brain.) To do this, they implanted a small electrode in a single retinal ganglion cell of a cat and counted the number of impulses generated by the cell as a function of the average number of quanta of light delivered to the cat's cornea.

Figure 1.5 shows the response of a single ganglion cell to a 10-msec flash containing an average of 5 quanta. The open bars give the distribution of the number of responses observed over a 200-msec period following the presentation of the stimulus. The shaded bars give the distribution of counts observed over a comparable period of time when no stimulus was present. The shaded bars thus represent the amount of "dark light" the system must deal with.

For simplicity, suppose in the Hecht et al. experiment the decision as to whether or not a flash was seen was based on a single ganglion cell. (In fact, at most a very few such cells probably serviced the region stimulated in the Hecht et al. experiment.) Moreover, suppose that the decision as to whether or not a flash has been presented is determined by the number of impulses generated by the ganglion cell. If there are enough impulses, the system will generate a visual experience of seeing a flash—otherwise no visual experience will result. We will let the number of responses required to generate a visual experience be called our *criterion*. Suppose, for example, that we set our criterion to be 10. In the case of the graphs shown in Figure 1.5 that would mean that we will "see" the flash about 23% of the time when it is presented and we will respond that we "see" a flash when none is presented about 4% of the time. These numbers are derived easily from the diagram by simply counting the percentage of times 10 or more neural responses were observed—first under the condition that a signal was presented and then when no signal was presented. (A positive response when no signal was present is called a "false alarm.")

In general, we can describe the overall relationship between the two distributions by plotting the percentage of times the signal would be correctly detected versus the percentage of false alarms as a function of the criterion. Such a curve is called a receiver operating characteristic (ROC) curve. Figure 1.6 gives the ROC curve derived from the distributions shown in Figure 1.5. We have already seen how we get the point on the curve labeled 10. We observed that a criterion of 10 would lead to 23% correct detections and 4% false alarms. Thus, we plot a point at .23, .04 on the graph. Similarly, the point labeled 5, for example, was derived by plotting the percentage of times the signal generated at least 5 neural responses (about 63% of the time) versus the percentage of times 5 or more neural responses were counted when no signal was present (about 38% of the time). All other points can be derived in like manner to produce the entire ROC curve.

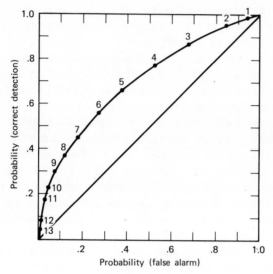

Figure 1.6
The ROC curve derived from the distribution shown in Figure 1.5. (See chapter discussion for explanation.)

This curve shows the tradeoff between the number of correct detections and the number of false alarms. The lower we set our criterion, the more correct detections we get, but the number of false alarms is also increased. If we set our criterion at 1, we would correctly detect a 5 quanta signal 99% of the time. On the other hand, we would make almost 96% false alarms. If we set our criterion to 14 neural responses, we would only make .025% false alarms, but we would also only detect our 5 quanta signal 4% of the time.

In any threshold experiment such as the ones we have been discussing, a subject must *choose* a criterion level that will allow him to detect as many signals as possible without making "too many" false alarms.

An interesting experiment by Barbara Sakitt (1972) would seem to indicate that subjects *can,* if properly trained, count every rod signal generated (either by dark light or by the signal). In this experiment, subjects were presented with one of three signals. They were given either a *strong* stimulus (an average of 55 photons at the cornea) or a *blank* stimulus (no photons at the cornea). On each trial, the subject was asked to give a number between 0 and 6 indicating how bright the signal presented on that trial appeared to be. The numbers were to be assigned as follows:

> 0 meant that nothing was seen;
> 1 meant that it was very doubtful if a light was seen;
> 2 meant that it was slightly doubtful if a light was seen;
> 3 meant a dim light;
> 4 meant a moderate light;
> 5 meant a bright light;
> 6 meant a very bright light.

(*Note:* since all lights were in fact very dim, it should be understood that the terms *bright* and *very bright* are considered relative to the range of lights presented in the experiment.)

Before turning to Sakitt's results, let us consider the results we would expect from an idealized subject. Suppose we have a subject who is able to count his actual number of neural firings and report to us a numerical rating value equal to the number of firings he observed on a particular trial. Moreover, suppose that 4% of the quanta which we sent to the cornea were absorbed and that, on the average, there was 1 neural response due to "dark light" on any given trial. What results would we expect from this subject?

Figure 1.7a illustrates the results expected from plotting the average rating value versus the average number of quanta delivered to the cornea. Note first that when no quanta are delivered to the eye, we still get an average rating of 1. Since no quanta are coming from the outside in this case, the firings are entirely due to "dark light." The value 1 indicates that, on the average, 1 rod fires spontaneously on any 1 trial. Observe further that, for our ideal subject, every additional 25 quanta that are delivered to the eye add 1 additional neural response and thus increase the average rating response by 1. This follows because we have assumed that 4% of the quanta delivered to the cornea lead to firings of the rods. Since .04 x 25 = 1, we see that 25 additional quanta at the cornea amount to 1 additional firing.

Thus, we see from our idealized subject that if our rating scale can be used so precisely as to indicate each neural firing we should observe a straight line when we plot average rating value versus average number of quanta at the cornea. Moreover, the intercept of the straight line tells us how many neural firings are due to dark light, and the slope tells the percentage of the quanta delivered to the cornea that generates neural responses.

Figure 1.7b shows the actual data from Sakitt's subject BS. In this case we find a straight line with intercept roughly .36 and slope about .03. These results (along with other more complex analyses) lead to the conclusion that (1) subject BS could respond differentially to 0, 1, 2, . . ., 6 neural firings, (2) for this subject we have an average of .36 firings per trial due to dark light, and

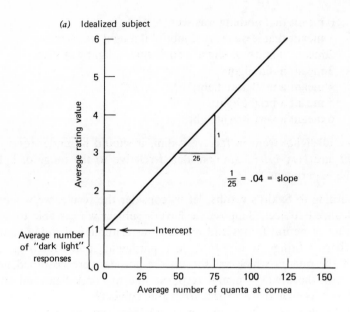

(a) Idealized subject

$\frac{1}{25}$ = .04 = slope

Average number of "dark light" responses

Intercept

Average rating value

Average number of quanta at cornea

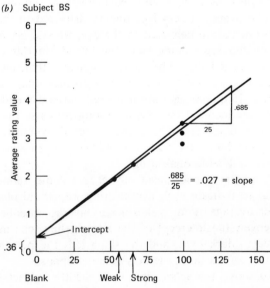

(b) Subject BS

$\frac{.685}{25}$ = .027 = slope

.685

25

Intercept

.36

Average rating value

Blank   Weak Strong

Figure 1.7
The average rating value as a function of number of quanta presented to the cornea. (a) Data expected for an idealized subject. (b) Data from Sakitt's subject B. S.

16

(3) roughly 3% of the quanta striking the cornea lead to neural responses. This experiment, along with that of Hecht et al., graphically illustrates the remarkable sensitivity of the visual system and our remarkable ability to monitor minute changes in our visual environment.

Let us summarize the view of the visual process we have developed thus far. A light source directed toward the eye emits light quanta at irregular intervals, and some strike the eye. Of those that strike the eye, only a fraction ever reach light sensitive receptors in the retina. Somewhat less than 10% of the incident quanta are finally absorbed by the light sensitive pigment of the receptors. The absorption causes a chemical process in the pigment which results in a response by the receptor. Similar chemical changes can also occur without the absorption of light quanta resulting in "dark light." The responses of the receptors are transferred through the bipolar cells to the ganglion cells where they generate neural responses which are then relayed to the brain. Although a single quantum of light can initiate a neural response, it is not enough to generate a visual experience. The reason for this would appear to be the "dark light." If we are not to make too many "false alarms" we must respond only when we have a significant number of neural impulses. Moreover, this strict criterion coupled with the fluctuations inherent in the nature of light will cause us to miss flashes at or above threshold level. In fact, the data of Hecht et al. and that of Sakitt taken together suggest that the primary determinants of our responses in this situation are (1) the fluctuation in the number of absorptions and (2) the existence of "dark light." We have thus developed a very simple model in our attempt to understand the behavior of the visual system at threshold. We have seen that the visual system is able to transform remarkably small variations in its physical environment into usable neural information.

The threshold experiment just discussed is a special case of the intensity discrimination experiment mentioned earlier. The threshold, in this case, is the j.n.d. (just noticeable difference) when one element of the comparison is total darkness. It is possible of course to have a comparison stimulus of any intensity. Consider, as an example, the problem for the system to descriminate between a stimulus that delivers an average of 100 quanta to the cornea and one that delivers an average of 200. Figure 1.8 shows the number of firings we would expect at the retinal ganglion cell under the assumptions that each absorbed quantum leads to an average of 1.5 firings at the retinal ganglion level (this assumption is consistent with the findings of Barlow, Levick and Yoon) and that there is an average of 4 firings due to dark light during a single 200-msec observation period (also from Barlow, Levick and Yoon).

Now, suppose that we determine whether the more or less intense target

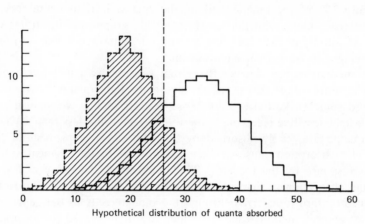

Hypothetical distribution of quanta absorbed

Figure 1.8
Hypothetical distribution of quanta absorbed for 2 different light sources. The figure shows the number of firings expected at the retinal ganglion cell under the assumption that each absorbed quantum leads to an average of 1.5 firings at the retinal ganglion level and that there is an average of 4 firings because of dark light during a single 200-msec observation period. These assumptions are consistent with the findings of Barlow, Levick and Yoon. The curve on the left is that expected for a light source that delivers an average of 100 quanta to the cornea. That on the right is from a light source that delivers an average of 200 quanta.

has been presented by the number of firings observed at this cell. If we get 26 or more firings, we respond "brighter," otherwise we respond "dimmer." This is an optimal decision rule inasmuch as it leads to the highest percentage of correct responses. In this case we would expect the data presented in Table 1.2. The subject would be correct 84.5% of the time. Nineteen percent of the time he would make a "dim" response to the 200-quanta stimulus and 12% of the time he would make a "bright" response to the 100-quanta stimulus.

Suppose that we now made the brighter stimulus somewhat dimmer, until

Table 1.2

Stimuli	"Bright" Response	"Dim" Response
200 quanta source	81%	19%
100 quanta source	12%	88%
Percentage correct responses = 84.5%		

the subject was correct just 75% of the time. How many quanta would we have to deliver to make the two stimuli just noticeably different? Using the assumptions outlined above we can calculate that it would take a flash of about 175 quanta in 100 msec to yield just 75% correct responses. This amounts to an absorption of an average of 7.5 more quanta. In an intensity discrimination experiment such as the one under discussion, it is usual to plot the intensity difference, ΔI, as a function of the intensity of the dimmer stimulus, called I. Thus, in this case ΔI is 75 quanta (on average) and I is 100 quanta.

With more intense signals we expect somewhat larger values of ΔI. This increase in ΔI is to be expected solely because of the physics of the photon emission process. The variance of the number of photons emitted in a brief time period is identical to the mean of that number. Thus, as the mean number of quanta is increased (i.e., the signal becomes more intense), the variability in the signal must also increase. The greater the variability, the further the two signals must be from one another to insure 75% correct detection.

The solid line in Figure 1.9 illustrates the expected value of ΔI as a function of I. Notice that when the dimmer stimulus is below or near threshold, the

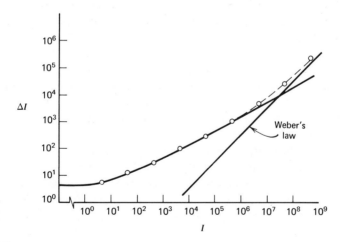

Figure 1.9
Expected value of ΔI as a function of I. The open circles come from an experiment by van den Brink and Bouman (1957). Notice that as the intensity of I approaches the normal reading level (more than 10^7 quanta per 100-msec), the data begin to deviate from the predicted line and to approach the 45° line labeled Weber's law.

value of ΔI is about constant. This results because the to-be-discriminated signal is small relative to the dark light and since the dark light doesn't increase with increased values of I we get little increase in ΔI. Then, as the dimmer alternative comes above threshold, the effect of the dark light becomes minimal and the major determiner of the function becomes the variability in the number of quanta absorbed or emitted.

The open circles come from an experiment by van der Brink and Bouman (1957). In this experiment they presented very small stimuli for very brief time periods. The open circles coincide, to a remarkable degree, with the results expected by our very simple model. It should be noticed, however, that as the intensity of the comparison stimulus, I, approaches the normal reading level and rises above (over 10^7 quanta per 100 msec) it begins to deviate from the predicted line and to approach the 45° line labeled *Weber's law*.

Weber's law is said to hold when the needed incremental intensity, ΔI, is proportional to the comparison intensity, I. This is often stated as

$$\frac{\Delta I}{I} = k$$

The ratio $\Delta I/I$ is called the *Weber fraction*. Figure 1.10 shows the expected values of the log of the Weber fraction as a function of intensity. Again the data shown in Figure 1.9 are plotted. In this figure Weber's law is denoted by the flat line representing a constant Weber fraction. The line extending on below the flat line is the prediction derived from the simple view of the visual system thus far outlined. Although it may not be clear from this experiment, numerous other experiments show that the Weber fraction does not continue to decrease, but does "level off" and follow Weber's law for more intense signals. Thus as the intensity of the signal grows, factors other than those thus far discussed enter in.

In our analysis thus far, we have demonstrated how sensitive the visual system really is. It appears that, after the initial loss of about 90% of the quanta before the receptors are reached, the eye manages to preserve nearly all of the information in the stimulus flash for flashes ranging from 100 to 1,000,000 quanta per 100 msec. The discrimination difficulty (i.e., ΔI) among flashes in this range is determined entirely by the fluctuations in the physical signal. As the signal level increases, and Weber's law begins to hold, the sluggishness of the visual system itself finally begins to intervene and our Weber fraction becomes constant. The ratio $\Delta I/I$ no longer continues to decline as it would if the physical signal were being perfectly transmitted.

The exact reasons why Weber's law begins to hold are unknown. However, it is known that the loss of information represented by the flattening of the

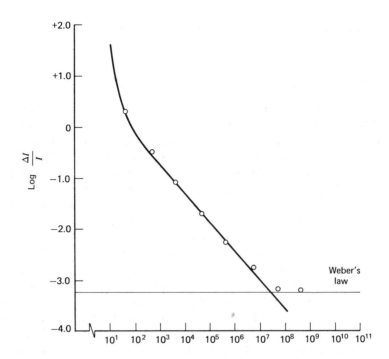

Figure 1.10
The log of the Weber fraction $\Delta I / I$ as a function of the intensity I.

Weber fraction occurs very early in the system, before the ganglion cells. It is considered most probable that it occurs at the level of the bipolar cells (see Figure 1.1). It would appear to be the result of an *inhibitory* effect of the transmission of one impulse on the transmission of later pulses.

Although one might imagine that such a loss of information through inhibition is a detriment to the system, we will see in the following section and in the next chapter that the balance of excitation and inhibition is a basic mechanism whereby the neural system manages to maintain essential information while discarding that which is inessential.

Perhaps the main lesson to be drawn from our discussion thus far is that the visual world (as far as the eye is concerned) does not consist of objects and relationships among them. Rather, it is a rapidly fluctuating configuration of tiny quanta of light. Much of the information about these light quanta is preserved and sent to the brain as a sequence of neural pulses. It is the brain and our higher neural processing which must laboriously construct the world of objects and relations among objects that seem so apparent to us as we view the world.

SEEING COLOR

To this point we have discussed the process whereby the visual system transforms information about *rate* of emission of quanta from a light source into rate of neural impulses sent to the brain. However, the photon stream entering the eye is characterized not only by rate, but also by *wavelength*. Variations of wavelength are reflected in our perceptual system by variations in color. The eye is sensitive to quanta varying from roughly 400 nanometers (nm) in length (such lights look blue or violet) to about 700 nm (these lights look red). We now want to consider the process whereby the visual system detects variations in wavelength and translates this information into a usable neural code which is finally realized by our perceptual system as the experience of color.

To this point we have discussed the visual system as if it were a homogeneous system. It is not. To begin, there are several different kinds of receptors. One kind of receptor, called a *rod,* relays no color information, but is responsive to very small amounts of light. Most of the data we have discussed thus far has been concerned solely with rod vision. In dim illumination, only rods are operative. Thus, we have no color perception at low illumination levels.

As the illumination increases, the rod system becomes inoperative and a new system, called the *cone* system, comes into play. It is the cone system that generates a neural code from the wavelength of the absorbed quanta. How do the cones abstract wavelength information from the photon stream? In principle there are many ways that the cones could transform wavelength information into a neural code. One possibility would be that the cones are all identical, but on the absorption of a quantum of a particular wavelength a particular pattern of neural impulses would be set up which would, at higher levels, be interpreted as color. In fact, this seems not to be the case. Ordinarily the neural system codes information either by an increased or decreased rate of responding. There seems to be no mechanism for either coding or interpreting other sorts of configurations. Another possibility would suggest that there were several types of cones. Perhaps one for each important wavelength. Then we could imagine that different wavelength information would be sent through different input channels to the brain. It appears that the latter possibility is closer to the truth.

Perhaps the most characteristic aspect of quanta of different wavelengths is that they are differentially absorbed (and reflected) by different kinds of pigments. Some pigments absorb short wavelength quanta and reflect long wavelength quanta. Since such pigments reflect light which looks to us orange or red we say that these pigments are *colored* orange or red. In general, a pigment will appear to be the color associated with the wavelength it reflects. The human visual system makes use of the differential absorption characteristics of different pigments to extract wavelength information from the photon stream. There are at least three different kinds of cones. These cones differ in that the pigment associated with each of them has different absorption characteristics. For example, one kind of cone—call it the red receptor—absorbs only quanta with relatively long wavelengths. A second kind of cone—call it the blue receptor—absorbs mostly quanta of short wavelengths. A third kind of cone—call it the green receptor—absorbs quanta of intermediate wavelength but neither long nor short wavelength quanta. Since it is the absorption of a quantum of light that sets off a neural response, these different absorption characteristics allow differential responding to different wavelength configurations among the incoming quanta.

Figure 1.11 illustrates the relative probabilities that each of the three receptor types will absorb a quantum striking the receptor as a function of the wavelength of the quantum. These curves are called the *spectral absorption curves* of the three receptor types. The blue receptor has its peak sensitivity around 445 nm, the green receptor at about 535 nm, and the red absorbing receptor at about 570 nm.

To determine how these three different kinds of receptors can help us see colors of different hues, consider the presentation to the eye of 3,000,000 quanta of 500-nm monocromatic light (this will look a little bluish green). Suppose that one third of the quanta fell on each of the three types of receptors (i.e., 1,000,000 on each receptor type). Now, from Figure 1.11 we see that about 10%, or 100,000, of the incident quanta are effective on the red-absorbing receptors. About 15%, or 150,000, of the quanta falling on the "blue-absorbing" receptors are effective, and about 25%, or 250,000, of the responses are generated by the "green-absorbing" receptors. Similarly, if the stimulus had been at 600 nm we would have had no blue responses, 120,000 green responses, and about 650,000 red responses. Thus, for every configuration of wavelength and intensity we would get a different configuration of responses.

The scheme that we just outlined appears to be correct as far as it goes. Information of the sort that I just mentioned could be sent to the brain, and the brain could then interpret it in terms of color and intensity. Interestingly, it turns out that the eye itself goes to the trouble of sorting out the color information and the brightness information independently. In fact, intensity and color information are sent to the brain from the retinal ganglion cells along different paths.

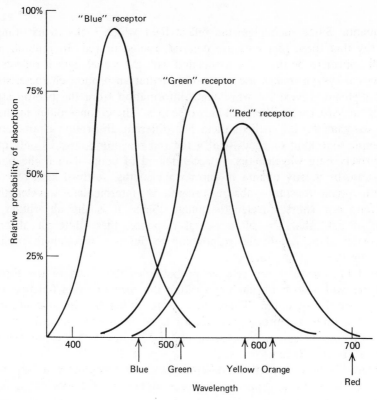

Figure 1.11
The relative probabilies that each of the three receptor types will absorb a quantum striking a receptor as a function of the wavelength of the quantum. These curves are called the spectral absorption curves of the three receptor types. (Based on data from Thomson and Wright, 1953)

Figure 1.12 (adapted from Boynton, 1971) illustrates, in schematic form, the probable connections from the various kinds of cones to the brain. Here again, we have essentially three channels of information to the brain, but now the three channels represent (1) the ratio of blue absorptions to red absorptions (2) the total amount of red plus green absorptions and (3) the ratio of green to red absorptions. (Evidence would also seem to indicate that the logically redundant ratio of red to blue and ratio of red to green information is also transmitted.) The blue-red channel carries information about the relative contents of blue or yellow in the stimulus. The green-red summation channel carries information about the intensity of the stimulus, and finally, the

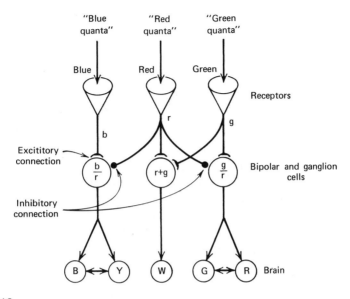

Figure 1.12
A schematic of the probable connections from the various kinds of cones to the brain. (Adapted from Boynton, 1971.)

green-red ratio channel carries information about the degree of green versus red in the stimulus.

One of the real virtues of this system is that taking the ratio on the two "color channels" generates color information entirely independently of intensity information. Consider again our example of a 3,000,000-quanta 500-nm stimulus. In this case the numbers we gave before would represent output of the receptors (i.e., 150,000 blue-receptor responses, 250,000 green-receptor responses and 100,000 red-receptor responses). The three channels illustrated in Figure 1.12 would thus have an output of 150,000/100,000 = 1.5 for the blue over red channel, an output of 350,000 on the red + green luminance channel, and an output of 2.5 on the green over red channel. Thus, we would conclude that the signal was a bluish-green signal of high intensity.

Suppose, now we present only 3000 500-nm quanta. In this case, we still get a blue over red ratio of 150/100 = 1.5 and a green over red ratio of 250/100 = 2.5 (just as before), but now we get a reading on the luminance channel of only 350. Thus, we have maintained the wavelength information as before, and only changed the intensity information.

Although the model outlined here is not complete and has glossed over numerous aspects of the color system, it does give a fairly satisfactory picture of the mechanisms used in the human visual system to extract and differentiate wavelength information from the rate information in the incoming stream of photons. (More details are given in Boynton, 1971, and in Cornsweet, 1970.)

To summarize the view we have developed thus far, a primary characteristic of quanta of different wavelengths is that they are differentially absorbed by different pigments. This fact allows the different receptors in the retina to fire selectively in response to certain wavelengths of quanta and not to others. There are apparently three kinds of pigments in various receptors of the eye. These are called (1) red-absorbing, (2) green-absorbing, and (3) blue-absorbing. Rather than send these three channels of wavelength information directly to the brain, the wavelength information is abstracted by the eye. The output of the cone system consists of three outputs: one corresponding to intensity information, one corresponding to the ratio of green to red quanta absorbed, and one corresponding to the ratio of blue to red quanta absorbed. Together, these three channels provide the brain with all it needs to construct color.

It should be emphasized again that the eye is a mechanism for abstracting from the stream of photons impinging on it those characteristics that the system preserves. We abstract information about intensity and we abstract information about wavelength. From these two independent bits of information the brain constructs unified perceptions of colored objects. The process is constructive, and these complex constructions occur at high cognitive levels where (as we shall see) many variables other than simply the carefully preserved information from the eye enters in.

THE AUDITORY TRANSDUCTION PROCESS

Whereas the visual system uses the absorption of a quantum of light to initiate a *chemical* process which ultimately leads to an experience of seeing, the auditory system uses *mechanical* means to convert tiny vibrations among air molecules into a neural code. Figure 1.13 illustrates, in schematic form, the primary mechanisms which accomplish this transduction. Some object in the world, such as a tuning fork or our vocal chords, begins to vibrate. This sets up pressure waves in the air—periods of high compression followed by periods of low compression. If the source produces a pure tone, the peaks and valleys of the pressure wave follow a simple sine wave. When these variations in pressure contact the tympanic membrane (eardrum) they cause it to move back and forth with the waxing and waning of the pressure wave. Attached to the tympanic membrane are the ossicles (the three small bones of the middle ear).

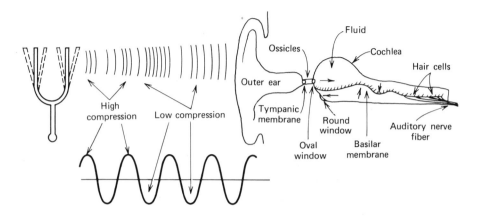

Figure 1.13
A schematic of the primary mechanisms involved in the auditory transduction process. The process begins with the vibration of some object in the world such as a tuning fork. This sets up pressure waves in the air. Then, these variations in pressure contact the tympanic membrane, causing it to move back and forth. Attached to the membrane are the ossicles (three small bones in the middle ear) which are attached on the other end to a membrane called the oval window. The ossicles act as a plunger pushing against the oval window and thereby transform the pressure waves impinging on the tympanic membrane into a pressure wave surging through the fluid of the cochlea. This pressure wave sets up a traveling wave along the basilar membrane suspended in the cochlea. Attached to this membrane are hair cells that are connected to the auditory nerve.

These bones are attached on the other end to a membrane called the oval window. The oval window covers an opening to a fluid-filled compartment called the cochlea. The ossicles act as a plunger pushing against the oval window and thereby transforming the pressure waves impinging on the tympanic membrane into a pressure wave surging through the fluid of the cochlea. This pressure wave sets up a *traveling wave* (like the wave which travels down a whip when you snap it) along the basilar membrane suspended in the cochlea. Attached to the top of this membrane are tiny hair cells. Each hair cell is connected to the auditory nerve bundle. As the traveling wave moves across the basilar membrane and the hair cells are stimulated, impulses are sent along a fiber of the auditory nerve to higher processing centers. The basilar membrane is so constructed that the maximal displacement of the traveling wave occurs at different places depending on the frequency of the input signal. If a high frequency stimulus is put in, maximal displacement occurs near the end of the basilar membrane closest to the oval window. If low frequency tones are presented, the maximum displacement occurs near the far end of the membrane. Intermediate frequencies cause maximum displacement at intermediate points along the membrane. Thus, depending on the frequency of the input stimulus, different hair cells are maximally stimulated and different fibers of the auditory nerve send information to the higher processing centers.

We now want to take a more careful look at the nature of the impulses initiated by the hair cells and of the relationship between these and the input signal. The input signal is a continuously varying pressure wave, whereas the neural impulses are a discrete series of neural firings. Important information about these patterns of firing have recently become available through microelectrode recordings from single fibers of the auditory nerve. It is to these results that we now turn.

THE NEURAL CODE

In a remarkable set of experiments Jerzy Rose and his colleagues at the University of Wisconsin (cf. Rose, Brugge, Anderson, & Hind, 1967; Hind, Anderson, Brugge, & Rose, 1967; Brugge, Anderson, Hind, & Rose, 1969; Rose, Brugge, Anderson, & Hind, 1969) have carefully measured the detailed structure of the response of single fibers of the eighth nerve[2] of the monkey to simple sine wave stimuli. The results yield a rather clear picture of the auditory signal relayed to the brain. We can summarize their results by the following four statements.

1. Fibers are tuned to particular frequencies. A particular fiber responds best to tones at its characteristic frequency. Tones of higher or lower frequency lead to less firing. Different fibers are tuned to different frequencies. Thus, the entire frequency range is spanned not by any particular fiber, but by a set of fibers.
2. The firing of the fibers is *phase locked* to the input stimulus. That is, fibers fire no more than once per cycle. Moreover, they always fire at the same point in the cycle.
3. A fiber has a refractory period. That is, once a fiber fires it cannot fire again for an average of about 0.5 msec.
4. After it recovers from its refractory period, a fiber fires on the very next cycle of the input tone with probability p. If it should fail to fire, it fires on the next cycle with the same probability p. On each successive cycle it has

[2]The eighth nerve, or auditory nerve, is in fact a bundle of nerve fibers leading from the cochlea to the higher brain centers. All auditory information must pass through the fibers of this nerve.

probability p of firing until it finally does fire. The value of p depends on (a) the intensity of the signal—the more intense the signal the greater the probability of firing—and (b) the frequency of the signal. The closer the signal frequency to the "best" frequency for the fiber the greater the probability of firing.

To make this more concrete, consider the following situation (illustrated in Figure 1.14). We are measuring the responses of a fiber whose "best frequency" is a tone of 1000 Hertz (Hz)—i.e., cycles per second—to a 1000-Hz tone. (Note: The high note on a piano is about 4000 Hz, "middle C" is about 260 Hz). Suppose that we are at an intensity so that $p = .5$.

If the fiber fires once (call the time of the firing time 0), when do we expect it to fire again? According to statement 2 above, it cannot fire again until the next cycle of the signal. Since we are presenting a 1000-Hz tone, it will cycle again in $1/1000$ sec, or 1 msec. Hence, it will have its next opportunity to respond just 1 msec later. (Since this is substantially greater than the refractory period of 0.5 msec, the limitation mentioned in 3 above will not be a factor.) Since we are assuming that at the present intensity it will fire with probability .5 on each opportunity we expect that 50% of the time it will fire after exactly 1 msec. If it should fail to fire, then it has a 50% chance of firing on the next cycle, 1 msec later. Therefore, we expect 25% (half of the remaining half, $.5 \times .5 = .25$) of the time the fiber will fire after exactly 2 msec, and 12.5% of the time it should fire after exactly 3 msec, etc. Figure 1.14b illustrates the effects of reducing the intensity of the 1000-Hz tone. Reducing the intensity reduces the probability, p, that the fiber will fire on any given opportunity. In the example, I assumed that we reduced p to .25. In this case we expect only 25% of the firings to occur after 1 msec; 18.75% (25% of the remaining 75% of the times) of the time it will fire after exactly 2 msec, etc. Figure 1.14c illustrates the expected result of changing the frequency of the input signal. Since the best frequency of our hypothetical fiber is 1000 Hz, presenting a 1333-Hz tone will reduce p, the probability of firing on any cycle. Thus, even though in the example the 1333-Hz tone has the same amplitude as the 1000-Hz tone, the probability of responding on any cycle has been reduced to .25.

Now, however, since we have a higher frequency stimulus with only a 0.75-msec period, the fiber gets more opportunities to fire. After only 0.75 msec it has a 25% chance of firing. At 1.5 msec we expect to find 18.75% of the firings etc. Finally, Figure 1.14d illustrates the expected effects of presenting a 500-Hz tone. In this case the value of p is reduced (I have arbitrarily set it to .25), but now the fiber gets an opportunity to fire only every 2 msec.

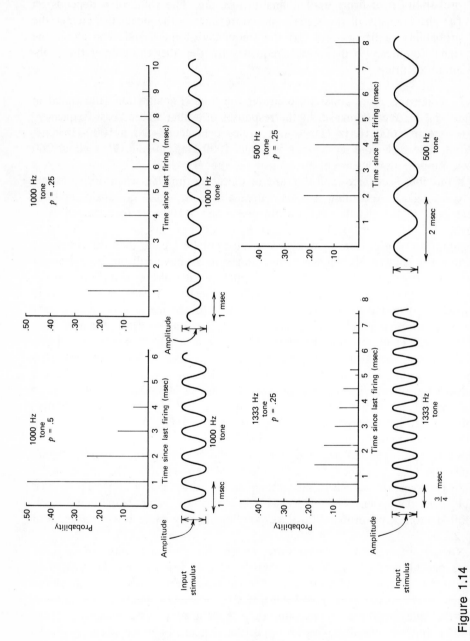

Figure 1.14

The hypothetical distribution of inter-spike intervals (i.e., the time between successive firings of a particular fiber) as a function of frequency and intensity of the pure tone stimulus. (See chapter discussion for further explanation.)

Figures 1.15 and 1.16 show the analogous plots from the data of Rose et al. (1967). Figure 1.15 shows the effects of changes of frequency on a fiber whose best frequency is about 1000 Hz. Figure 1.16 illustrates the effect of changes in intensity on the firing pattern of another fiber. The results clearly follow our expectations with two minor differences. (1) Firings do not *always* occur at *exactly* the same place during the cycle. They vary a few tenths of 1 msec from time to time which leads to a slightly smeared version of what we would have expected. (2) When the frequencies get low enough that the fiber becomes non-refractory while still in the upward moving portion of the cycle, it may fire twice in the same cycle. Thus, in Figure 1.14a and b, we get a few responses immediately after it recovers. Nevertheless the large bulk of the responses follow the expected pattern.

We have charted the flow of information from a continuously varying time waveform into a pattern of neural responses. The pattern is remarkably clear and well behaved. However, we have not answered the question of how this information is used by the brain to give us our perceptions of the loudness (intensity) and the pitch (frequency) of an input stimulus. The data are suggestive in two respects. (1) The fact that the overall rate of firing increases with the intensity of the stimulus leads to the suspicion that in the ear, as with the eye, it is the overall rate of firing (or number of firings observed in some small interval of time) that carries intensity information. (2) Frequency information comes from two sources. The firings are phase locked to the signal; hence, the time between firings on a single fiber are multiples of the cycle time of the stimulus. Second, different fibers respond maximally to different frequencies. Hence, the fibers with the maximal firing rate could signal pitch information.

SIGNALING INTENSITY

One problem with the view that the firing rate of an individual fiber indicates the intensity of a signal comes from a comparison of the range of an individual fiber with that of the ear. Although we can discriminate intensities ranging from 0.0002 dynes/cm² to 20 dynes/cm² (a factor of 100,000), individual fibers vary in their probability of firing over only a limited range and "saturate" at a rate of only 100 to 500 responses per sec. Figure 1.17 shows the probability of firing, p, as a function of intensity for one fiber. (Data from Rose et al.) Here we see the probability rising and reaching a maximum value of about .125. With further increases in intensity, the probability remains constant; for the highest intensity it even falls slightly.

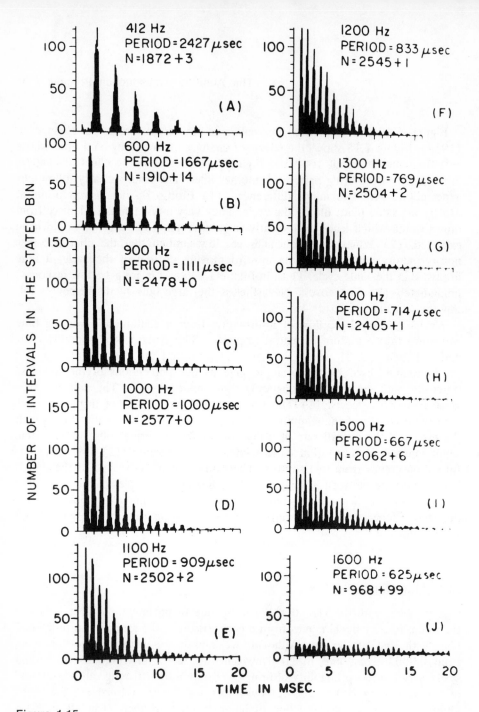

Figure 1.15
Observed distribution of inter-spike intervals for pure tone stimuli of different frequencies. The measurments were taken from a single neuron of a cat. (Data from Rose, Brugge, Anderson and Hind, 1967.)

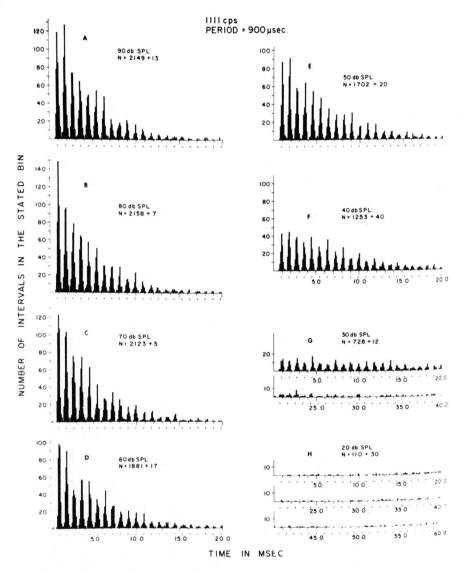

Figure 1.16
Observed distribution of inter-spike intervals as a function of intensity of a pure tone stimulus. The measurments were taken from a single neuron of a cat. (Data from Rose, Brugge, Anderson and Hind, 1967.)

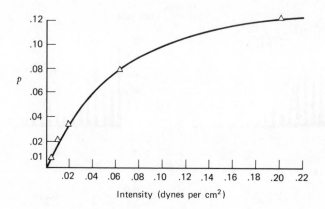

Figure 1.17
The probability that a single neuron will fire as a function of the intensity of the input stimulus. The smooth curve is generated by a negative exponential function. (Data are from Rose et al., 1967.)

Notice, here, that after the fiber saturates (i.e., begins firing at its maximum rate) it can no longer serve to signal variations in tone intensity. Thus, single fibers cannot carry intensity information concerning higher intensities. Instead, the firing patterns of aggregates of fibers must carry our intensity information. It is an interesting side effect of the frequency response of a fiber that all fibers do not saturate simultaneously to a given tone. Instead, after those fibers responding "best" to the input frequency saturate, there are still other fibers (those with other best frequencies) that are still firing below their saturation rate. Figure 1.18 illustrates the point. Suppose we are playing a tone of frequency f_0 at intensity I. Those fibers whose best frequency is f_0 will be stimulated according to the nominal intensity I. However, those fibers whose best frequencies differ from f_0 will not be receiving full stimulation. Consider, for example, a fiber whose best frequency is $f_0 + 200$. According to the hypothetical function of Figure 1.18 it will be stimulated at only about 40% of the nominal intensity. Thus, as the intensity increases and the "center" fibers begin to saturate, the effective intensity stimulating the "outer" fibers will increase more slowly and they will continue to provide intensity information.

As the intensity continues to increase, a broader and broader range of fibers will become saturated; but as they do, more and more peripheral fibers will receive more and more stimulation and continue to provide intensity information. Figure 1.19 illustrates the spreading and flattening of the probability of response curve for a single fiber (Rose et al., 1967) as a function of increasing intensity.

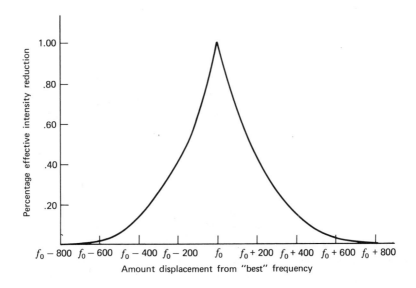

Figure 1.18
Hypothetical percentage of effective intensity as a function of the distance of the stimulus in frequency from its "best" frequency.

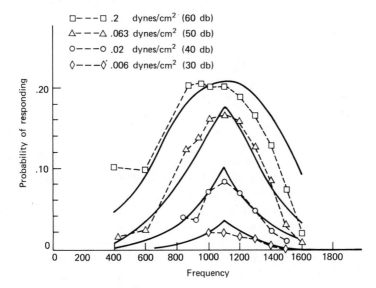

Figure 1.19
Observed and predicted probability of a single neuron firing as a function of the frequency and intensity of the pure tone stimulus. (Data are from Rose et al., 1967.) The theoretical lines were generated on the basis of Figure 1.18 and the assumption that the function relating P to "effective intensity" is the negative exponential, as in Figure 1.17.

At low and moderate intensities the probabilities of firing are shaped much like the hypothetical curve illustrated in Figure 1.18. However, as the intensity increases and the central fibers saturate, the response curve becomes flatter and broader. This is because the firing rates of the peripheral fibers can continue to increase after the central fibers have saturated. The solid lines is the distribution expected on the basis of Figure 1.18 and the assumption that the function relating p to "effective —intensity" is a negative exponential (as in Figure 1.17).

To summarize, it appears likely that the overall rate of firing is the essential neural code for intensity information. However, since an individual fiber cannot fire more than about 200 times per sec, aggregates of fibers must be used. At low intensities most firing comes from those fibers "tuned" to the frequency of the input signal. Then, as the intensity increases, the fibers "tuned" to the signal become saturated and can no longer respond differentially to increases in intensity. As this is happening, the burden for carrying relevant information falls on the more peripheral fibers which are receiving less effective stimulation and thus have not yet reached their saturation point.

We have shown how the auditory fibers of the eighth nerve *can* code intensity information. How can we get evidence on whether or not we *do* use such information in our judgments of intensity? Consider tthe following experiment. We choose a tone of some frequency (say, 1000 Hz). On some trials, we present the tone at intensity I. On others, we present it at $I + \Delta$. We ask our subject to tell us which tone he or she thought we presented. We then adjust Δ until the subject can make the correct discrimination 75% of the time. This experiment should be familiar. It is the exact analog to the intensity discrimination experiment described for vision. Consider the following model. Suppose that our subject is able to monitor and count the number of firings, over all fibers, resulting from the presentation of each stimulus. If that number is greater than some criterion he or she will respond that the "louder" stimulus was heard, otherwise it will be the "softer" of the two.

These assumptions should also be familiar, for they are the exact analog of the intensity discrimination model described for vision. From the assumptions we have already discussed, we can calculate the increase in intensity (and therefore in firing rate) required to detect a difference 75% of the time. Figure 1.20 is a plot of the expected relationship between log ΔI and log I. This plot, again, is the exact analog of the plot, shown in Figure 1.9, for a visual discrimination experiment. Figure 1.21 gives the Weber fraction expected on the basis of these assumptions. It is clear that the major aspects of the observed data are accounted for by our simple neural model. Therefore, it would seem that for audition, as well as vision, the basic information already available at

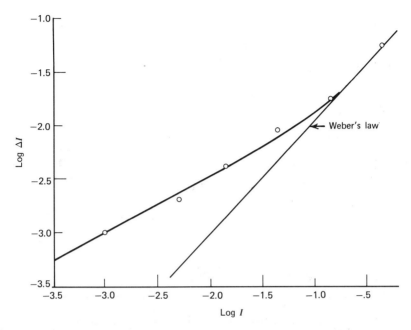

Figure 1.20
The logarithm of values of Δ*I* as a function of the logarithm of the intensity of a 1000-Hertz sine wave stimulus. Intensity is measured in dynes per cm². (Data from Riesz, 1928.)

the receptor level sets the basic limits of intensity discrimination—as observed in psychophysical experiments. Similar arguments could be made concerning frequency information (cf. Siebert, 1968; and Green & Luce, 1974). We will not, however, develop those ideas further here. The major structure of the neural transduction system for vision and audition has already been laid out. Similar analyses could be given for the other sense modalities. In each event some disturbance in the environment is translated into a stream of neural pulses sent off to the brain. With some modalities, such as with audition and our sensitivity to pressure, the transduction process is mainly accomplished by mechanical means. With other senses, as in the case of taste, smell, and vision, the transducer is primarily chemical. In every case the transduction process is remarkably sensitive (as compared to machines designed to accomplish the same task) and remarkably well tuned to the kinds of stimulation they are designed to detect. I will not however move into a detailed discussion of these other sensory modalities. The basic processes are the same for the other modali-

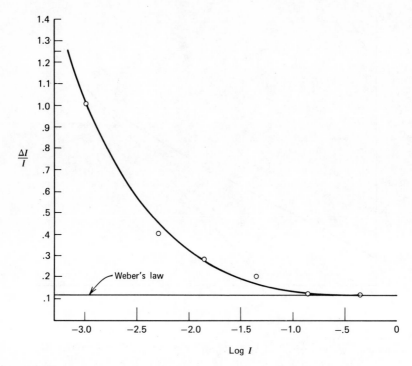

Figure 1.21
The Weber ratio $\Delta I / I$ as a function of the log of intensity. The data are the same as those illustrated in Figure 1.20.

ties. Rather we will now turn to an analysis of the means whereby this rudimentary information available at the receptor level is combined with information from other sources to allow us to perceive patterns and make sense out of the world around us.

2
RECOGNIZING PATTERNS

In the preceding chapter we saw how the rate of photon flow onto the cornea is transformed into a rate of firing from retinal receptors and thus into brightness information. Normally, of course, we are interested in much more than brightness. We must not only interpret the rate of photon absorption, but also its spatial distribution. It is ordinarily more important to know the *pattern* of stimulation than to know the absolute brightness of any part of the stimulus. Thus, we must monitor the relative firing rates of millions of receptors in order that the patterns of stimulation may be discovered and identified with representations of such patterns stored in our memories. Continual fluctuations due to eye movements as well as the fluctuation inherent in the visual stimulation make pattern identification a complex task. To complicate the problem further, patterns arising from stimuli whose physical characteristics differ substantially must frequently be recognized as the same object. Consider, for example, the various drawings in Figure 2.1. We have little trouble recognizing them all as representing the same English words, yet they obviously differ

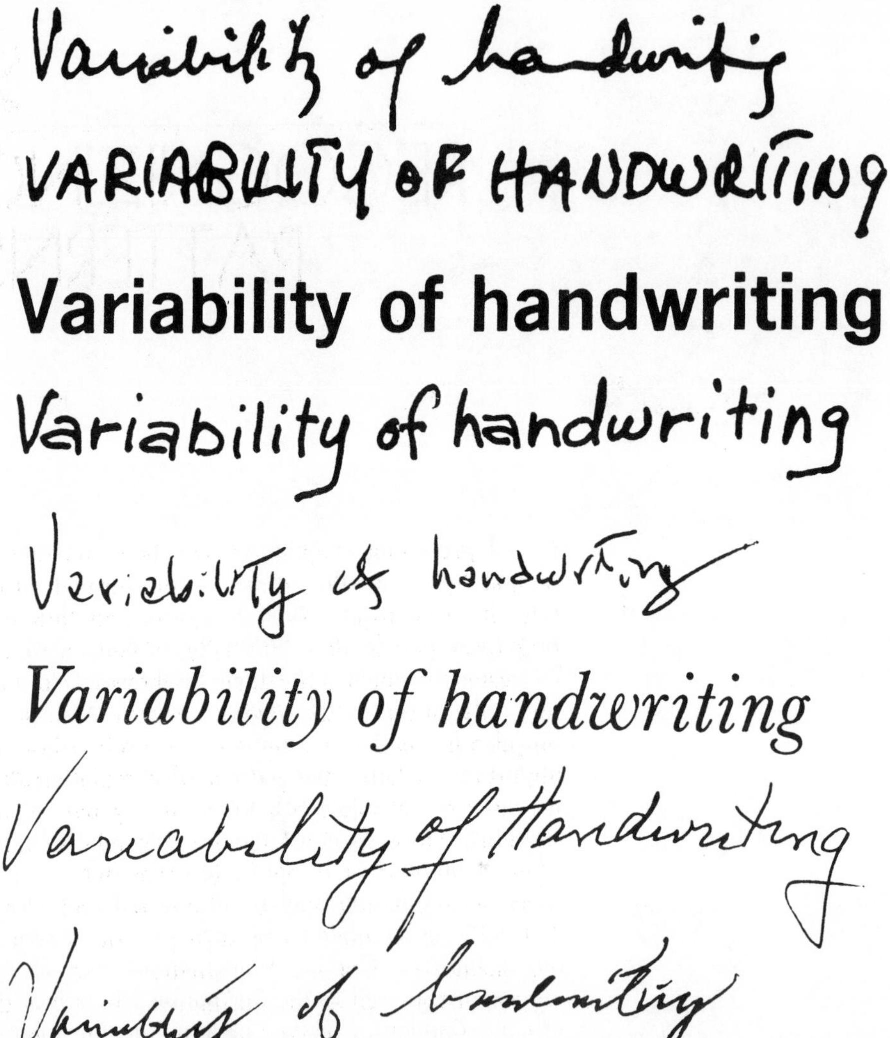

Figure 2.1
A detailed analysis of even simple visual patterns shows incredible variation.
(Drawing from Lindgren, 1965.)

considerably in detail. Moreover, we are able to recognize these words as the same patterns in spite of substantial changes in size and orientation. The problem of recognizing patterns, then, is that of reliably discovering and applying the same name to patterns of stimulation which are in some sense similar to one another.

Applying the same name to different objects implies that some sort of abstraction from the retinal image must occur. Little is known about the mechanism whereby this abstraction occurs in the human organism. Nevertheless, physiological experiments with cats and monkeys and work with pattern recognition machines have been suggestive and have led to theories which make considerable sense out of the data on human pattern recognition.

PHYSIOLOGICAL EVIDENCE

Perhaps the most suggestive physiological evidence for mechanisms of pattern recognition comes from the work of Hubel and Wiesel (1959, 1962, 1965, 1968). (For a review of their earlier work, see Hubel, 1963.) Hubel and Wiesel attempted to trace the visual pathways from the retina to the cortex of the brain. They accomplished this tracing by means of single-cell recordings in the cat. They placed electrodes in cells at a given point in the visual pathway, flashed lights and other stimuli in the cat's eye, and then watched for activity in the chosen cell. In this way, they were able to discover the portion of the retina to which their cell was most sensitive (that most sensitive portion is called the *receptive field* of the cell), and in addition, the kind of stimulation within the sensitive area that caused the greatest activity.

The first important integrative stage after the retinal receptors is the retinal ganglion cells. These cells generally receive inputs from a number of receptors spread over a rather large area of the retina. The organization of the receptive fields of these cells was first mapped by Kuffler (1953). Within the receptive field of the retinal ganglion cell there are usually two readily distinguishable areas: the so-called "on" and "off" areas. Light flashes into the "on" area of the field cause the cell to fire; when the flash is turned off, the cell ceases firing. Flashes into the "off" region of the receptive field cause the cell to cease firing. When the light is turned off, the cell almost always fires briefly, that is, gives an "off" response. When lights are shined in both the "on" and "off" regions of the receptive field, the cell will either not respond at all or respond weakly. Thus, the "off" region plays an inhibitory role on the effects of flashes in the "on" region. Flashes that cover the entire "on" region and leave the "off"

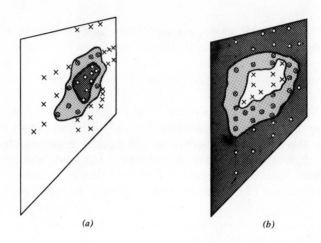

(a)   *(b)*

Figure 2.2
Diagrammatic representation of receptive field response pattern of an on-center
(a) and an off-center *(b)* ganglion cell of a goldfish retina. The fields shown were
mapped with small circular points of light. X = "off" response; O = "on" response.
Pure "on" regions are shown in black, pure "off" regions are shown in white, and
"on-off" regions are hatched. (Data from Wagner, MacNicol, and Wolbarsht,
1963.)

region of the receptive field completely unilluminated lead to maximum response
of the cells.

    There appear to be two distinct organizational patterns of such cells, the "on-
center" and the "off-center" patterns. These two organizational patterns are
shown in Figure 2.2*a* and *b*. The "on-center" type cell (2.2*a*) is arranged
with its on receptors forming a small, roughly circular disk with a ring of "off"
receptors. This type of cell responds maximally to a small disk of light on a
dark background (see Figure 2.3). The second type of cell, the "off-center"
cell, has just the reverse pattern, a small disk of off receptors encircled by a
ring of on receptors. This configuration responds most vigorously to a small
black dot just covering the off receptors on an otherwise lighted background.
These two configurations of receptive fields in the retinal ganglion cell are very
widespread and occur in animals from the goldfish to the monkey.

    Before proceeding with a discussion of the "higher" processing levels, it is
useful to consider some of the consequences of the processing already accomplished at the retinal ganglion level. The pattern of excitatory centers surrounded by inhibitory regions serves to accentuate edges and discontinuities in
the light pattern. Figure 2.4 illustrates, in schematic form, how this is accom-

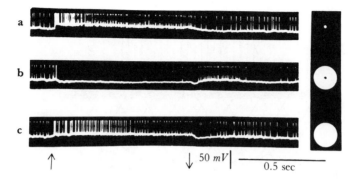

Figure 2.3
The responses of a retinal ganglion cell of the cat to various visual stimuli. Onset and offset of illumination are marked by arrows. The area illuminated to obtain each record is shown at the right of the figure. Part *(a)* shows the high rate of responding generated in this cell by a small spot of light, 1° in diameter; Part *(b)* shows the suppressed responding of the cell to a small black dot surrounded by a 12° illuminated area. Part *(c)* shows the response of the cell when the entire receptive cell is illuminated. This pattern of responding is typical of the "on-center, off-surround" receptive field. (Data are from Wiesel, 1959.)

plished. The upper portion of the figure illustrates (in cross section) the intensity pattern of light striking the retina as a result of the presentation of a white bar against a dark background. The receptor responses from a small region are pooled and then relayed to the retinal ganglion cells. The schematic diagram shows each pool passing information on to three such cells. To one it sends excitatory information. To the adjacent cells it sends inhibitory information. Thus, the cells illustrated are "on-center, off-surround." They receive excitatory information from a central region and inhibitory information from the surrounding regions. To see how this configuration "sharpens" the edges of the image consider first cells numbered 1 and 9. These cells are unaffected by the light bar since their responses are determined entirely by the dark region of the stimulus. Thus, they respond at a rate only slightly above the spontaneous rate for that cell. Cells 2 and 8, on the other hand, actually show a depression *below* their spontaneous rate. This can be understood simply by noting that each cell's excitatory region is almost entirely in the darker region of the image, but half of its inhibitory field is in the light, and thus the output of those cells is suppressed. Cells numbered 3 and 7 receive nearly all of their excitatory input from the white portion of the stimulus, but half of their inhibitory field is in the dark. Thus, each cell fires well above the rate it would

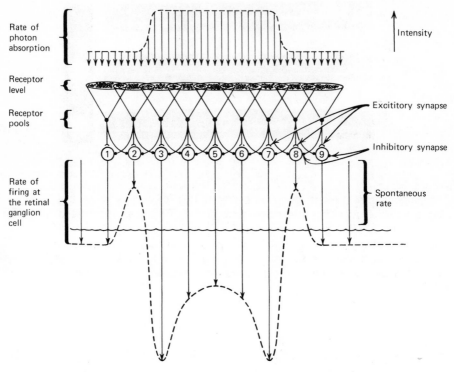

Rate of photon absorption

Intensity

Receptor level

Receptor pools

Excititory synapse

Inhibitory synapse

① ② ③ ④ ⑤ ⑥ ⑦ ⑧ ⑨

Rate of firing at the retinal ganglion cell

Spontaneous rate

Figure 2.4
A hypothetical organization of receptive fields that leads to the "sharpening" of the edges of a visual image. (See chapter discussion for explanation.)

under steady illumination. The excitatory-inhibitory interaction allows the system to accentuate the discontinuities in the spatial distribution of light on the retina and send this information on to the higher centers.

It is interesting that we can get *behavioral* evidence for these neural interactions by use of the *increment threshold procedure* outlined in the previous chapter. A recent experiment by Springer (1973) will serve to illustrate the logic behind such experiments. As an example, suppose we present a subject with a visual field which is light on one side and dark on the other. Figure 2.5*a* illustrates such a field. Figure 2.5*b* is a plot of the intensity of the light as a function of position across the field. The critical region here is the sharp discontinuity near the center of the field. It is there that the neural interactions will become most noticeable. Now, let us determine the pattern of neural activity set up by such a field. Figure 2.6*a* shows, in schematic form, the sorts of neural responses

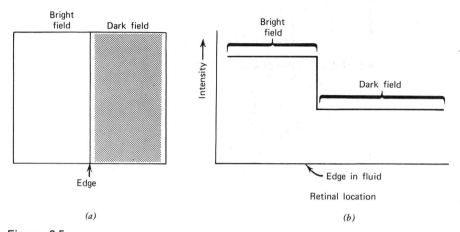

Figure 2.5
(a) Schematic of a split field with the left-hand "light" and right-hand "dark."
(b) A plot of the intensity of the field illustrated in *(a)* as a function of retinal location.

we expect at the level of the retinal ganglion cells. In this figure, as in Figure 2.4, we see that the effect of inhibition is to increase the rate of responding as we get nearer to the edge of the bright portion of the field and to depress the rate of responding as we near the edge in the darker portion of the field. Figure 2.6*b* plots an idealized rate of responding as a function of retinal location superimposed on the initial intensity plot (2.5*b*). Note that the neural responses do not mirror exactly the input signal. Rather they serve to "sharpen" the edge. That is, they serve to accentuate the difference between the light and dark sides of the field.

Now consider what would happen if we flashed a tiny spot of light at various places on the field. Recall from the previous chapter that the more neural activity at a given location, the harder it is to see a tiny spot of light focused at that location. Thus, we expect, for example, that the light will be more difficult to perceive when flashed on the bright portion of the field than when flashed on the darker portion. More significantly, since the amount of neural activity *increases* near the edge of the light region of the field, *we expect that the light will become even more difficult to perceive near the edge of the bright field.* Similarly, since the amount of neural activity *decreases* near the edge of the dark field, *we expect the spot of light to actually become easier to see near the edge of this field.*

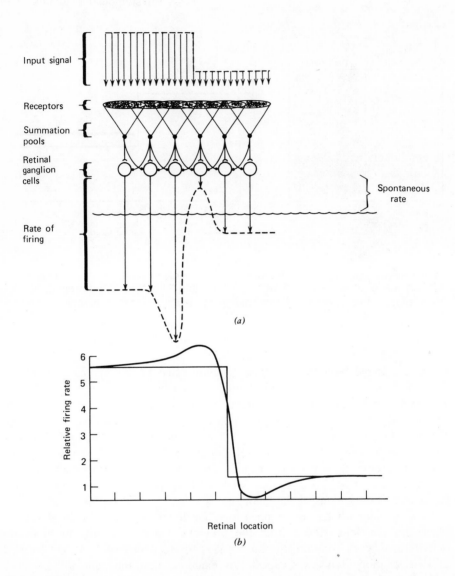

Input signal

Receptors

Summation pools

Retinal ganglion cells

Spontaneous rate

Rate of firing

(a)

Relative firing rate

6

5

4

3

2

1

Retinal location

(b)

Figure 2.6
(a) A schematic of the sorts of neural responses expected at the level of the retinal ganglion cell to the split field illustrated in Figure 2.5. The expected variation in rate of firing is illustrated by the length of the arrows pointing from the retinal ganglion cell. *(b)* An idealized rate of responding as a function of retinal location superimposed on the initial intensity plot.

Figure 2.7 shows the results reported by Springer for this experimental situation. The figure gives threshold values for the spot of light as a function of retinal location. It is clear that our expectations are fulfilled. The threshold (our measure of the difficulty of seeing the spot) rises on the bright half of the field as it approaches the edge of the field and it decreases in the dark band as it approaches the edge. Thus, Springer's experiment would tend to indicate that we *can,* through careful analysis, observe the detailed effects of the neural interactions observed by the neurophysiologists. As we shall see in our discussion below, the neural system not only uses this excitatory-inhibitory tension to "sharpen" edges and other intensity discontinuities, but it makes general use of this scheme in selectively responding to "important" aspects of the stimulus configuration.

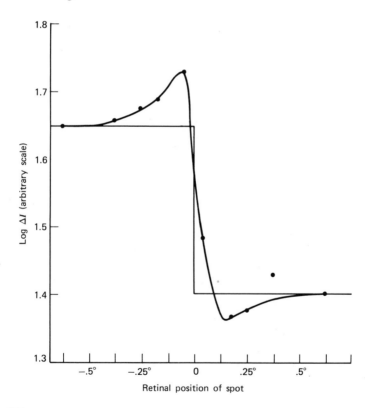

Figure 2.7
Observed values of log Δ*I* as a function of retinal position. (Data from Springer 1973.)

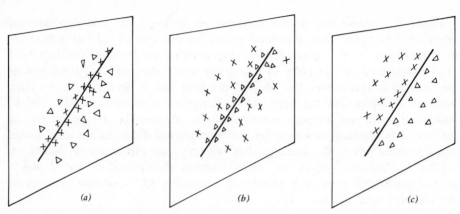

Figure 2.8
Arrangements of cortical receptive fields. *(a)* Receptive field that is maximally sensitive to a white line on a dark background. *(b)* Receptive field that is maximally sensitive to a black line on a white background. *(c)* Receptive field that is maximally sensitive to an edge. In all figures, X denotes areas giving excitatory responses ("on" responses); △ denotes areas giving inhibitory responses ("off" responses). In the figure, all lines are oriented at 45°, but each arrangement occurs in all orientations. (Data replotted from Hubel and Wiesel, 1962.)

The output of the retinal ganglion cells feeds into the lateral geniculate body. Since the receptive fields of lateral geniculate cells mirror very closely those of the ganglion cells, they are assumed to have little integrative importance in pattern processing beyond that of the retinal ganglion cell.

The cells in the visual cortex, the site of the next stage of processing, show a great many types and degrees of complexity of receptive fields. Figure 2.8 shows three of the several different arrangements of cortical receptive fields that Hubel and Wiesel (1962) discovered in the cat. A receptive field of the type shown in Figure 2.8*a* would respond maximally to a small slit of light arranged at a 45° angle on the retina. The one in Figure 2.8*b* responds maximally to a black bar on a light background oriented at 45°. Finally, Figure 2.8*c* shows a receptive field which responds maximally to an edge of light against a dark background oriented, again, at 45°. Although all of the configurations shown here require a 45° orientation to give maximal responses, fields responsive to vertical, horizontal, and other orientations were found as well.

In addition to these various configurations, Hubel and Wiesel were able to classify the receptive fields as simple or complex. Fields were classified as simple when "(1) they were subdivided into distinct excitatory and inhibitory regions; (2) there was summation within the separate excitatory and inhibitory parts; (3) there was antagonism between excitatory and inhibitory regions; and (4) it was possible to predict responses to stationary or moving spots of various shapes from a map of the excitatory and inhibitory areas" (Hubel & Wiesel, 1962). Complex cells, however, have no simple retinal projections. They do not respond well to small dots of light regardless of where they are flashed on the retina.

Instead, a particular complex cortical cell might be found to respond maximally to a slit of light of an appropriate orientation anywhere in an area covering as much as 5 to 10° on the retina. Whereas simple cortical cells are line and orientation detectors at a particular point on the retina, complex cortical cells are general line or orientation detectors which respond to the same stimulus wherever it may occur over a large area. Therefore, even though small eye movements radically change the behavior of simple cortical cells, the behavior of a complex cell is virtually unaffected.

Hubel and Wiesel noticed that these complex cortical cells behaved as if they had input from only simple cells. Figure 2.9 illustrates a set of connections which would lead to a complex cell which would detect narrow horizontal slits of light over a region of the retina. In this diagram "on-center" retinal ganglion cells integrate activity over a small region of the retina, giving maximal response to small patches of light striking the center of their receptive fields. A row of such cells then feeds into a simple cortical line detector which gives its maximum response when the sum of all of the ganglion cells feeding into it is at a maximum. This will occur when the slit of light is directly superimposed on the row. Finally, all of the simple cortical cells responding to horizontal lines feed into a complex horizontal line detector which responds to a horizontal line anywhere on the surface of that area of the retina. Although there is no evidence against this account of simple cells, it now seems that Hubel and Wiesel's hypothesis about complex cells is inaccurate. Recent physiological measures have indicated that the latency of responses of the complex cell is no more than that for the simple cell—thus indicating that complex cells are as directly related to the retina as are simple cells. Figure 2.9b indicates the change required in our wiring diagram to conform with this finding.

Cells of the type they have found are very suggestive. They show us how simple attributes of patterns can be abstracted very early in the stimulus processing and thus show us the nature of some of the information that the system has to work with at higher levels in pattern recognition.

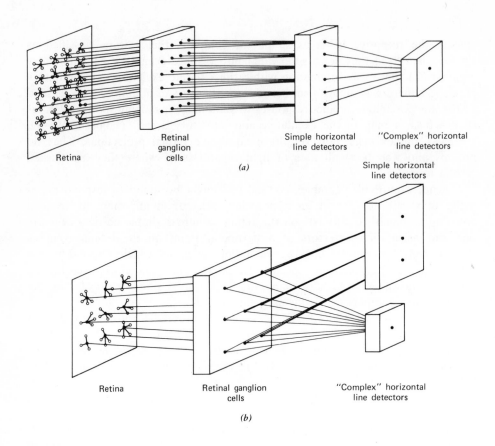

Figure 2.9
Schematic diagram showing possible wiring schema for explaining the organizatino of cortical receptive fields. *(a)* Small areas of the retina map on to single retinal ganglion cells, and a number of these cells arranged in a horizontal row, for example, map on to single "simple" cortical cells. The figure shows four such cells each of which respond maximally when stimulated by a horizontal line on the retina. Complex line detectors can be generated by connecting several simple detectors. *(b)* A possible alternate organization consistent with observations that complex and simple cells respond equally quickly to presented lines. In this example, complex line detectors are not generated by connecting simple detectors but, instead, depend directly on imputs from the retinal ganglion cells.

ARTIFICIAL SYSTEMS

Another source of information about pattern recognition systems comes from those who have tried to build mechanical devices to recognize patterns. Many of the basic ideas which now permeate the field were set out very early in the pioneering work of Oliver Selfridge. His model, called Pandemonium, is really a complex computer program which has been applied to the recognition of hand-sent Morse code (Selfridge, 1959) and to the recognition of handwritten letters (Selfridge & Neisser, 1960). Its primary value to psychology has not been in its successes or failures as an operating pattern recognizer, but as it offers an analogy to human pattern recognition processes.

The structure of the model is shown in Figure 2.10. The model is arranged hierarchically with the output at each higher level dependent on that of the

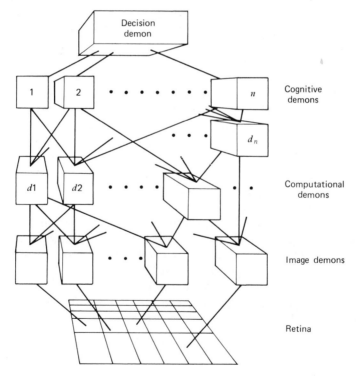

Figure 2.10
Parallel processing in Selfridge's (1959) Pandemonium program. (Redrawn from Selfridge, 1959.)

lower levels. Each possible pattern (for example, each letter of the alphabet) is represented by a so-called cognitive demon. Each demon is constantly looking for evidence that it is present in the data which are presented to Pandemonium. This evidence is obtained from computational demons who themselves are searching for evidence that they are present in the data. This evidence may be obtained directly from the image demons or, in turn, from still more primitive computational demons. Each time any demon, cognitive or computational, finds evidence that it is indeed present in the image, it gives a shout. The more evidence it finds, the louder it shouts. The decision demon merely sits above it all and listens to the shouts of the cognitive demons. When it is time to make a decision, the decision demon merely chooses the name corresponding to the demon that is shouting the loudest and applies that name to the pattern. All demons at a given level of the hierarchy work independently (in parallel) in that the shouts of a demon's neighbors have no effect at all on the shouts of the demon itself. A particular demon's shouts depend only on the outputs of the demons on the lower levels of the hierarchy.

The computational demons correspond to what are elsewhere called analyzers (Sutherland, 1959) or critical feature detectors. These demons search for important features of the stimulus configuration. The features may be as simple as vertical or horizontal line segments or as complex as closed perimeters, parallel lines and even more global stimulus characteristics.

Initially, a scheme like this in which analysis at each level is independent of all of the other activity at that level appears very inefficient. It would certainly seem that a careful, systematic search in which each computation depended on the outcomes of all previous computations would be more effective. In practice, however, this does not seem to be true. The noise inherent in the stimulus and its neural representation would frequently lead to wrong decisions being taken. As a rule of thumb, no possibility should be absolutely eliminated at any level of analysis prior to the final decision. A parallel scheme, of the sort proposed by Selfridge, has that characteristic. There is another consideration that leads to a preference, in machines at least, for parallel as opposed to a serial or sequential computation at each level, and that is time. If characteristics were found and analyzed serially, the time needed to reach a decision would often be longer, even though it might take fewer computations. This is particularly true when the data are somewhat noisy and wrong branches are sometimes taken.

The primary alternative to a feature extraction model of the kind Selfridge proposed is the so-called template matching model. According to this view, pattern recognition is accomplished by goodness of fit between the retinal image and a memorial prototype of the object. The pattern corresponding to the template that best matches the image is chosen as the correct perception. This view has the obvious problem that characters of different sizes or ones at slightly different orientations would frequently give very bad fits to even the appropriate template (Figure 2.11a). This problem can be overcome by various size and rotational normalizations before the template match is made. The primary disadvantage of such a model, as opposed to a feature analysis technique, is that small but critical aspects of characters are given no more weight in the decision than are deviations of a nonessential nature. Consider, for example, the drawings in Figure 2.11b. Suppose the A on the left is the template and the R on the right or the As below were presented. A template model judging which was the A would choose the R because it has more overlap with the template than the actual As of different fonts. To human observers, however, the distinction is clear. The crossbar and the sloping sides designate an A, not an R, no matter what the degree of overlap.

From these considerations, many investigators have been led to accept the view that pattern recognition involves a process of extracting abstract features (such as contours, lines, angles, etc.) from the retinal image and comparing these abstracted qualities with those sets of qualities that are known to characterize the items that the observer expects.

Inherent in tthe information processing point of view is the notion that everything takes time. There have been many studies whose purpose has been to study the temporal characteristics of the feature extraction and comparison process. We turn now to a discussion of these findings.

TEMPORAL PROCESSES—THE ICON

Thus far we have only incidentally considered the temporal characteristics of sensory processing and character recognition. There are well known aftereffects of one visual stimulus on the next as a function of the delay between the two stimulus presentations. Sometimes there is interference: the presentation of the second stimulus interferes with the perception of the first (backward masking), or the perception of the second is interfered with by the earlier presentation of the first (forward masking; see Raab, 1963). The mechanism of these temporal interactions is in some dispute. In some cases interference seems to result from simple retinal integration over time; in other cases it appears to result from more central interactions. However, one thing is clear; processing doesn't stop as soon as the physical stimulation is turned off. There appears to be a more or less veridical image, called the icon by Neisser (1967), which persists

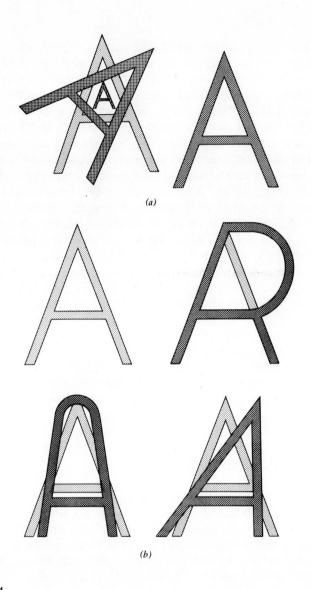

(a)

(b)

Figure 2.11
(a) Size and orientation normalizations must be made before a template matching procedure can succeed. *(b)* An incorrect match may occur even when the target letter has been converted to standard form. Here *R* matches the *A* template more than do samples of correct letter. (From Selfridge and Neisser, 1963.)

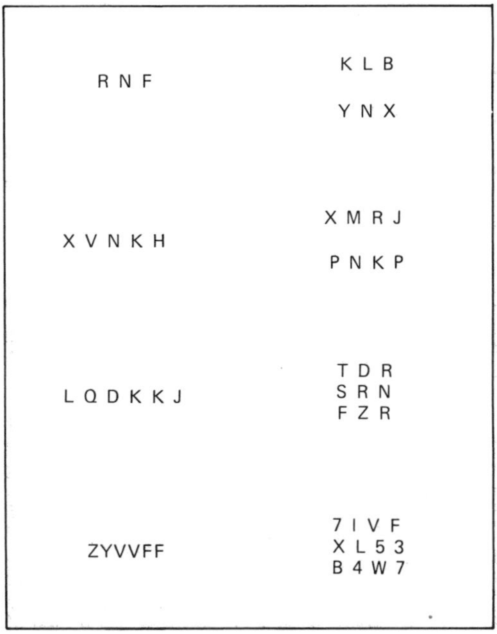

Typical stimulus materials. Column 1: 3, 5, 6, 6—massed.
Column 2: 3/3, 4/4, 3/3/3, 4/4/4 L and N.

Figure 2.12
Examples of stimulus materials used by Sperling (1960).

for some period of time after the stimulus is turned off and from which features can be extracted just as from the physical stimulus. In fact, subjects sometimes have difficulty determining exactly when the physical stimulus is turned off (Sperling, 1963).

Sperling (1960) has carried out a particularly nice set of experiments which illustrate some of the temporal characteristics of the icon as it functions in letter recognition. In these experiments subjects were given 50-msec views (much too short for voluntary eye movements to occur) of a matrix of letters (some examples are shown in Figure 2.12). Then, sometime either just before or just after the offset of the physical stimulus, the subjects were cued by a tone to report one of the three rows. If a high tone was played they were to report the top row, if a medium tone was presented they were to report the middle row, and if a low tone was presented they were to report the bottom row. Figure 2.13 shows the percentage correctly recognized as a function of delay of the cue tone in one condition for Sperling's five subjects. The clear decline in

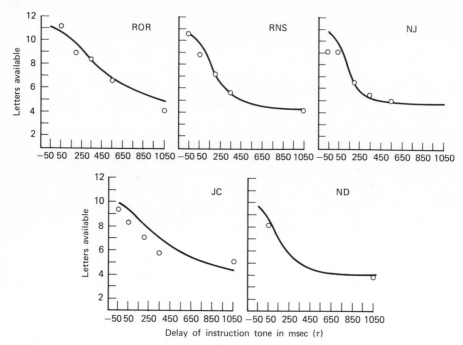

Figure 2.13
Number of letters available as a function of delay of cue tone. (From Rumelhart, 1970.)

probability of correct recognition over about a second reflects the decay of information in the icon. The closer the cue is to the actual stimulus presentation, the more it is as if the cue were given while the stimulus actually remained on the retina. Essentially similar results have been obtained by Averbach and Coriell (1961) and by Keele and Chase (1967).

Another source of evidence on the transitory iconic store comes from an experiment by Eriksen and Collins (1967). Examples of the kinds of materials used in their experiment are shown in Figure 2.14. The upper two dot patterns in the figure represent two halves of the stimulus. When these two halves are superimposed as shown in the lower dot pattern the nonsense syllable VOH can be read. In their experiment, Eriksen and Collins presented the two dot patterns separated in time so that the only way the two patterns could be superimposed was to bring them together in the form of some sort of iconic memory store. They then varied the interval between the presentation of the two halves from 0 to 500 msec. The results are shown in Figure 2.15. The

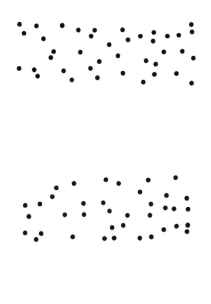

Figure 2.14
The upper two dot patterns, when superimposed, result in the bottom stimulus pattern in which the nonesense syllable VOH can be read. (From Erickson and Collins, 1967.)

temporal decay evident in these graphs mirrors very closely the decay found by Sperling (1960) in his partial report study. Essentially similar results have been found by Fraisse (1966). Apparently a similar temporary sensory store exists in the auditory domain. This store, called by Crowder and Morton (1969) the precategorical acoustic store (PAS), and by Neisser (1967) echoic memory, can be shown to behave much like the iconic store we have been discussing. In one experiment Darwin, Turvey, and Crowder (1972) carried out an auditory analog to Sperling's partial report experiments. The general design of their experiment was to present simultaneously a different list of items from each of three different spatial locations (right, left, and middle). The subjects were then required either to report all of the items in their correct spatial location (the whole report procedure) or to report one set of three items (the partial report condition). The particular location from which items were to be recalled on any trial was indicated by a visual cue. The visual cue was delayed either zero, 1, 2, or 4 sec after the end of the stimulus presentation.

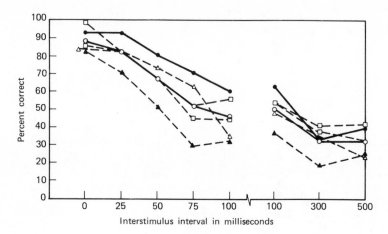

Figure 2.15
Accuracy of nonsense syllable perception as a function of interstimulus interval between corresponding stimulus halves (the open circle function represents the average, while the other functions are for individual subjects). (From Erickson and Collins, 1967.)

Figure 2.16 illustrates the procedure whereby Darwin et al. were able to produce impressions of three different spatial locations. One list of three items was presented to the left ear (e.g., Q,6,3). One list of three items was presented to the right ear (e.g., 9,R,5). The third list (the middle list) was presented to both ears (e.g., 2,B,F). This results in the impression that the third list is localized in the middle of the head.

From what we know about the visual icon and Sperling's experiments, we can predict pretty well the results of this experiment. If we present the visual cue immediately the subject will be able to respond with most of the items in the cued list. If we delay the visual cue sufficiently the subject will be able to respond with no more items from that list than in the whole report procedure. The results are illustrated in Figure 2.17. The results manifest two variables which affect response probability. One of the variables, delay of the cue, behaves just as we have expected. The number of items reported from a cued list drops monotonically with the delay of the visual indicator. It appears to level off at the whole report level as we would expect. (The inset in the figure shows the average number of items available.) However, there is one effect here not apparent in the visual experiment. Namely, the last item of a list is significantly better recalled than the first two items of the list. This is presumably due to a sort of masking that results from the necessarily sequential

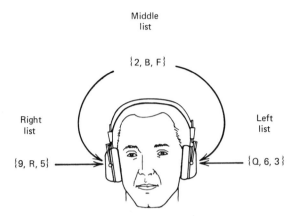

Figure 2.16
Procedure whereby Darwin et al. were able to produce impressions of three different spatial locations. One list of items was presented to the left ear. One list of items was presented to the right ear. And a third list was presented to both ears resulting in the impression that the third list is localized in the middle of the head.

nature of the list presentations. Each successive item "writes over" the item preceding it in the list, thus reducing performance on the earlier items. In retrospect, this is exactly the result we would expect from a sequential rather than a parallel presentation. Thus, it would appear that there is, in fact, an auditory sensory buffer strictly analogous to the iconic store discussed above. Perhaps the only significant difference is that the decay rate of the echoic store seems to be somewhat slower than for the icon (about 4 sec in the Darwin et al. experiment as opposed to about 1 sec for Sperling's experiments).

To summarize the view of visual pattern recognition we have developed thus far, we begin with the photon fluctuation in time and space as emitted or reflected from the physical stimulus onto the cornea of the eye. Some of these photons make their way through the ocular medium to the retinal receptors themselves. Those that are absorbed by receptors initiate a chemical reaction ending in a spike in the nerve connecting the receptors to the retinal ganglion cells. Each such cell collects impulses from a relatively large number of receptors. Some of these impulses cause the cell to fire, others inhibit its firing. These patterns of stimulation are relayed through the lateral geniculate body to the visual cortex. It is presumably the function of these cells to begin the process of abstraction of characteristics of the patterns of firing at lower levels. These features which are abstracted from the visual image are then to be matched

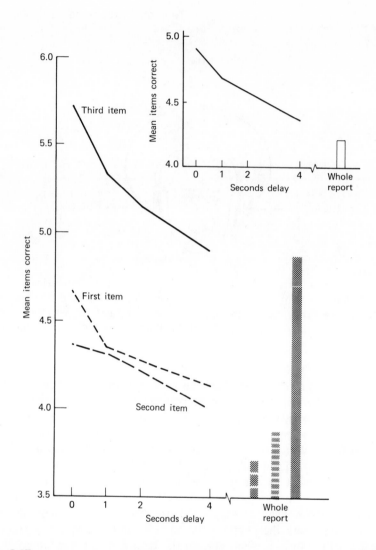

Figure 2.17
Partial report accuracy as a function of delay in the visual cue. The three curves correspond to the temporal order of the three items in the channel. The bars on the right are the whole reports made with no indicator. The inset is the average of the three curves together with the average report. (Darwin et al.)

against memorial representations of the possible patterns, thus finally eliciting a name to be applied to the stimulus pattern, and making contact with stored information pertaining to the item.

The process of auditory pattern recognition follows a similar course. In this case we begin with air molecules pushing against the tympanic membrane. Motions in the membrane are eventually transformed into neural responses in the auditory nerve. This nerve carries the signal to higher levels where presumably features analogous to those of the visual system are abstracted. These acoustic features then serve as input to be matched against memorial acoustic representations.

In either system this all takes time. For some milliseconds after the physical stimulation is lifted from the cornea, or the tympanic membrane, further processing and feature extraction continues. Finally, the sensory trace of the stimulus fades or is supplanted by another. That information extracted from the trace before it fades may be stored in memory. The rest is lost.

INFORMATION ACCRUAL

We may think of information as being gathered in time. The longer one is allowed to process the stimulus the more information one will gather about it and the more accurate one will be in identifying it. Results showing this effect are rather common; two examples will be discussed here.

The most straightforward means of studying this question is to vary systematically the duration of a tachistoscopic stimulus exposure of the type used by Sperling (1960) and see if the number of letters correctly recognized increases with duration. The problem is complicated slightly by the existence of the visual icon from which information can be obtained after the offset of the stimulus. This problem can be overcome by exposing a pattern of visual "noise" at the offset of the stimulus exposure. This "noise" has the effect of overwriting the image in the icon and thus rendering it nearly unusable following stimulus offset. Sperling (1963) has run such an experiment. Figure 2.18 shows examples of his stimulus materials for the two conditions he had in the experiment. In one condition the pre-exposure field is dark, in the other it is "noise." In either case, the post-exposure field contains noise. Figure 2.19 shows the mean number of letters reported as a function of the duration, numbers of letters in the display, and pre-exposure field. The apparent delay before the onset of processing in the prenoise condition is interpreted as the time required to clear the icon of extraneous noise and begin processing the letters themselves. Sperling took these data to indicate that alphabetic characters can be processed at

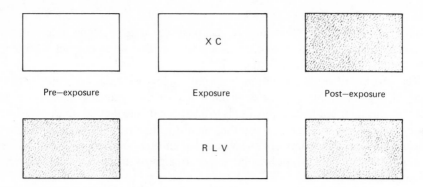

Figure 2.18
Two kinds of stimulus presentations used by Sperling, 1963. The sequence of stimuli on a trial is indicated from left to right.

a rate of about 10 msec per letter. Neisser (1967) has argued that this estimate is in error because it assumes that the noise completely halts processing and that the true estimate is somewhat higher. In any case, these results unequivocally show a rapid and measurable increase in information obtained as a function of processing time.

Another line of evidence on the information accrual process in pattern recognition comes from the so-called "speed-accuracy" tradeoff observed in experiments measuring reaction time. As subjects are paid more and more to respond quickly in these experiments, their accuracy of response declines. The interpretation of this result from an information accrual model is that when forced to respond quickly, people are able to respond on less than a complete analysis of the information and therefore respond more quickly but less accurately. There is, of course, at least one other interpretation of this kind of result. It is possible that people do not really have access to information until the pattern is completely processed and have available to them only two strategies: (1) they may elect to process the figure fully or (2) they may elect not to process it at all. When they process it fully they are very accurate; when they do not process it they respond just to the onset of anything and have merely chance performance on the discrimination task.

If responses in these experiments were actually determined by a combination of these two strategies, and if the percentage of times the subjects elected to make a "fast guess" increased as more emphasis was placed on a speed response, the speed-accuracy tradeoff would be observed, but for the wrong reasons. It would not reflect the temporal course of processing. In a very care-

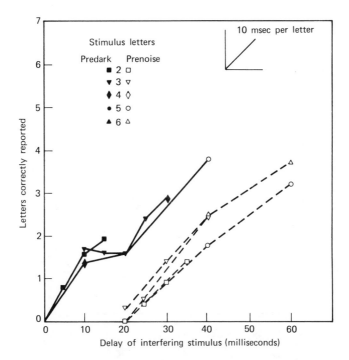

Figure 2.19
The number of letters correctly reported as a function of the delay between the
onset of the lettered stimulus and an interfering "noise" stimulus. The number of
stimulus letters was also varied. The pre-exposure field was either dark or "noise."
(From Sperling, 1963.)

fully done study, Swensson and Edwards (1971), while looking for a tradeoff
in the sense of partial processing, found a tradeoff of the second kind. Further
investigation by Swensson (1972) showed in a particularly elegant way the
source of their difficulty.

In order to obtain good control over the subjects' strategies in this situation,
Swensson employed high monetary payoffs and penalties (as was done earlier
in the Swensson & Edwards study). For example, subjects were charged for
observation time at a rate of $1.38 per sec, were charged $1.25 for each
anticipation response (i.e., a response that was executed before the figure to
be discriminated was presented), and, in some conditions, could win or lose
as much as $10.00 for a single correct or wrong response. Under these condi-
tions it is rather easy to see the accuracy and speed strategies when they are.

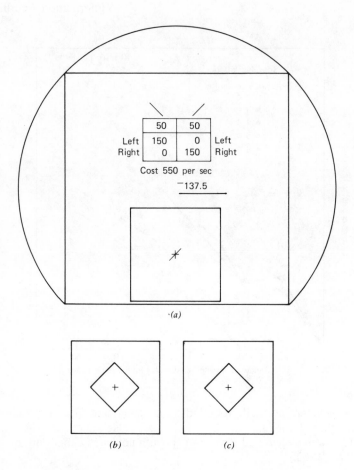

Left
Right

	50	50	
Left	150	0	Left
Right	0	150	Right

Cost 550 per sec

⁻137.5

·(a)

(b)   (c)

Figure 2.20
The stimulus display used in the experiments of Swensson (1972). *(a)* The stimulus display as it appeared in one of the experiments midway through the feedback sequence after a correct response with reaction time of 250-msec (cost = 137.5). The matrix in the upper half of the screen illustrates the values paid for correct responses to the right or to the left. *(b)* and *(c)* A pair of stimuli used in one of the experiments. Part *(b)* required a left-finger response, and part *(c)* required a response with the right finger. (From Swensson, 1972.)

applied. The stimulus materials and display are shown in Figure 2.20. The task in this experiment was to make a left-hand response if the rectangle displayed in the square was oriented to the left and to make a right-hand response if it was oriented to the right. The difficulty of the task was manipulated by varying the length to width ratio of the rectangle. Rectangles were chosen so that with unlimited time subjects could make a correct response about 98% of the time.

Figure 2.21 shows the performance for six subjects who were tested in this experiment. The data points were segregated as to whether or not the reaction time was under 250 msec. When it was, subjects responded at a chance level; when it was over 250 msec, subjects were about as accurate as they could ever be. These data clearly support the fast-guess model of the speed-accuracy tradeoff. That is, when subjects were paid enough for accuracy, they employed the accuracy strategy and responded as accurately as they could. When cost for time exceeded the value of making a perfectly accurate response, they responded very quickly but were wrong half the time. Under these conditions, information accrual appears to be all or none. However, when the payoff structure was modified only slightly the problem became apparent.

In a second experiment, subjects were charged just as before but were given a "free" 250 msec before the clock started and began charging them at a rate of $1.38 per sec. This made all of the difference. Under these conditions the speed-accuracy tradeoff was easily obtained. Figure 2.22 shows the curve relating the error rate to the reaction times. The interpretation given to these results is that information is not accrued linearly with time. When subjects are charged linearly for time starting from time zero, it is never advantageous to partially process the figure. There is apparently a dead time of some 200 msec before information relevant to the discrimination in this task could be collected. That, with a linear charge for time from time zero, always led the subject to choose one of the complete strategies. When subjects were given some "free time," however, a "true" speed-accuracy tradeoff occurred.

A MODEL

Rumelhart (1970) has suggested a quantitative model with explicit assumptions about the time course of the feature extraction or information accrual process. A schematic diagram of the events which are assumed to occur is given in Figure 2.23. At time zero, the target stimulus is illuminated; it remains so until time T, when the illumination is turned off and the stimulus is no longer visible. Shortly after the onset of the illumination the image of the figure registers in a transitory iconic store. The clarity of the image soon reaches a maximum at which it remains until the illumination is turned off.

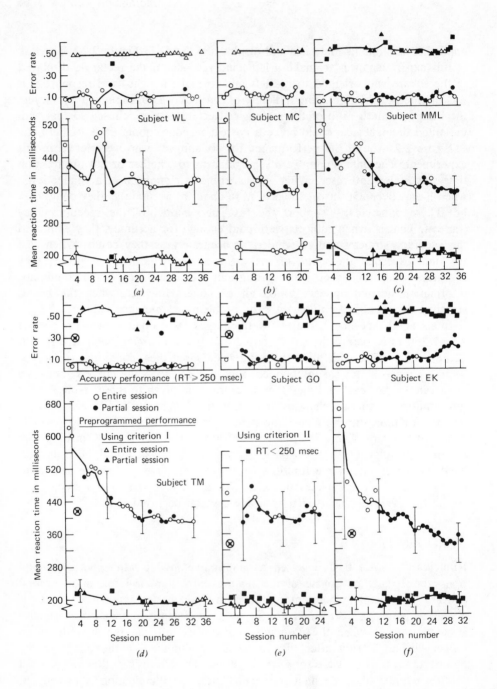

66

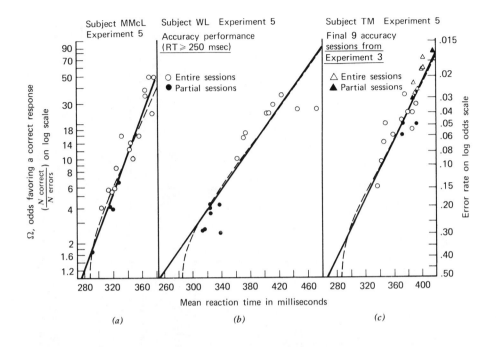

Figure 2.22
Speed accuracy operating characteristic functions for each of the three subjects in this experiment. These plot the ratio of the number of correct responses to the number of errors on a log scale as a function of mean reaction time for each subject's reactions greater than or equal to 250-msec. Open points represent conditions with reaction time greater than or equal to 250-msec on all 350 trials. Filled points represent conditions in which some preprogramming occurred. (From Swensson, 1972.)

Figure 2.21
Mean reaction time (lower panels) and error rates (upper panels) for accuracy (reaction time greater or equal to 250-msec) and preprogram strategy performance of six subjects in one experiment. Open and filled circles differentiate entire sessions under the same strategy from mixed sessions, in which the subject used both strategies. Triangular points represent preprogram trials identified by one procedure and solid square points represent all trials faster than 250-msec. Solid lines indicate moving averages over adjacent sessions, and vertical lines indicate reaction time variability; the single performance indicated by a circled asterisk for three subjects does not separate easily into two strategies. (From Swensson, 1972.)

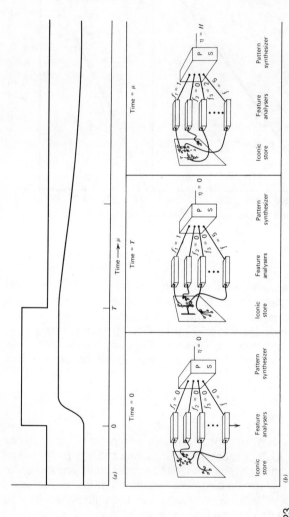

Figure 2.23

(a) The hypothetical relationship between the contrast of the figure on a screen and the clarity of the iconic image as a function of time. Note that the clarity of the image rises and falls more slowly than the contrast of the figure. (b) A schematic illustration of the feature extraction and pattern synthesis process. (1) The state of the feature analyzers and pattern synthesizer at times 0, that is, just as the figure is illuminated on the screen. Notice that no image of the figure is visible in the iconic store; thus far, the feature analyzers have found no features (i.e., f_1 through f_n all equal 0) and the pattern synthesizer has no output. (2) The state of the iconic store, feature analyzers, and pattern synthesizer at time T just as the figure is turned off. Note that there is still a clear image of the figure in the iconic store and some of the feature analyzers have values, but the pattern synthesizer has not yet output the name of the object. (3) The iconic store feature analyzers and pattern synthesizer at some time after the offset of the stimulus. Note that the figure is still faintly visible in the iconic store, more features have been discovered, and the pattern synthesizer has output the name, H, as a plausible correspondence to the pattern.

At that time, the clarity of the image decays until it finally fades away. During the entire time, a large number of feature analyzers are searching the image looking for critical features of the stimulus. The rate at which they find such features depends on the clarity of the image. As the clarity of the image decays, the rate of feature analysis also slows down. It is assumed that the time required for any one of the feature analyzers to find the feature for which it is searching is a function of the momentary clarity of the image. The results of these feature analyzers feed into a pattern synthesizer that compares the obtained feature list with those in memory. When enough features are found so that the pattern synthesizer has reasonable confidence as to what object the image represents, it outputs an abstract characterization of the object. This abstract representation is assumed to include such things as the *name* of the object as well as its *canonical* (standard) sensory characteristics.

One particularly powerful experimental way to observe the temporal properties of the character recognition process is to make use of the masking paradigm. The model described above has been applied to data from experiments of this type. Thompson (1966) has studied a situation in which a target consisting of a single letter was masked by a homogeneous flash of light. In his study, Thompson presented one of three letters followed, after delays of 0, 5, 10, 25, 50, or 75 msec, by a homogeneous 100-msec flash of 0.039, 0.067, 0.102 or 0.200 footlamberts (ft-L). To apply the model, we simply assure that the flash has the effect of degrading the information in the iconic store, thus reducing the clarity of the information and hence the rate at which features can be discovered. Figure 2.24 shows the predicted and obtained percentage of correct recognitions as a function of delay of flash in milliseconds and brightness of the mask. The estimated parameters indicated that it required about two features for recognition, that features were discovered at a rate of about one every 12 msec, that the decay constant of iconic store is about 50 msec, and that it had a rise time of about 16 msec.

The model not only suggests that information should be accrued over time, but it also suggests that the unit of information is something we call a critical feature. If we are to take the idea of a feature extraction model seriously, we must have some idea of what a feature might be like. Thus far, our best view of what features might be like comes from the physiological evidence. As described earlier in this chapter, Hubel and Wiesel (1962) have suggested that oriented line segments may be good candidates for underlying features. To test the viability of this view, Rumelhart (1971) extended the model described above with the explicit assumption that underlying features correspond to oriented line segments. The model was then used to predict the nature of the confusions among briefly exposed alphabetic characters. Figure 2.25 illustrates

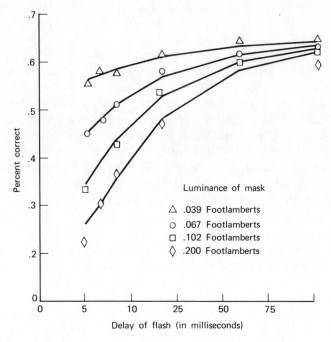

Figure 2.24
Percent correct identifications as a function of delay of a homogeneous mask.
(Figure from Rumelhart, 1970; data from Thompson, 1966.)

the six characters used in the experiment along with an analysis of these characters into a set of seven underlying features.

According to the model, on a brief presentation of one of these characters the subject is able to discover some subset of the features actually available from that stimulus. If that subset is sufficient to uniquely determine which character had been presented (for example, features f_5 and f_7 uniquely determine a B in this font), then the subject responds correctly. Otherwise, the set of observed features is used to eliminate those responses which could not have given rise to the observed features (for example, feature f_5 eliminates all possibilities except B and D), and the subject then guesses from the remaining candidates.

Figure 2.26 illustrates the results from one of the subjects. The close match between the "theory" and the "data" indicates that the assumption that features are line segments is sufficient to account for the kinds of confusions that occur

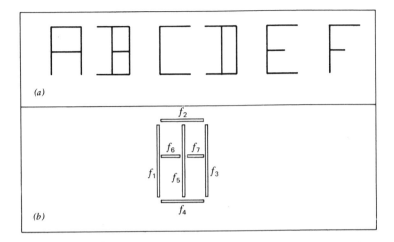

Figure 2.25
Panel *(a)* shows the letters *A* to *F* in the font used by Rumelhart, 1971. Panel *(b)* indicates that these characters can be constructed from seven straight-line segments. The segments, called functional features, are labeled F_1 to F_7.

in identifying these sorts of characters. Of course, it is clear that in more complex forms which include curving lines, additional kinds of features must be postulated. Nevertheless, to a first approximation it appears that the sorts of analyzers for which we found physiological evidence could easily serve as a basis for the recognition of simple geometric patterns.

Now consider how, within the context of the current model, we might accept or reject the hypothesis that a character we are looking at is some particular target character. Recall that the only information we get is a set of features discovered by some feature analyzers. It should be clear that it would take less time to reject the hypothesis than to accept it. To reject it we need only one disconfirming feature—to accept it we must find an entire configuration of features that are unique to the target letter in question. This reasoning also leads to the expectation that it will take longer to reject a character containing many features in common with the target than one with few or no features in common. Neisser and his colleagues (Neisser, 1963; Neisser & Beller, 1965; Neisser & Lazar, 1964) have developed techniques for measuring the time required to accept or reject the hypothesis that a particular character is or is not some specified target.

These experiments involve the search through a list of characters for some specified target character. The subject is shown a list of the sort illustrated in

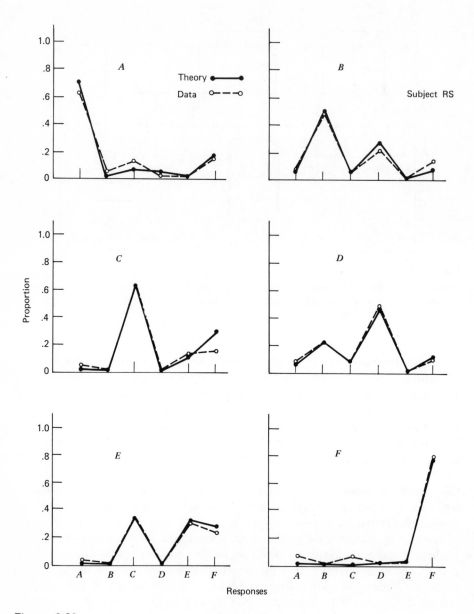

Figure 2.26
The predicted and observed proportions of responses made to each of the six stimuli by subject R. S.

a	*b*	*c*
ZVMLBQ	ODUGQR	IVMXEW
HSQJMF	QCDUGO	EWVMIX
ZTJVQR	CQOGRD	EXWMVI
RDQTFM	QUGCDR	IXEMWV
TQVRSX	URDGQO	VXWEMI
MSVRQX	GRUQDO	MXVEWI
ZHQBTL	DUZGRO	XVWMEI
ZJTQXL	UCGROD	MWXVIE
LHQVXM	DQRCGU	VIMEXW
FVQHMS	QDOCGU	EXVWIM
MTSDQL	CGUROQ	VWMIEX
TZDFQB	OCDURQ	VMWIEX
QLHBMZ	UOCGQD	XVWMEI
QMXBJD	RGQCOU	WXVEMI
RVZHSQ	GRUDQO	XMEWIV
STFMQZ	GODUCQ	MXIVEW
RVXSQM	QCURDO	VEWMIX
MQBJFT	DUCOQG	EMVXWI
MVZXLQ	CGRDQU	IVWMEX
RTBXQH	UDRCOQ	IEVMWX
BLQSZX	GQCORU	WVZMXE
QSVFDJ	GOQUCD	XEMIWV
FLDVZT	GDQUOC	WXIMEV
BQHMDX	URDCGO	EMWIVX
BMFDQH	GODRQC	IVEMXW

Figure 2.27

Figure 2.27. He is then asked to scan the list for the presence or absence of a target character on each line of the list. He presses a button as soon as he finds a line meeting the specifications. The time is measured from when he begins to scan the list until he presses the button. The time needed to process each line of the list is estimated by dividing the total time required by the number of lines a subject must scan to reach the target. The results are just as we would expect. When searching lists like list *a* for the line which does not contain a Q, the subject is slow. This is expected since he must in fact confirm that each of the lines before the critical line in fact contains a *Q*. Subjects are much faster searching for a letter containing only straight line segments (such as Z) against a background of letters containing primarily curved features (such as list *b*). On the other hand, it is much harder to find a Z against a background of similar characters as in list *c*. The estimated times

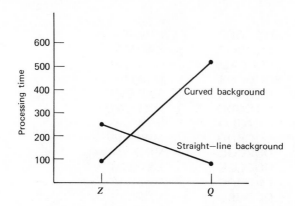

Figure 2.28
Processing time per letter for Z and Q against backgrounds of characters made up of primarily curved and primarily straight-line noise elements. (Data from Neisser and Bellar, 1965.)

for processing each line when searching for either a Z or a Q against either a curved- or straight-line background is given in Figure 2.28.

Let us summarize the model we have developed thus far. When a complex stimulus pattern is presented to the eye of the human, it causes a pattern of firing in the retinal receptors. Feature extraction devices begin abstracting characteristics, such as lines, edges, etc., from the visual image. These features then feed into a pattern synthesizer which compares the extracted features to memory representations, and a pattern is synthesized which is then sent on for further processing.

The results discussed above suggest that certain decisions can occur in the pattern synthesizer, prior to the level of naming. For example, we can apparently reject a character as being a target faster than we can identify it as a target. Other sorts of decisions require a fully synthesized pattern. Posner and his colleagues (Posner, 1969; Posner, Boies, Eichelman, & Taylor, 1969; Posner & Keele, 1967; Posner & Mitchell, 1967) have carried out a series of experiments to study the nature of the pattern synthesizer, what decisions can be made at that level of analysis and which must wait until after synthesis is complete.

The basic procedure for these experiments is illustrated in Figure 2.29. First a letter (A in the example) is displayed for about 100 msec (plenty of time to be recognized). Then, following a variable delay a second letter is

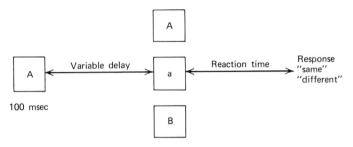

Figure 2.29
Schematic of experimental procedure employed by Posner et al. *A* is presented for 100-msec. Then, following a variable delay, a second letter is presented. The second letter may be either physically identical to the first, may have the same name but be physically different, or have a different name than the first. Subjects are instructed to respond "same" whenever the two letters have the same name, and to respond "different" otherwise.

presented. The second letter may be either physically identical to the first (AA); physically different but have the same name (Aa); or have a different name than the first (AB). The subjects are instructed to respond "same" whenever the two letters have the same name and to respond different otherwise. The basic results for "same" responses are given in Figure 2.30. The differences in reaction times for physically identical and the same-name pairs are plotted as a function of the delay interval. When the intervening interval is zero we find that physical identity can be judged a full 100 msec faster than name identity. This would seem to indicate that physical identity can be judged earlier in the system than name identity—perhaps at the level of the pattern synthesizer. The judgment of name identity, on the other hand, clearly requires that the stimulus be processed to the level of the name before a decision can be made. When the delay is increased to 1 sec, we find that the time for physical matches has increased to within about 30 msec of the name matches. It would thus appear that subjects are increasingly making both judgments at the name level.

Posner has employed this general technique to measure the time required to determine whether two letters are vowels or consonants, whether two words are in the same category, etc. Furthermore, he has compared match times for "real" and "imagined" stimuli. The model we are developing is not yet sophisticated enough to encompass all of these effects. We will return to Posner's experiments later. First we must consider the effects of context on pattern recognition.

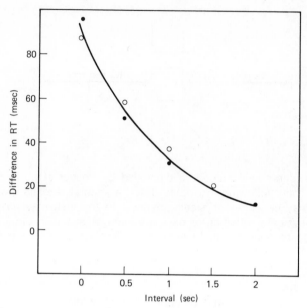

Figure 2.30
The difference in reaction times between physically identical and same name responses as a function of the variable delay interval. (Data from Posner and Mitchel, 1967.)

CONTEXTUAL EFFECTS

In our discussion up to now we have assumed that there was a small set of possibilities which were known to the subject and that there was enough information "contained in the stimulus" to unambiguously identify the stimulus pattern. Rather surprisingly, this is frequently not the situation in human pattern recognition. Consider, for example, the sequence of symbols in Figure 2.31.

THE CAT

Figure 2.31
The effect of context on letter recognition. (After Selfridge, 1955; from Neisser, 1967.)

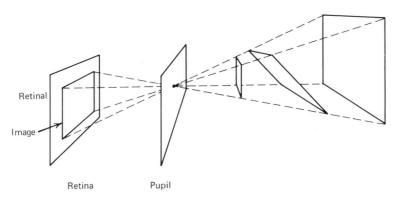

Figure 2.32
There are an infinite number of possible three-dimensional objects corresponding to each retinal image.

Most people read this easily as two English words, THE CAT. However, inspection shows that the middle symbols of the words are the same. When it occurs between a T and E it is interpreted as an H, and when it occurs between a C and T it is interpreted as an A. Thus, our interpretation of the symbol Η depends strongly on the context in which we find it. We apparently do not construct letters independently and see what word we have. Rather, we use information about the entire configuration to deduce its probable meaning. In fact, as illustrated in Figure 2.32, every retinal image could have been caused by an infinity of possible objects, yet we usually have little trouble settling on one or another of these interpretations which seem probable to us. (That we do sometimes have difficulty is attested to by the "ambiguous" pictures in Figure 2.33.)

The degree to which our perception of an object is determined by what we think is probable as opposed to what is "out there" is sometimes surprising. For the most part, the features which we abstract from the visual image act merely as *constraints* on what we see rather than as *determiners* of what we see. As Neisser (1967) puts it, the features we abstract from the visual image are much like the bones a paleontologist digs out of rubble from which we constructs a full-blown dinosaur. The bones act as constraints on the paleontologist which, along with his beliefs about dinosaurs (what they ate, where they lived, how they evolved, how they became extinct, etc.) allow him to reconstruct the dinosaur. Likewise, the perceiver uses his knowledge about what sorts of events should be happening in conjunction with the relatively few features which he finds to construct a representation of what must be

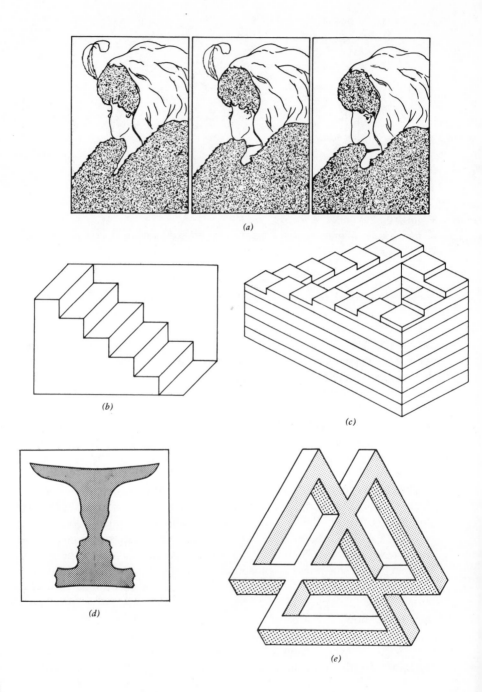

(a)

(b)

(c)

(d)

(e)

happening and what he must be "seeing." We seldom make sharp distinctions between those aspects that are at the moment constraining our perceptions and those that we are "filling in." Thus, we are sometimes surprised, as in the case of Figure 2.33c & e, to discover that our reconstructions of an object are internally inconsistent.

It is therefore not surprising to find numerous experiments reported in the literature showing dependence of pattern recognition on nonsensory factors. A wide variety of these results comes from the literature on word recognition. For example, it is known that more letters per unit time can be perceived when a word is presented than when a string of unrelated letters is presented (Huey, 1908). Other things being equal, words which occur frequently in the language are more easily perceived than those which occur less frequently (Broadbent, 1967). The more closely a letter string approximates the arrangement of letters we expect in a word, the better the perception of the letter string (cf. Miller, Bruner, & Postman, 1954). The more predictable a word is within a sentence, the more easily it is perceived (cf. Tulving, Mandler, & Baumal, 1964).

CONTEXTUAL EFFECTS ON RECOGNIZING ALPHABETIC STRINGS

The model of pattern recognition that we have provided to this point leaves little room for effects such as these. How can we incorporate these sorts of results into a unified view of the pattern recognition process? Perhaps the simplest answer is suggested by experiments by Pillsbury (1897). In these experiments subjects were presented with words that either had a single letter deleted or replaced by an incorrect letter (e.g., FOYEVER or FO EVER). Subjects in these experiments frequently reported perceiving the entire word (e.g., FOREVER). This suggests that subjects might be receiving visual information about some few of the letters and then guessing the missing letters in an appropriate fashion. This basic strategy would readily account for the results mentioned above. According to this view, it is not that we see any

Figure 2.33
We are sometimes surprised when our perceptual reconstructions are incomplete or inconsistent. (a) The panel in the center can be seen as either the young woman on the left or the old woman on the right. (After Boring, 1930; Leeper, 1935.) (b) The staircase can be seen either as upright and ascending or as inverted. (c) The figure can be seen either as a vase or as two faces. (After Rubin, 1915.) (d), (e), and (f) These represent impossible figures. (From Penrose and Penrose, 1952.)

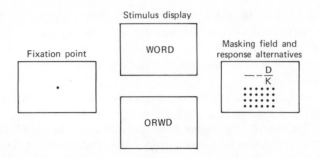

Figure 2.34
Schematic diagram of Reicher's experiment. First fixation point is presented followed either by a word or a nonword. After they are presented, a mask and an
alternative pair are presented. The subject must respond as to which of the two
alternate letters appeared in the indicated position of the stimulus display.

more letters on being presented with words than nonwords, it is merely that
we can guess better from the letters we do see.

Although this general explanation is appealing, it is nevertheless incorrect.
A clever set of experiments initiated by Gerald Reicher in 1969 and continued
by Johnston and McClelland (1973) and others has put this explanation to
rest. The general procedure employed in these experiments is illustrated in
Figure 2.34. Subjects are asked to fixate a small fixation point. They are then
presented with either a word (such as WORD) or a nonsense string of characters (such as ORWD). Following this presentation a mask blanks out the
stimulus and the subjects are presented with two response alternatives posi-
tioned above one of the letters in the display. One of the alternatives appeared
in the display (D in this case) and one did not (K). The subject must respond
with the name of the letter that he feels most certain occupied that position in
the display. The important consideration in choosing the response alternatives
is that both alternatives form words. Thus, guessing a word when the critical
letter was not seen will not help in the choice. Nevertheless, in this experiment
subjects were almost 15% more accurate when a word was presented than
when a nonsense string of letters was presented. Hence, guessing of the correct .
letter could not account for the difference between words and nonwords. How
then can we account for these results?

Rumelhart and Siple (1974) have provided a model which is consistent with
the view of pattern recognition presented here and which appears to offer a
reasonable account of the phenomena discussed above. The basic view is illustrated in Figure 2.35. When a complex signal, such as the word WORK, is

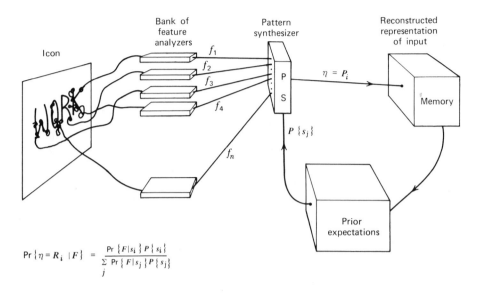

Figure 2.35
Schematic diagram of the effects of prior expectation and memory on the pattern synthesis process. The equation shows that the pattern that is reconstructed depends on the set of features found, F, the prior probability of the stimulus, S_i and on the set of alternatives, J.

registered on the icon, a bank of feature analyzers begins processing the image. The features extracted from the image are input to the pattern synthesizer. The pattern synthesizer also receives as inputs the expectations of the system at the time of the features input. It then produces as output some reconstructed representation of the input target which is then passed into memory. The memory system, in turn, uses both the immediate input and the permanently stored knowledge to determine a new set of expectations. According to their view, expectations simply consist of an a priori probability distribution over the set of possible stimuli $[P(s_i)]$. Rumelhart and Siple assumed that the pattern synthesizer operated by combining the feature information (denoted F in the equation) with the prior expectations by outputting perception P_i with probability proportional to the a posteriori probability that s_i in fact gave rise to the feature set F. The equation for this probability is given in the figure. The important point about the equation is to observe that, all other things being equal, the greater the expectation for stimulus s_i [i.e., the bigger $P(s_i)$], the more probable that percept P_i (corresponding to stimulus s_i) will be seen.

Table 2.1
Verbal Contexts and Target Words

Countries in the United Nations form a military   *alliance.*
The political leader was challenged by a dangerous   *opponent.*
A voter in municipal elections must be a local   *resident.*
The huge slum was filled with dirt and   *disorder.*
The ten Canadian provinces united to form a   *dominion.*
The light bulb was discovered by an American   *inventor.*
June sixth was the date of the allied   *invasion.*
The talented young violinist eventually became a professional   *musician.*
Occupationally his lack of education was a serious   *obstacle.*
He was sentenced to hang as a convicted   *murderer.*
A deadly type of bomb is made of   *hydrogen.*
Her closest relative was appointed as her legal   *guardian.*
The hermit retired to a place of lonely   *solitude.*
Many ethnic groups were represented at the folk   *festival.*
Honesty and courage are qualities which merit wholehearted   *approval.*
The first of the seven deadly sins is   *jealousy.*
Baseball games are covered by the newspaper's sports   *reporter.*
He built his new house in a desirable   *location.*

Now, how does this model account for the variety of nonsensory effects on recognizing patterns that we catalogued above? Its account, of course, depends on the expectations that a subject actually holds about the experimental materials. Our expectations about strings of alphabetic characters should depend on at least the following four components. (1) The frequency of the string considered as a word in the language (nonwords are considered to have zero frequency). (2) The frequency of this string considered as a syllable or sequence of syllables. (3) The frequency of this string considered as a sequence of letters. (4) Moreover, in the context of a sentence, one would imagine that the predictability of that string in that particular sentence would also contribute to the overall expectancy for that string. We can illustrate the use of this model by applying it to the recognizability of words in a sentence context. These studies typically manipulate the amount of contextual information surrounding the to-be-recognized word by varying the number of words preceding the target word in a sentence. An experiment by Tulving, Mandler, and Baumal (1964) will serve to illustrate the results.

    Table 2.1 shows the materials used by Tulving et al. in their experiment. The subjects were given either the preceding eight, four, two, or zero words in the sentence and then shown the target word for either 0, 20, 40, 60, 80,

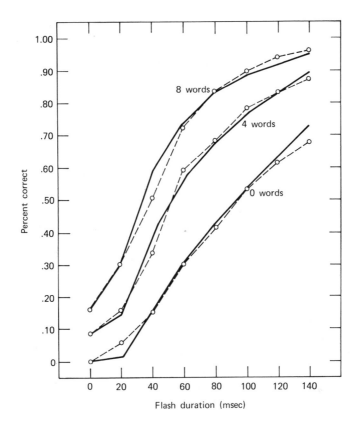

Figure 2.36
Percent correct responses as a function of flash duration and number of words of context. (Data from Tulving, Mandler and Baumal, 1964.) Smooth lines from theory described in the text.

100, 120, or 140 msec. The probability of a correct response was calculated for each of the conditions. The results for zero, four, and eight words of contextual information are shown in Figure 2.36. The results clearly show that there is some sort of tradeoff between sensory input (exposure duration) and information gathered through context. A 50-msec exposure duration and eight words of context lead to the correct perception more often than a 140-msec exposure and no words of context. The solid lines in the figure are calculated from the model discussed above. It is assumed that contextual information simply has the effect of increasing the expectation of the critical word and thereby reducing the number of stimulus features that must be extracted before the pattern synthesizer has enough information to find a satisfactory interpretation of the discovered input. Rumelhart and Siple have given similar accounts of word frequency and approximation to English (letter predictability) experiments.

Now consider how this model accounts for the results of the word-nonword experiment discussed above. To understand how it might work, suppose that the word WORK had been presented. Further suppose that enough features have been extracted to uniquely identify the first three characters of the stimulus. Now, if our subject managed to perceive only the \ part of the final character he would nevertheless be able to uniquely determine that the word WORK appeared. Then, when he receives the choice between the D and the K he will be certain that the K had been presented. Now consider the same situation except that the letters ORWK were presented. We suppose, as before, that the letters ORW have been identified and further that only the feature \ has been extracted from the final character. Now, instead of being certain of the response, the subject still has four possibilities among which he must choose: ORWK, ORWR, ORWX, and ORWQ. Since, according to this model, the subject cannot preserve feature information, the perceptual system must output either ORWK, ORWR, ORWX, ORWQ, or ORW?. Only one of these alternatives will lead with certainty to a correct response. In other cases, the subject can only guess as to the correct alternative in the forced choice. [The notion that feature information is not preserved is consistent with the finding by McClelland (1975) that when subjects are asked to both give a whole report and make the forced choice response (for example, between the D and K), their forced choice response is almost perfectly predictable from their whole report response.]

A recent experiment by Johnston (1974) suggests that the sort of explanation given here accounts for only part of the observed effect. There is, it would seem, an additional source of information that accounts for the rest. This is the information about order of letters. Although we have not mentioned it to this point, results obtained by Estes (1975) and by McClelland (1975) show that our knowledge about relative location of letters is less accurate with nonwords than with words. Thus, even if enough features are discovered to accurately identify the characters in the string, the letters may well be misordered in the nonword string leading to likely error on the forced choice response. If we assume that there is uncertainty in the position information coming into the pattern synthesizer, our model will again account for the observed responses. There are many fewer ways a string can be reordered and still form a word than there are ways that a string of random letters can be reordered.

Ordinarily, when we are reading words in the context of sentences we cannot predict with great assurance exactly the next word in a sentence, but we can, with high probability, predict the general *meaning* of the next word. Thus, it should not be surprising that we have developed strategies of increasing our expectancy for a whole set of semantically interrelated words at once. Ordinarily, this will allow us to process semantically meaningful prose more quickly. In an ingenious experiment, Graboi (1974) has demonstrated that even when searching for a particular word in a list, we tend to activate our expectations for a whole class of semantically related words.

In one of his experiments Graboi employed a variation on Neisser's search procedure described earlier. First, subjects were trained to search for the occurrence of any one of five target words among a list of semantically unrelated nontargets. Half of the subjects searched for any one of the words labeled "Experimental Target Set" in Table 2.2, scattered among lists constructed from the "Unassociated Nontargets." The other half searched for occurrences of any of the "Control Target Set" against the same background. Notice that neither target set is semantically related to the nontarget background in which it was searched for. Subjects were trained in this task for an hour a day for 14 days. After this much training the experimental group could scan their lists at a rate of 182.2 msec per word. The control group scanned at a rate of 180.0 msec per word. On the fifteenth day, the background lists were changed. Now both the groups were searching for targets against a background of the nontargets labeled *Associated Nontargets*. Notice that the experimental subjects are now searching for their targets against a semantically related background whereas the background is unrelated to the control target set. Now we find that the control group is not slowed down at all by the switch and scans the new lists at a rate of 179 msec per word. The experimental group, however, scanning through words semantically related to the target set was slowed to a rate of 197.4 msec per word—i.e., they were slowed down over 1.5 sec per 100 words scanned.

Why should it slow subjects down to scan through a list of semantically similar nontargets? After the switch one subject reported, "Before the [target] words would stick right out, and I was just moving right over all the other ones. The only ones that would give me problems were words which were letter-by-letter similar, like SUNNY and MONEY. This time, for some reason, I was slowing down by word content too. Synonyms slowed me down, like COIN–MONEY." One might argue that subjects were just surprised to see related words in the context and slowing down a few times accounted for the entire difference. However, in that case one would expect the difference to soon disappear. But this did not happen. Through five additional hours of searching (they searched through 2000 words during an hour session), the

Table 2.2
Target and Nontarget Stimuli in Search Experiment

Experimental Target Set	Associated Nontargets	Control Target Set
BIRD	WORM CHICK NESTS ROBIN CHIRP WINGS FLY EAGLE PARROT SONG	ROCK
COLOR	BLACK GRAY PURPLE BROWN GOLD BLUE RED YELLOW GREEN PAINT	CHAIR
MONEY	SAVE SPEND COINS DIME BANK SILVER DOLLAR CASH PENNY PEARL	HOUSE
LEARN	BOOKS SCHOOL READ CLASS WRITE TEACH EXAM NOTES GRADE STUDY	SPORT
FRUIT	ORANGE NUTS GRAPE SWEET PLUM APPLE PEACH PEAR FRESH LEMON	CLOUD

	Unassociated Nontargets	
	HUG PEN SLEEP NIGHT BRIDGE STAPLE LAMP RULER LEADER ROAR	
	SUNNY PLACE CORNER ALBUM ABOUT RATE WEEK POINT SWITCH ANKLE	
	TOWN DIAL SPOON TOWEL SHEET STOVE CRUST BRUSH GLASS ROAD	
	WHICH AFTER PASS STORY SIGN CHURCH MURAL PHONE BOOTH CARD	
	STREET MOTOR RADIO KNOB PLUG DRIVE LINE TASK PRINT SHIFT	

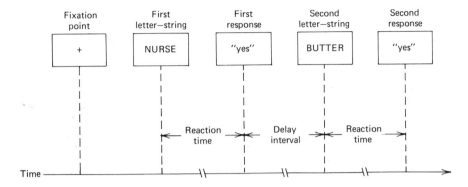

Figure 2.37
Schematic diagram of experimental methods for measuring the effects of the first letter string on the processing of the second letter string. (From Meyer et al., 1973.)

difference between the control subjects and experimental subjects remained at about 20 msec per word. It would thus appear that even when searching for particular words our expectations are based on meaning as well as visual form. As we shall see, a substantially different procedure leads to the same conclusion.

In a series of papers Meyer, Schvaneveldt, and Ruddy (Meyer & Schvaneveldt, 1971; Meyer, Schvaneveldt & Ruddy, 1972; Ruddy, Meyer, & Schvaneveldt, 1973; Schvaneveldt & Meyer, 1973; Meyer, Schvaneveldt & Ruddy, 1974) have reported effects of semantic context on word recognition. The basic procedure in these tasks involves measuring how quickly people can decide whether a string of letters is a word or nonword. Figure 2.37 illustrates the procedure used in one of these experiments. The subject was first presented with two fixation points. Following a 0.5 sec delay the top string was replaced by a string of letters (e.g., NURSE). The subject had to respond either YES if the string was a word or NO if it was not a word. Following another brief delay a second string of letters (e.g., BUTTER) replaced the lower fixation point and again the subject had to decide whether or not it was a word. The time required to make the decision was recorded in each case. The variable of primary interest was the effect of the first word on the recognition of the second. As Table 2.3 illustrates, some of the word pairs were associated (BREAD–BUTTER) whereas others were unassociated (NURSE–BUTTER). Of particular interest here is the effect of recognizing the word BREAD, for example, on the speed of recognizing BUTTER. Within the model we have discussed

Table 2.3
Examples of Stimuli in the Lexical-Decision Task

Type of Pair	Examples
Associated words	BREAD-BUTTER NURSE-DOCTOR
Unassociated words	NURSE-BUTTER BREAD-DOCTOR
Word-nonword	WINE-PLAME GLOVE-SOAM
Nonword-word	PLAME-WINE SOAM-GLOVE
Nonword-nonword	NART-TRIEF PABLE-REAB

thus far, this amounts to the question of whether reading BREAD increases our expectation for BUTTER. If it does, we can expect that the decision about BUTTER will be made somewhat faster than the same decision in the context of NURSE. The results of the experiment clearly implicate a context effect. It takes over 40 msec longer to recognize a word in an unassociated context than in an associated context. It thus appears that, upon reading a word, we are able to increase our expectation for related words and thereby increase the rate at which we can recognize those words.

To this point we have discussed contextual effects mainly as they relate to the processing of alphabetic strings. However, these effects appear to be universal and certainly not restricted to the processing of linguistic inputs. We now turn to a discussion of such effects.

PROCESSING VISUAL SCENES

Of course, context is as important for our processing of visual scenes as for linguistic units like words. In a recent paper, Palmer (1975b) has discussed the role of context in visual processing extensively. One particularly interesting contextual relationship discussed by Palmer is what he called "part-whole context." In the context of word perception it makes sense to ask whether the word or the letter is the unit of analysis. Do we perceive words as units and

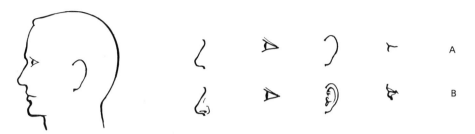

Figure 2.38
Illustration of part-whole context. Facial features recognizable in the context of a profile (left) are not recognizable alone (series A). If their internal part structure is shown (series B), the features are recognizable out of context. (From Palmer, 1975b.)

then derive the letters from our knowledge of how the word is spelled? Or do we perceive the letters first and then derive the word from the letters it contains? Our analysis of the word-nonword effect seems to suggest the latter. What about complex visual objects? Do we first see the parts and then construct the whole? (Do we recognize some drawing to be a face because we see a nose and eyes and ears?) Or do we recognize the parts because we know what we are looking at? (Do we know that some little mark is a mouth or a nose because we know we are looking at a face?) Palmer points out that the interpretation of parts and wholes must proceed jointly. The final interpretation is determined by consistency among various "part-whole" levels. As Figure 2.38 illustrates, at least two levels of detail are necessary. Consider, for example, how much better a nose must be drawn to be recognizable by itself than in the context of a face. As the figure illustrates, the same is true for all the other parts of the face. It is clear that the part-whole context is essential for our interpretations of ordinary line drawings.

The point that the recognition of objects is strongly affected by their surround is well made by consideration of a simple experiment of Palmer's (1975a). His experiment was a close analog of the Tulving, Mandler, and Baumal (1964) experiment described above. On some trials subjects were shown drawings of scenes like that illustrated in Figure 2.39. Following this they were given a tachistoscopic presentation of a target object like those shown in the lower portion of the figure. Target objects were constructed to be either (1) appropriate for the scene (e.g., the bread), (2) inappropriate for the scene but physically similar to an appropriate object (e.g., the mailbox), or (3) both inappropriate for the scene and dissimilar to the target object (e.g., the drum).

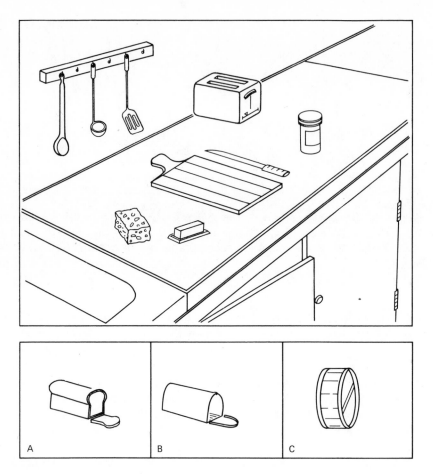

Figure 2.39

Drawings used in context experiment. Presentation of the scene shown in the upper part of the figure establishes the context for the identification of one of the three items shown in the lower part. When paired with this scene, the loaf of bread (item A) illustrates the appropriate context condition, the mailbox (item B) illustrates the inappropriate context condition in which the target is visually similar to the appropriate item, and the drum (item C) illustrates the inappropriate context condition in which the target is visually different from the appropriate item. (From Palmer, 1975a.) Percent correct responses and percent similar wrong responses are a function of context types. A is the appropriate context condition; N is a no context condition in which no context figure was presented; I_D is the visually differ-ent condition as, for example, when the drum is presented following presentation of the kitchen scene; and I_s is the condition in which the visually similar item was presented.

90

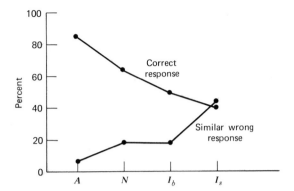

Figure 2.40

There were thus four types of context-object combinations: (1) *appropriate context, A;* (2) *no context, N;* (3) *inappropriate context, similar object, I_s;* and (4) *inappropriate context, different object, I_d.* Figure 2.40 shows the results of the experiment. The curve labeled "correct response" gives the percentage of times the subjects were correct as a function of context. In an appropriate context they were about 84% correct (e.g., seeing bread in the kitchen context), in an inappropriate context with a similar object they were only about 40% correct (e.g., seeing a mailbox in the kitchen context). The curve labeled "similar wrong response" indicates the number of times they responded wrongly with the similar object (e.g., responded mailbox when bread was presented). This goes from a low of 7% when the appropriate context was presented (i.e., 7% of the time they responded mailbox, when bread was presented in the context of the kitchen scene) to a high of over 40% when an appropriate context for the similar object was presented (e.g., responding mailbox when bread was presented in the context of a front-walk scene appropriate to a mailbox). In this case subjects actually gave the context-appropriate response slightly more often than the correct response.

It is clear from these and a wide range of similar results (cf. Biederman, 1972) that one's expectations are very important, both in the context of linguistic inputs and ordinary visual scenes. Although the expectations often help us perceive more accurately, they can also cause us to get distorted images of the world. If our prior beliefs play such an important role in our perception, how are we able to get a veridical view of the world? The answer is, of course, that we often don't. If we build up our beliefs about something on the basis of too little information, we may in fact be unable to get an appropriate view of the object when more information does become available—we may be victims of "a little knowledge being a bad thing."

A good example of this comes from an experiment by Bruner and Potter (1964). In this experiment, subjects were shown slides of familiar objects and asked to try to recognize them. At first, the slide was so badly out of focus that a blur was all that was visible on the screen. They then slowly brought the slide into focus. At each point subjects were required to guess as to the object in the picture. The subjects in this experiment nearly always failed to correctly perceive the pictured object until long after the point where it was readily identifiable to a naïve subject. Bruner and Potter interpret their results to mean that during the early exposures, when subjects are forced to make the best reconstructions they can with the few features available, they mistakenly identify the object but cling to this mistaken interpretation long after the sensory evidence is sufficient for a proper perception.

SPEECH PERCEPTION

All of the problems of visual pattern recognition are present in the perception of speech. The problems in speech perception are perhaps even more aggravated. For example, while it has proved possible to build a machine capable of recognizing typewritten characters, it has proved impossible to build a speech recognition device with equal capabilities. The physical stimulus is even noisier in speech than in visual pattern recognition. Different speakers saying the same words produce acoustic waveforms which bear little resemblance to one another. Even the same speaker speaking at different times with different intonations and stress patterns produces acoustic signals with few discoverable similarities. Figure 2.41 compares speech spectograms of the same person speaking the same sentence under several different conditions. The abscissa of the graph is frequency, from low to high. The ordinate shows time. The intensity of the various frequency components is depicted by the density of the spectrogram. In each of these cases, the words were plainly spoken and easily understood.

As with visual presentations, contextual cues play a critical role in speech recognition. Consider, as an example, the words I SCREAM and ICE CREAM; the acoustic signals corresponding to these two phrases can be made to be identical. Yet, we seldom confuse the two. This example is somewhat extreme, but experiments studying word recognition in noisy environments have shown that contextual information of all sorts plays a critical role in the perception of speech. An experiment done by Miller and Isard (1963) illustrates the point very well. They presented sentences masked by noise to subjects, and the

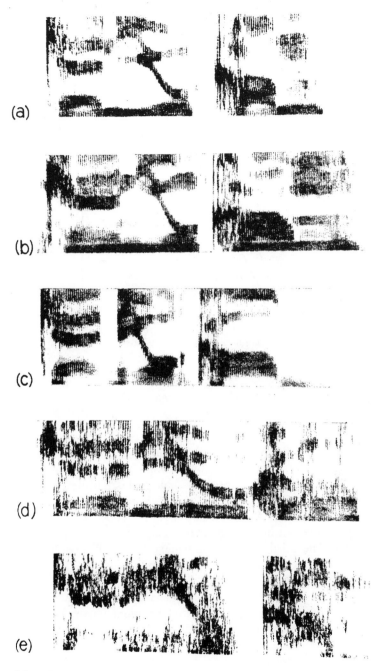

Figure 2.41
Speech spectograms of the question: Can you come? All samples are from the same speaker, using *(a)* normal intonation, *(b)* positive nasality, *(c)* negative nasality, *(d)* aspirate, and *(e)* whisper. (From Potter et al., 1947.)

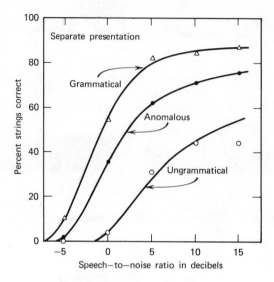

Figure 2.42
Proportion of strings heard correctly as a function of speech to noise ratio and type of string presented. (From Miller and Isard, 1963.)

subjects were supposed to repeat the sentences aloud. Some sentences they used were syntactically and semantically sensible: "A witness signed the official document," or "Sloppy fielding loses baseball games." Miller and Isard called these "grammatical" sentences. Other sentences were syntactically correct but semantically nonsensical: "A witness appraised the shocking company dragon," or "Sloppy poetry leaves nuclear minutes." These were referred to as "anomalous" sentences. The third category of sentences, called "ungrammatical" sentences, was neither syntactically nor semantically sensible: "A legal glittering the exposed picnic knight," or "Loses poetry spots total wasted." Correct perceptions of the ungrammatical sentences depend almost solely on the clarity of the sensory input. Correct perceptions of the anomalous sentences, however, can be aided by extrasensory syntactic knowledge, and correct perceptions of the grammatical sentences can be aided by both syntactic and semantic contextual cues. The percent of correctly perceived strings is plotted as a function of signal-to-noise ratio in Figure 2.42. These results with spoken word strings, as those of Tulving, Mandler, and Baumal (1964) with visual word recognition, show clearly that when grammatical constraints, both semantic and syntactic, are present, we are able to make good use of them in properly reconstructing sentences. When these constraints are not present and we must depend only on sensory information for our reconstructions, our performance suffers badly. Our knowledge of grammar is certainly an important variable in our everyday understanding of speech.

In addition to Miller and Isard's results, paralleling those of Tulving et al. (1964), effects similar to those of Bruner and Potter (1964) showing the negative effects of mistaken reconstructions on later perceptions have been reported. Fredrickson (1969) presented subjects with words embedded in white noise at signal-to-noise ratios so low that no word could be identified. He then increased the signal-to-noise ratio in small steps, requiring a response after each increase until the word was correctly identified. In this experiment, as in Bruner and Potter's, many subjects maintained a false reconstruction of the stimulus object long past the point at which the word was clear to naïve subjects. Here again we have evidence for a constructive mode of perception. When sensory cues are insufficient to determine the word exactly but an initial reconstruction is nevertheless made, the result is an inability to use the appropriate sensory cues when they do become available.

ATTENTIONAL PHENOMENA

There are two additional related phenomena which are frequently observed in considerations of pattern recognition. The first is man's apparent ability to focus on certain aspects of the world impinging upon him in order to increase the detail with which it is perceived. The second is his apparent inability to process deeply and simultaneously all aspects of stimuli exciting his sense organs. There actually appears to be a tradeoff between *depth of processing* and *breadth of processing*. This tradeoff has been subsumed under the name *attention*. When we focus on certain details, we are said to be attending to those aspects of the stimulus configuration; when we are unable to monitor a large number of such details simultaneously it is said that "We can attend to only one thing or a limited number of things at a time."

These two facts have led to two different kinds of questions about the mechanism of attention. First, how much do we know of things not attended to, and, second, how many things can be attended to at once? The early information processing models (see Broadbent, 1958) took an extreme point of view on both of these questions. They proposed that there is but one input channel (we can attend to only one "thing" at a time) and that we know nothing about those things to which we don't attend. We occasionally shift our attention from one channel to another (this was assumed to take a reason-

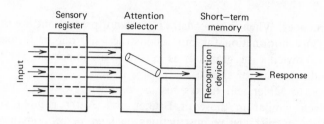

Figure 2.43
Illustration of single-channel model of attention where multiple input channels enter and leave the sensory register. An attention selector chooses one channel and funnels it into the short-term memory system. (Figure from Shiffrin et al., 1974.)

able amount of time). Thus, we have some information about the "unattended" channels, but in general only information through the attended channel is processed. This simple point of view was bolstered by numerous experiments in which subjects were to repeat (shadow) a verbal message played into one ear while another message was played into the other ear. Subjects had no trouble following the message in the attended ear completely, but had only the most rudimentary knowledge about the message in the unattended ear. They knew, for example, whether a man or a woman spoke the message, but they failed to notice when the speaker in the unattended ear changed from English to German speech (Cherry, 1953).

Figure 2.43 illustrates in schematic form Broadbent's view. A vast array of information impinges on our receptors at one time. However, all of the sources of input cannot be monitored simultaneously. Rather, an attention selection device chooses one of the channels and only passes information from that channel on to be processed and passed into short-term memory.

Later experimentation has shown that this simple model is inaccurate. Although subjects neither recall nor recognize irrelevant messages presented as many as 35 times to their unattended ear, they frequently hear their own name when it is presented to the unattended ear (Moray, 1959). Similarly, when prose messages are switched back and forth from one ear to the other, subjects will occasionally involuntarily follow the passage rather than continue shadowing the disjointed messages coming to the attended ear (Treisman, 1960). Analysis apparently proceeds to some extent even when the channel is not being attended to.

The view that some, but not all, of the information from all channels is processed led Treisman (cf. Treisman & Geffen, 1967) to develop a so-called "attenuator" view of attention. Figure 2.44 illustrates this view. Here, instead of

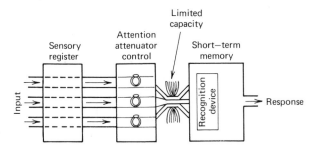

Figure 2.44
Diagram of limited capacity attention model. Multiple channels of information enter and leave the sensory register. The attention device is an attenuator that reduces all of the signals and passes through the limited capacity channel more-or-less information from each of the channels. (Figure from Shiffrin et al., 1974.)

a single channel over which information can be input there is a limited capacity channel, but inputs from various sources can use the channel simultaneously. However, since there is a limited capacity, inputs from some of the channels must be "attenuated." There is one primary channel that is being attended to and all other channels are passing information only in reduced amount. Nevertheless, whenever important information comes across one of the unattended channels it can be discovered and responded to.

Perhaps the results most strongly favoring the "attenuation" view of attention comes from an experiment by Treisman and Geffen (1967). In this experiment subjects had to shadow one of two dichotically presented prose passages. Simultaneously they had to monitor *both* channels for the occurrence of a specific target word. Whenever the target occurred on either channel the subjects had to tap. Thus, on the primary channel the subject had to perform two responses for each target word: repeat the word (shadow it) and tap. When a target occurred on the unattended ear the subject needed only to tap. The results showed that whereas almost 90% of the target words were detected in the primary channel, only about 9% were heard in the unattended channel. These results then would seem to argue strongly for a limited- capacity channel view of attention.

However, a recent experiment by Shiffrin, Pisoni, and Casteneda-Mendez (1974) would seem to challenge that view. In this experiment they found no difference in the recognizability of a consonant played in noise between a condition in which the subject had to divide his attention between the two ears and one in which he knew the ear to which the consonant was being presented. Similar results have been found for the detection of a tone in noise

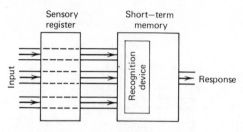

Figure 2.45
Parallel channels model. Information enters and leaves the sensory register from many channels, and there is no attentional reduction at the level of short-term memory. (Figure from Shiffrin et al., 1974.)

(cf. Sorkin & Pohlman, 1973). Shiffrin et al. have interpreted these results to support an independent channels model of the sort illustrated in Figure 2.45. In such a model attention is not a perceptual effect at all. Instead, all information passes into short-term memory and is analyzed by the recognition device. All selection comes at the level of short-term memory. Some information may be selectively rehearsed, encoded, and responded to; the other information is forgotten from short-term memory.

We are thus faced with contradictory models and apparently contradictory results. In order for the attenuation model to account for the Shiffrin et al. results, it has to be assumed that we can process consonants embedded in noise as well when we are dividing our attention equally between two channels (thus attenuating each by 50%) as when we are attending fully to one channel. On the other hand, in order for the Shiffrin et al. independent channels models to account for the Treisman and Geffen result, it has to be assumed that "the target word in the nonshadowed ear was perceived, entered into short-term memory, and then forgotten, all before an overt tapping response could be made" Shiffrin et al., (p. 200). This is exactly what Shiffrin et al. assume. On the face of it, it would seem an odd use of the term perception to argue that we could perceive a target, but not realize it, particularly when our task required us to be "on the lookout" for the target.

A recent paper by Norman and Bobrow (1975) perhaps shows us a way out of this dilemma. Norman and Bobrow have distinguished between what they call *resource-limited* and *data-limited* processing tasks. Consider, as an example, the performance of some complex task—such as playing a game of chess. Up to some level of performance the harder we try (i.e., the more we attend to what we are doing), the better we will perform. Up to this level our performance is said to be *resource-limited*—the quality of our performance is determined by the amount of resources we devote to the task. Thus, "whenever an increase in the amount of processing resources can result in improved performance, we say that the task (or performance on that task) is *resource-limited*" (p. 46). On the other hand, not all tasks are resource limited. Norman and Bobrow define a data-limited task in the following manner (p. 46).

> Consider the task of detecting a superthreshold sound: for example, the sound made by striking a piano key in a quiet room. The detection task is straightforward: the processing is limited by the simplicity of the data structure. Consider now the task of determining whether or not a particular signal has occurred within a background of noise. Suppose the recognition mechanism uses all the most powerful techniques at its disposal—matched filters, correlational techniques, and so on. In either of these two tasks, once all the processing that can be done has been completed, performance is dependent solely on the quality of the data. Increasing the allocation of processing resources can have no further effect on performance. Whenever performance is independent of processing resources, we say that the task is *data-limited*.

More tasks that we ask our subjects to do are resource-limited up to a point, and thereafter, once all of the effective processing has been completed, they are data-limited. It is important to notice that perfect performance is not required for a task to be data-limited.

How then does this distinction help us out of the dilemma proposed earlier? How can we simultaneously account for the result of Treisman and Geffen and of Shiffrin et al.? Suppose that there is a limited central processing capacity as assumed by both the single-channel model and the attenuator model. Suppose, further, that when trying to perform two or more simultaneous tasks, a subject can flexibly allot his resource capacity among the tasks being performed. Depending on the demands of the experiment, the subject will presumably allocate his capacity so as to maximize his performance on all of the tasks he is instructed to perform. Thus, if one or more of the tasks are data-limited, they will be given the minimal amount of resources necessary to reach the data-limited level of performance. The additional resources will be allocated to any resource-limited task that may be competing for this processing capacity. Thus, to interpret the Treisman and Geffen experiment we must assume that the process of shadowing and the process of monitoring for a target word both require a reasonable amount of processing. Since the primary task involves shadowing, enough attention must be devoted to that task to perform it at a high level of proficiency. This leaves only enough capacity to perform at a low or mediocre level to the unattended ear. The process of detecting a consonant in noise, on the other hand, is very likely a task that is data-limited and requires a relatively low level of processing capacity. (As pointed out above, detecting a signal in noise can easily be data-limited at less than perfect performance.) It is thus not unreasonable that we should find no decrement in performance when we have to monitor two channels instead of one. The process of monitoring one channel requires nowhere near half of the available resources before it is data-limited.

SUMMARY

We are now in a position to construct a general diagram of the pattern recognition system consistent with all of the data we have discussed thus far. Figure 2.46 is such a diagram. The physical stimulus, either photon fluctuations required for a visual pattern or molecule vibrations serving as auditory input, impinges on the receptors and modifies their pattern of firing. This pattern is then registered in a transient sensory memory (iconic or echoic memory) where it can be stored briefly for further processing. At this point of analysis, the extraction of critical features is carried out. The outputs of the feature analyzers feed into a pattern synthesizer. This device uses the constraints imposed by

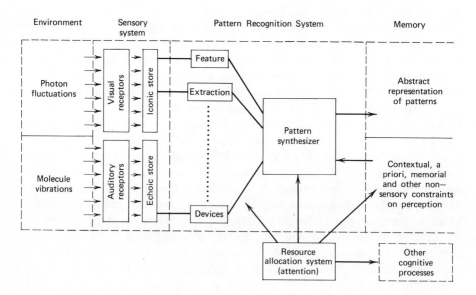

Figure 2.46
Diagram illustrating the interactions among environment, sensory system, pattern recognition system, and memory system.

the extracted features, contextual information (semantic, syntactic, and other), and memorial information to reconstruct an abstracted image of the sensory input. This abstract representation is then stored in memory with a tag indicating that it has just occurred. All of this processing requires resources. Depending on the attentional priorities of the system, each of these various processing devices (or subprocesses within them) is allocated processing capacity. As long as the processing demands of any given process are not too great, we can monitor all relevant inputs. However, when some part of the system demands too many resources, processing in the other parts of the system must suffer.

Although the general nature of the pattern recognition system is outlined in the figure, we have been vague on how the pattern synthesizer operates, how the expectancies are determined, and how the attentional priorities are to be determined in complex processing tasks. In general, of course, the answer is that we don't know. Nevertheless, in certain limited domains we are beginning to get some ideas as to how these critical aspects of the system work and interact. In the following chapter we will look at the special case of language comprehension and illustrate how these critical aspects of the human information system might work.

3

UNDERSTANDING LANGUAGE

Of all the complex tasks the human information system carries out, perhaps the most sophisticated is language processing. Like perception, language processing usually proceeds so smoothly and efficiently that we hardly realize the remarkable feats we are performing. Only when we stop and analyze the intricate reasoning that appears to underlie even the simplest cases of language comprehension can we begin to appreciate the complexity of the language understanding process. Consider the following ordinary sentences:

I know John claims he can read French. He told me he read several classics in the original French.

Most of us read these sentences without difficulty. Yet, in one context we see the letters r-e-a-d as representing a word pronounced 'reed,' in the second we see the same sequence of letters as representing a word pronounced 'red.' Of course we all know that the tense of the verb "read" changes its pronunciation. Somehow we must have been computing the tense of the verb and using that in the processing of the sentence. Thus our knowledge of *grammar* or *syntax* enters into our language processing at an early stage.

Similarly, consider the following pair of sentences:

I saw the cow grazing in the pasture.
I saw the Grand Canyon flying to New York.

Again with these two examples, we usually have no difficulty realizing that in the first sentence it was the cow, not the speaker, that was grazing, but that in the second example the speaker, not the Grand Canyon, was flying to New York. Here we somehow automatically use our knowledge of the meaning of words, or *semantics,* to help us sort out which of the two possible meanings we should take.

How does our syntactic and semantic knowledge combine with the information we get from the written page or, in the case of speech, from the speech wave form? The present chapter will focus on just that question. How does the human information processing system combine information from the sense organs with our knowledge of language to determine our interpretation of speech or written language?

We are only now beginning to collect evidence on this issue and develop a picture of these processes. As with the work on pattern recognition it is often useful to look at the problems of a machine attempting a human task to get insights into the problems encountered by the human.

As mentioned in the previous chapter, the acoustic input in speech is extremely noisy, and all direct attempts at machine speech recognition have ended in failure. It has become conventional wisdom that the source of the failure for their earlier attempts has been their reliance on analysis of characteristics of the speech waveform without regard for the various contextual and other nonsensory aids to knowledge available to the human interpreter of the language. Thus, the most recent attempts at computer speech understanding have emphasized the use of a variety of sources of knowledge in determining the meaning of a speech signal. The researchers were thus directly faced with the major problems of the pattern synthesizer: How can information from a wide range of disparate sources combine in an efficient way to "work cooperatively" in the determination of the "meaning" of an incoming signal? We now turn to a discussion of one of those systems.

THE HEARSAY SYSTEM

The HEARSAY system is a computer program developed at Carnegie-Mellon University by Raj Reddy and his associates (Reddy, Erman, Fennell, & Neely,

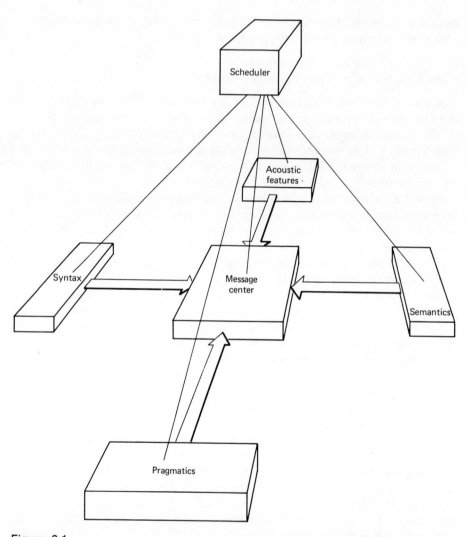

Figure 3.1
Diagram illustrating interaction of knowledge sources through a central knowledge center in HEARSAY.

1973; Lesser, Fennell, Erman, & Reddy 1974). It is particularly interesting because of its strong reliance on nonsensory information. Figure 3.1 gives a general overview of the system. At its most general, it consists of a set of *knowledge sources,* a *scheduler* which determines processing priorities, and a *global message center* through which the knowledge sources interact.

There are four basic sources of knowledge that are considered relevant: acoustic features, syntactic knowledge, semantic knowledge, and pragmatic knowledge. The acoustic features provide a preliminary analysis of the acoustic waveform. The syntactic component contributes knowledge of the grammar of the language. The semantic domain pertains to the *meaning* of the utterance. Pragmatics involves the likelihood of the utterance in the current context.

Within the HEARSAY system each knowledge source consists of a set of processes. Knowledge sources propose and/or evaluate hypotheses about the nature of certain aspects of the input. Proposed hypotheses are written into the message center, together with a preliminary evaluation of each hypothesis (i.e., how likely it is to be correct), by a knowledge source. Whenever a new hypothesis comes into the message center all relevant knowledge sources are called in to evaluate that hypothesis and possibly propose new hypotheses. All of this processing makes demands on the total processing capacity of the system. The scheduler allocates the processing capacity to those knowledge sources acting upon the most promising hypotheses at the moment. When the system finally comes up with a highly rated hypothesis which encompasses all aspects of the utterance it ceases processing and assumes that it has properly interpreted the utterance.

The HEARSAY system is designed around the message center. Hypotheses stored in the message center differ with regard to (1) the segment of the wave form they are presumably accounting for, (2) the rating of the hypothesis, and (3) the *level* of the hypothesis. Level refers to the degree of abstractness of a hypothesis. Some hypotheses, such as those suggested by the semantic and pragmatic knowledge sources, are very abstract and may suggest that a reference to a certain concept should be found in the input (this is called the conceptual level). Others are more concrete and suggest that a certain segment of the speech waveform corresponds to a word in some particular syntactic class (e.g., a noun). Still others suggest that a segment of the speech waveform corresponds to some particular word (the lexical level). And still others are at an even more concrete level and suggest, for example, that the phoneme /s/[1] is present in some segment of the waveform. (A list of the levels

---

[1]A phoneme is the speech unit associated with a single sound. Thus, "sit" and "bit" differ by one phoneme. Although one might mainly associate phonemes with letters in the alphabet, they are not the same. Sometimes combinations of letters (such as "ph") will

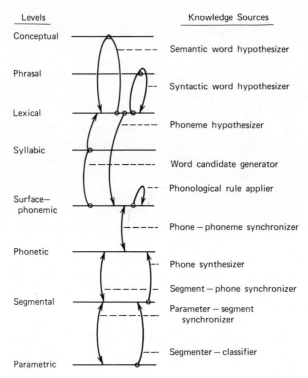

Levels   Knowledge Sources

Conceptual

          Semantic word hypothesizer

Phrasal

          Syntactic word hypothesizer

Lexical

          Phoneme hypothesizer

Syllabic

          Word candidate generator

          Phonological rule applier

Surface—
phonemic

          Phone — phoneme synchronizer

Phonetic

          Phone synthesizer

          Segment — phone synchronizer

Segmental   Parameter — segment
                            synchronizer

          Segmenter — classifier

Parametric

Table 3.1
Interaction of levels and their associated knowledge sources in HEARSAY II. The
levels that interact with each other are illustrated by directed arrows.
(*Source.* Reddy et al., 1974.)

used in one version of the **HEARSAY** system is given in Table 3.1) The
message center thus represents proposed hypotheses in terms of an essentially
three-dimensional space. One dimension correspond to time, the second corresponds to level of the hypothesis, and the third corresponds to the alternative
hypotheses that are under consideration. The following example will illustrate
how these various knowledge sources can work together to aid in the perception of a simple sentence.

---

indicate a single phoneme; sometimes different letters will indicate the same phoneme
(e.g., the "c" in "comb" and the "k" in "kind" both indicate the phoneme /k/); and at
still other times the same letter will represent different phonemes (e.g., "c" in "comb"
and the "c" in "city").

EXAMPLE

One of the primary applications of the HEARSAY system to date has been in the context of "voice chess." In this game a human plays chess against the machine. The human enters his move by speaking into a microphone. The computer then interprets the spoken input and responds with a counter move. In the example to be discussed here the speaker is playing white. The board configuration and a list of the forty-six legal moves, ordered by the semantics and pragmatics of the HEARSAY system, are given in Figure 3.4. In this example, the speaker elected to move his queen's bishop to his king's knight five. He spoke the words "BISHOP MOVES TO KING KNIGHT FIVE." The actual time waveform along with the associated speech sound is illustrated in Figure 3.2. In the versions of HEARSAY that carried out this example a rather minimal analysis of the speech-waveform itself took place. The system first segmented the waveform and then labeled each segment as one of three feature types. A segment could be primarily a vowel sound (i.e., characterized by a period of relatively constant frequency), or a fricative (sounds like /s/ or /f/ characterized by high frequency noise), or a period of silence (associated with so-called stop consonants such as "p" or "t"). Figure 3.2 illustrates the segments produced by HEARSAY and the labels given to each segment. These segment labels then act as a temporarily ordered set of features. They are written into the message center as the lowest level set of hypotheses about the nature of the speech waveform. As these features begin to move into the message center, the other knowledge sources are activated and begin to gen= erate hypotheses at other levels of abstraction.

Figure 3.3 illustrates the state of the message center after the first few hypotheses have been postulated. In this diagram hypotheses are represented as boxes. The level of the hypothesis is represented by the height of the box—i.e., the higher the box the more abstract the hypothesis. Time is represented from left to right—i.e., hypotheses about the contents of earlier parts of the utterance are further to the left. Whenever there are alternative hypotheses at the same level for the same part of the utterance, those alternatives are represented in depth in the same plane. The relationships between hypotheses are indicated by lines between the boxes. In the figure we see that the highest level hypothesis, suggested by pragmatics, is that the utterance will be a chess move. This hypothesis is entered as soon as the first acoustic features are being entered. Syntax believes that chess moves have the grammatical form <piece> <action> <position> and thus postulates that the first portion of the waveform should be a description of a piece. Consulting the ordering of moves (as given in Figure 3.4) semantics concludes that the two most likely pieces to

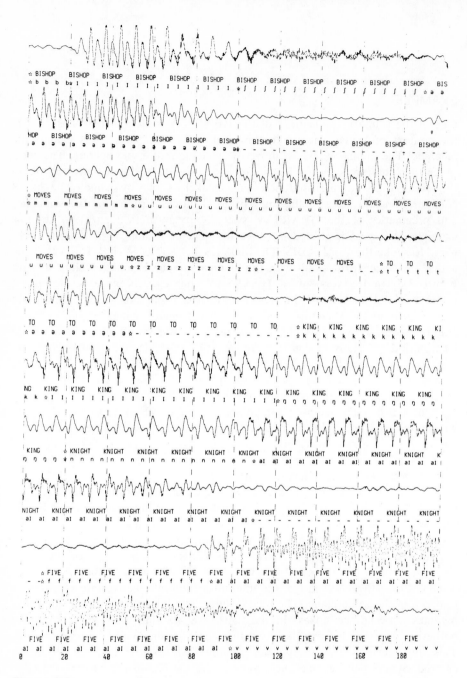

Figure 3.2
Waveform of the utterance, "Bishop moves to King Knight 5." Actual word and phoneme boundaries are illustrated below the waveform. (From Reddy et al., 1974.)

108

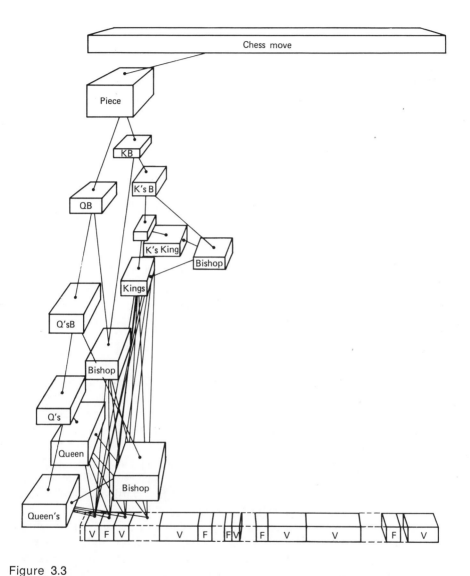

Figure 3.3

An illustration of the state of the message center in HEARSAY at a point early in the processing of the phrase, "Bishop moves to King Knight 5." Each box represents the hypothesis of some level about the interpretation of the incoming featural data. The lines between the boxes illustrate dependencies among the hypotheses.

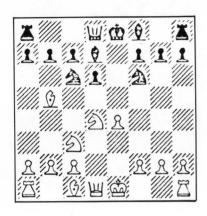

MOVE	MOVE
O–O	KNP/KN2–KN3
QB/QB1–K3	QNP/QN2–QN3
QB/QB1–KB4	QRP/QR2–QR3
QB/QB1–KN5	KN/Q4–K2
KB/QN5–QB4	KN/Q4–QN3
KR/KR1–KB1	QN/QB3–Q5
Q/Q1–Q3	KP/K4–K5
KB/QN5 × QN/QB6	K/K1–K2
QBP/KB2–KB4	QN/QB3–K2
KR/KR1–KN1	KNP/KN2–KN4
KBP/KB2–KB3	QNP/QN2–QN4
Q/Q1–Q2	QN/QB3–QR4
QR/QR1–QN1	QN/QB3–QN1
K/K1–KB1	QB/QB1–Q2
KB/QN5–K2	KB/QN5–Q3
KN/Q4–KB5	Q/Q1–KB3
KB/QN5–QR4	Q/Q1–K2
KN/Q4xQN/QB6	QB/QB1–KR6
KN/Q4–KB3	K/K1–Q2
KRP/KR2–KR4	KN/Q4–K6
QRP/QR2–QR4	KB/QN5–QR6
KR/QN5–KB1	Q/Q1–KN4
KRP/KR2–KR3	Q/Q1–KR5

Figure 3.4
The chessboard position and the ordered list of legal moves for white. (Reddy et al., 1974.)

move are the queen's bishop and the king's bishop (designated **QB** and **KB** in the diagram). Syntax realizes that the names for these two pieces can be expressed either by the word BISHOP or by a phrase indicating which bishop. In the latter case we could have either the word QUEEN'S or the word QUEEN followed by the word BISHOP or we could have either the word KING or KING'S followed by the word BISHOP. The acoustic component contains knowledge about the features required for each word. There are thus four lexical candidates to be compared against the first portion of the acoustic input: QUEEN'S, QUEEN, BISHOP, KING'S, and KING. It turns out that the feature maps of each of these words is available in the speech waveform. Thus in the case of QUEEN'S, QUEEN, KING, and KING'S additional effort is made to find the word BISHOP in the following waveform. No satisfactory fit can be found—thus the hypothesis that the first word is BISHOP is the most strongly supported and the scheduler suspends processing on the other hypotheses.

Figure 3.5 illustrates the state of the message center after the next round of processing. Syntax postulates that the next segment of speech will name some action. Semantics determines that the most plausible action for either the queen's bishop or the king's bishop to take is to *move* (rather than capture another piece). Syntax suggests the two most probable ways of expressing a

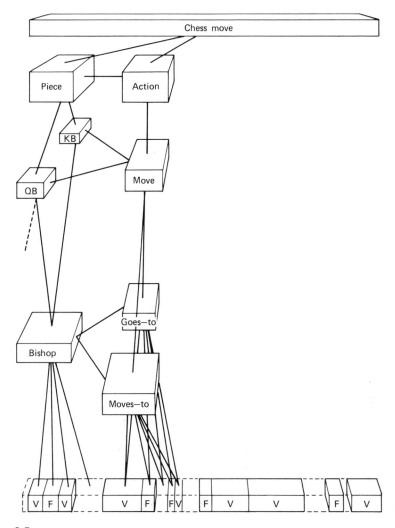

Figure 3.5
The message center at a later point in the processing.

move—MOVES TO and GOES TO. A match against the speech waveform finds both possibilities supported (although MOVES TO fits somewhat better than GOES TO); thus no choice is made and the two possibilities are continued in parallel.

Figure 3.6 illustrates what happens when a wrong track is taken. Here syntax suggested that a position would be described. Semantics suggests that the two

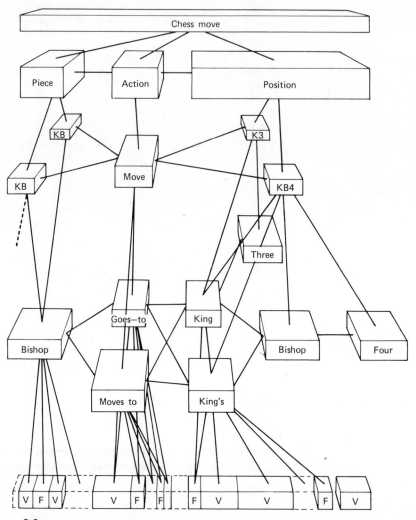

Figure 3.6
Message center at a still later point in the processing. At that point, the positional
hypothesis that the statement ended "King Bishop 4" is being seriously considered.

most likely places to move a bishop are to the king three (K3) or the king's bishop four (KB4). Thus the lexical items KING or KING's are next searched for in the acoustic waveform. Support is found for both. Then a search is carried out for a THREE or a BISHOP following KING or for BISHOP following KING'S. All of these searches result in very poor fits so the higher level hypothesis are abandoned. We thus have the configuration illustrated in Figure 3.7. We have found either KING or KING'S in the waveform and need to find a position. Thus a search is made for the most likely move not yet tested that ends on a square whose name can begin with KING or KING'S. The next most likely move (as illustrated in Figure 3.4) is to king's knight five (KN5).

Figure 3.8 illustrates the final state of the system. KN5 was hypothesized as the position; a search was carried out for KNIGHT followed by FIVE. These words were found following KING, but not following KING'S. Moreover, FIVE was at the end of the utterance. Thus, we have the statement of a complete utterance coinciding with the end of the waveform and conclude that we have properly decoded the message. Since the hypothesis involving MOVES TO is slightly better than GOES TO our final interpretation of the sentence reads BISHOP MOVES TO KING KNIGHT FIVE—the original input.

A number of points should be made about this example. First, in spite of a very primitive acoustic analysis the HEARSAY system is among the best systems ever built for recognizing connected speech. The primary reason for its success is that it makes use of a number of sources of information and attempts to find an interpretation of the input that satisfies all of these sources. Second, expectations are explicitly represented in the system as "hypotheses derived from above" without special support from below. Thus, expectations are embedded into the system because it asks the question "Could this segment of speech be a such and such?" as well as "What does this segment of speech represent?" A third point of interest is that the notion of *attention* and the allocation of attention is explicitly represented in the scheduler with its decisions on what hypotheses should be followed up. Finally, the entire system runs in parallel; that is, it works on a set of plausible hypotheses simultaneously. The example presented here was in fact made somewhat sequential for purposes of exposition—in reality the system runs in parallel with the scheduler determining where the processing gets done.

To summarize, we think of language comprehension as an extension of the process of recognizing patterns (perceiving). The pattern synthesizer does not stop when it has found a reasonably good match between a portion of the

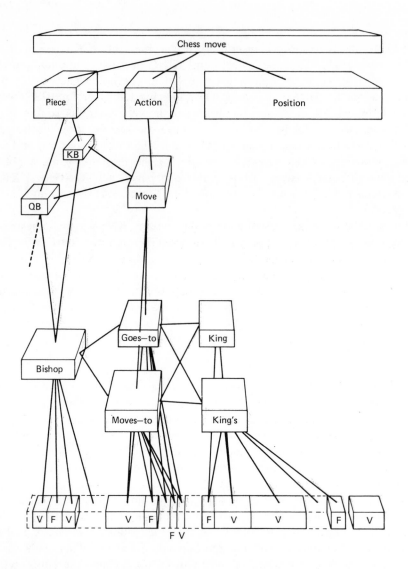

Figure 3.7
Message center at a still later point in time after the hypothesis that the position was "King Bishop 4" was rejected.

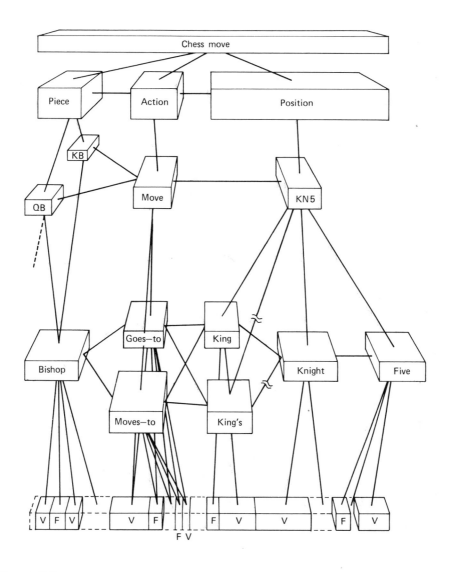

Figure 3.8
Message center in its near final state in which the reading, "Bishop goes to King Knight 5," has been accepted.

input and known word or letter. Instead, it continues to process the input until it finds sufficiently meaningful interpretation of as large a portion of the input as possible. In carrying out this processing it makes use of as many sources of information as possible. It uses the physical features extracted from the input signal, knowledge about the grammar of the language, knowledge about the meaning of sentences, and knowledge about the current context in which the input is arising, all as simultaneous constraints on the hypothesis that will ultimately constitute our *interpretation* of the input. The HEARSAY system is interesting primarily because it demonstrates how all of these various sources can be made to work together in a meaningful way to limit the total number of hypotheses tested to a reasonable number. Of course, the natural language problem is much more complex than the "Voice Chess" problem of our example. Natural language allows much more freedom in its grammar; the sets of concepts that must be understood are much broader than the few necessary to understand chess moves and board configurations; and, perhaps more important than any of the other simplifications used by HEARSAY is the way in which *context* was represented as the set of likely moves. In ordinary situations the contextual constraints are much weaker and very much harder to specify. Nevertheless, the HEARSAY system represents one of the most sophisticated attempts to specify the operation of the pattern synthesizer in the context of linguistic inputs, and it does appear to capture most of what is known about the way humans actually do use multiple sources of knowledge to interpret what they see and hear.

The remainder of this chapter will be devoted to a discussion of what is known about the way syntax, semantics, and pragmatics affect the way people actually analyze and understand natural language.

THE ROLE OF SYNTAX IN LANGUAGE UNDERSTANDING

Syntactic knowledge is knowledge about the *form* rather than the *content* of a linguistic message. Not all strings of words form sentences, and as the data of Miller and Isard (1963) presented in the previous chapter indicate strings of words that have the form of English sentences, albeit meaningless, are easier to perceive than strings of words that do not have the form of English sentences. (E.g., "Accidents carry honey between the house," is easier to perceive than "Around accidents country honey the shoot.") The fundamental explanation for this, within the general view of language understanding developed here, is that our knowledge of the *form* (syntax) of language is an important source of information on which we can draw in understanding language.

That syntactic knowledge is used in sentence processing is almost noncontroversial. There is not, however, a consensus about how syntactical knowledge is organized and applied during linguistic processing. Perhaps the most plausible model of the syntactic component is the *augmented transition network* (ATN). We now turn to a discussion of the ATN as a model of the syntactic component in language understanding.

THE AUGMENTED TRANSITION NETWORK AS A MODEL OF THE SYNTACTIC COMPONENT

The ATN was fiirst developed as a computational device for computer processing of natural language (cf. Bobrow & Fraser, 1969; Thorne, Bratley & Dewar, 1968; and Woods, 1970). It has since been developed and applied as a model for human language comprehension by Kaplan (1972, 1974), Stevens and Rumelhart (1975), and Wanner and Maratsos (1974). This section will first present a general description of an ATN and then illustrate its use as a model of language processing.

Not only does the syntactic component help us to perceive sentences by limiting the possible permutations of words we might reasonably expect, but, even more importantly, it allows us to determine the logical relationships among the words we discover in the string. At the simplest level, a sentence asserts that some relation, usually designated by a verb, holds among some set of objects, usually referred to by noun phrases. Consider the following sentences:

(1a) Dogs chase rabbits.
(1b) Rabbits chase dogs.
(1c) Rabbits are chased by dogs.
(1d) Dogs are chased by rabbits.

It is the syntax of the language that allows us to determine that the logical relationships underlying (1a) and (1c) are the same and can be represented by (2).
(2) [ACTION: chase, ACTOR: dogs, OBJECT: rabbits].
The logical structure underlying (1b) and (1d) on the other hand can be represented by:
(3) [ACTION: chase, ACTOR: rabbits, OBJECT: dogs].
It is the primary task of the syntactic component to take strings of words and construct representations like those illustrated in (2) and (3). An ATN is a device which takes a string of words as input and produces a structural description like those given in (2) and (3).

The basic structure of a very simple ATN capable of processing sentences

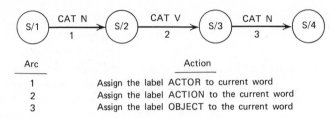

Arc	Action
1	Assign the label ACTOR to current word
2	Assign the label ACTION to the current word
3	Assign the label OBJECT to the current word

Figure 3.9
Simple ATN network for a sentence.

like (1a) and (1b) is given in Figure 3.9. The ATN illustrated in the figure consists of three kinds of elements: (1) *States*. There are four states, designated by circles in the diagram, illustrated here: S/1, S/2, S/3, and S/4. The analysis of a sentence consists of passing from one state to another. Processing begins in state S/1 and ends in state S/4. (2) *Labels*. States are connected to one another by labeled arrows. The arrows indicate the allowable movements between states. There is an arrow directly from S/1 to S/2. This indicates simply that during the analysis of a sentence the system may pass from S/1 directly to S/2. Since no direct arrow connects S/1 to S/3, S/3 may not follow S/1 directly in processing. The labels on the arrows indicate conditions which must be met for the transition from one state to another to occur. For example, the label CAT N (short for "category noun") indicates that a transition from S/1 to S/2 can occur only if the first word of the sentence is a noun. Similarly, the label CAT V indicates that a transition from state S/2 to S/3 can take place only when the next word is a verb. (3) *Actions*. In addition to the conditions determining moving from one state to the next, there are actions which are carried out whenever an arc is traversed. This action involves assigning the various parts of the sentence, discovered during the analysis, to their syntactical roles. Thus, the action associated with arc 1 (given at the bottom of the figure) is to assign the noun found at this arc to the role of ACTOR. Whenever a particular arc is traversed, the action associated with that arc is carried out.

To illustrate how our ATN works, consider how it would proceed with sentence (1a) above. The system begins in state S/1. At first the current word is the first word of the sentence, *dogs*. An attempt is made to traverse arc 1. The CAT N label on arc 1 indicates that the arc can be traversed only when the current word is a noun. In this sentence *dogs* is a noun so the system carries out the action associated with arc 1—that is, *dogs* is assigned to the ACTOR role. The next word *chase* then becomes the current word, and the

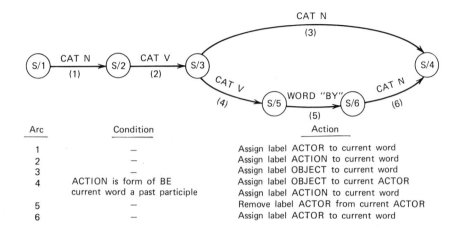

Arc	Condition	Action
1	—	Assign label ACTOR to current word
2	—	Assign label ACTION to current word
3	—	Assign label OBJECT to current word
4	ACTION is form of BE	Assign label OBJECT to current ACTOR
	current word a past participle	Assign label ACTION to current word
5	—	Remove label ACTOR from current ACTOR
6	—	Assign label ACTOR to current word

Figure 3.10
ATN sentence network including a provision for passive sentences.

system moves to state S/2. The CAT V condition requires that the current word is a verb. It is, so *chase* is assigned as the ACTION and the system moves into state S/3. Here it assigns *rabbits* to the OBJECT position and completes the sentence.

The system we have outlined thus far will, of course, fail to analyze passive sentences like those illustrated in (1c) and (1d). Figure 3.10 illustrates the additions required to make an ATN capable of parsing simple passives. Note that for arc 4, in addition to several associated actions, the ATN allows new conditions—in this case, the condition that a passive sentence requires a form of the verb *be* and a past participle form of the main verb. Moreover, in addition to CAT arcs we can also require that we have a certain word with a WORD arc. To illustrate how the system would proceed consider sentence (1c) again: "Rabbits are chased by dogs."

The system begins processing at the word *rabbits* in state S/1. As it traverses arc 1 it assigns *rabbits* to ACTOR. Then, as it traverses arc 2 it assigns *are* as the ACTION. It then attempts to traverse arc 3. Arc 3 requires that the current word be a noun. However, the current word is *chased,* thus the system *fails* to traverse arc 3 and tries the next arc from state S/3, i.e., arc 4. At the point it attempts arc 4 its partially constructed representation for the sentence is (4) [ACTION: are, ACTOR: rabbits].

Since *chased* is a verb the processor checks the additional condition that the current ACTION include a form of *be* and that the current word has a past

Sentence network

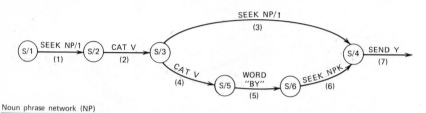

Noun phrase network (NP)

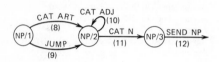

Arc	condition	Action
1	–	Set ACTOR to current phrase
2	Current word matches ACTOR in number	Set ACTION to current word
3	–	Set OBJECT to current phrase
4	ACTION = be, current word is past participle	Set ACTION to current word, set OBJECT to current SUBJECT
5	–	–
6	–	Set ACTOR to current phrase
7	–	Assemble sentence representation
8	–	Set DETERMINER to current word
9	–	Set DETERMINER to null
10	–	Set MODIFIER to current word
11	–	Set HEAD to current word
12	–	Assemble noun phrase

Figure 3.11
Sentence and noun phrase ATN networks.

participle form. Since both of these are satisfied in this example, the system carries out the designated actions and constructs a new representation. Thus producing

(5) [ACTION: chase, OBJECT: rabbits].

The system then proceeds with arcs 5 and 6 and completes the parse of (1c).

The system we have outlined thus far is still too rudimentary for all but the simplest sentences in the language. The most obvious defect is that it will only allow single nouns as subjects and objects. This defect can be easily remedied by introducing another feature of the ATN, namely the SEEK and SEND arcs. Within an ATN one can have CAT or WORD arcs which check to see if the current word is a member of some category or is some particular word. One can also use a SEEK arc which asks if the current word begins a particular sort of phrase. Figure 3.11 illustrates a version of our ATN which contains two networks, a sentence network of the sort we have been discussing and a noun phrase network which parses noun phrases. Notice that the noun phrase (NP) network is invoked from the sentence network through a SEEK arc. We can illustrate the operation of the SEEK and SEND arcs with another example. Consider the parsing of the following sentence.

(6) The small dogs are chased by large rabbits.

As before, the system begins in state S/1 looking at the first word in the sentence. In order to traverse arc 1 a noun phrase must be found. This is done by processing the initial portion of the sentence with the noun phrase network. Thus, the system transfers to state NP/1 and continues processing. Arc 8 is attempted. Since *the* is classified as an article it is labeled as DETERMINER and the processor changes to state NP/2 and shifts its attention to the word *small*. It then succeeds in traversing arc 10, setting *small* to be a MODIFIER and returns to state NP/2. The system then shifts its attention to *dogs* and attempts arc 10 again. This time it fails because *dogs* is not classified as an adjective. The system thus attempts arc 11 and succeeds assigning *dogs* as HEAD. The system then moves into NP/3 and attempts to traverse arc 12. This involves the action of constructing the noun phrase representation and SENDing it back to the place where the NP network was initiated—namely arc 1. The system thus has found a noun phrase and can complete the transition to state S/2. In traversing the arc the entire noun phrase was assigned as the ACTOR. Thus the representation of the sentence as the system enters S/2 is

(7) [ACTOR: [DETERMINER: the, MODIFIER: small, HEAD: dogs]].

The remainder of the parse proceeds as before until it reaches arc 6. Here it again enters the noun phrase network. At this point in time the current word is *small*. The processor attempts arc 8, but fails. It thus attempts arc 9 and succeeds setting the DETERMINER to null. Finally the parse is complete and generates the following final representation.

(8) [ACTION: chase,
      ACTOR: [DETERMINER: the, MODIFIER: small, HEAD: dogs],
      OBJECT: [MODIFIER: large, HEAD: rabbits]].

The ATN illustrated in Figure 3.11 is much more powerful than the previous ones we have discussed, but it too is still a long way from adequate for a grammar of English. Although no ATN grammar has ever been built capable of properly analyzing all of the English language, systems like that illustrated in the figure have been developed which can properly parse a significant proportion of English (cf. Woods & Kaplan, 1971). Rather than illustrate a more complex grammar at this point, we turn to a discussion of the general characteristics of an ATN that make it a plausible candidate for a psychologically valid model of the syntactic component and then discuss some experimental results which add to the credence of this general model.

There are a number of signifiicant features of the ATN which makes it a particularly promising model of the syntactic component of language processing. Perhaps its most important feature is the natural way that the *grammar of the language* fits together with the *rules for processing* the language. In more traditional approaches the structural rules of the language are stated quite independently of the processing rules (cf. Fodor, Bever, & Garrett, 1974). Much of the history of psycholinguistics has been tied to an attempt to take a grammatical theory developed without consideration of how it might be used in processing language and derive predictions about how its plays its role in language comprehension. The ATN is unique in that the grammar and processing rules can readily coexist. Moreover, as we will discuss in a later section, an ATN allows a variety of specific processing assumptions to be postulated and tested.

A second important feature of an ATN is the natural way the notion of expectation can be realized. A central theme of this book is the important role that our expectations and prior knowledge play in the details of our information processing. The ATN formalism allows us to develop specific theories about the syntactic aspects of our expectations. In a very real sense the arcs leaving a state in an ATN grammar represent expectations about the syntactic class of the words to follow. These expectations allow us to interpret naturally the *same word* as a member of different syntactic classes depending on the context in which the word occurs. Consider as an example the following sentences.

(9a) The sailors man the boats.

(9b) The old man rowed the boat.

(9c) The old man the boats.

Consider how each of these sentences would be processed by the ATN system illustrated in Figure 3.11. With (9a) the system would first find the noun phrase, *the sailors,* and would then check the next word to see if it could be a verb. Since *man* can serve as a verb it would immediately determine that the verb sense of *man* was desired and process the entire sentence. In this example the fact that *man* is more commonly a noun makes no difference to the system. It is *expecting* a verb when it encounters *man* and thus immediately interprets man as a verb. Now consider sentence (9b). As usual the system begins looking for a noun phrase. It finds a DETERMINER, *the,* checks for an adjective, finds *old* to be an adjective, checks for another adjective. There is no adjective sense for *man,* so the system checks for a noun sense for *man* and finds one. It then completes the parse of the noun phrase and proceeds to the remainder of the sentence. The normal noun sense of *man* is again found without any interference from the fact that it has a verb sense. Again, the system was *expecting* an adjective or a noun, but not a verb. Hence the noun sense of the term was found without any interference from its verb sense. An analysis of sentence (9c) illustrates the sorts of statements in which the existence of a noun sense of a verb *can* cause difficulties for the interpretation of the sentence. In this case the ATN will wrongly interpret tthe words *the old man* to be a noun phrase. Only later, after it has been unable to find a verb for the sentence, will it back up and discover that *old* was intended as a noun and *man* as a verb. The fact that the system has some trouble with sentence (9c) should not be taken as evidence against the ATN as a plausible model for human language processing. In fact, whereas people ordinarily have no difficulty with (9a) and (9b), (9c) is often found a difficult sentence to understand. This, then, should be taken as additional evidence favoring the ATN processing system we have been developing.

Sentences are naturally processed in a word-by-word, left-to-right order. This meets our intuitions about how we process sentences and is generally consistent with evidence from studies of eye movements which generally indicate that with the exception of a small number of regressions the eye jumps from left to right across the page, stopping for a quarter of a second or so every one to five words. The small number of regressions (i.e., right-to-left eye movements) may well be correlated with back up in the ATN. To date, no evidence exists on this point. However, evidence to be presented below shows clearly that *pauses* in reading aloud often correspond with periods of back up in an ATN. We now turn to a discussion of more detailed evidence which offers further support for the ATN.

The ATN and Comprehension Difficulty

Sentences differ in comprehension difficulty. Some sentences even though long can be relatively easy to understand. Thus, for example,

(10) The cat chased the mouse that lived in the house that Jack built.

Other sentences can be no longer, but much more difficulty to understand.

(11) The house the mouse the cat chased lived in was built by Jack.

The difficulty with (11) arises not from semantic complexity, but rather from the difficulty in unraveling the syntactic relationships. A number of experiments have been carried out to measure the complexity of sentences by assessing their comprehension difficulty. There have been three basic experimental methods. In the most straightforward method subjects are asked to judge the complexity or comprehension difficulty of a sentence. The data then consists of ratings of difficulty. A second method consists of asking subjects to paraphrase sentences and then measuring either the number of "correct" paraphrases or the amount of time required to form a paraphrase. A third method involves giving subjects a distracting task (such as a list of words to remember or a target to respond to) during the processing of the sentence and observing their ability to carry out this distracting task. Presumably the more difficult the processing of the sentence the poorer the performance on the distracting task.

Bever (1970) and more recently Fodor, Bever, and Garret (1974) have suggested a set of *perceptual strategies* that underlie the syntactic component of processing. An example of one such perceptual strategy given by Bever is *any non-verb-noun (NVN) sequence within a potential internal unit in the surface structure corresponds to "actor-action-object."*

This principle is, of course, already built into the ATN we discussed above. Whenever our ATN encounters an initial noun phrase, it assumes that it represents the ACTOR. As we have already observed, this makes the processing of passive sentences somewhat more difficult. That is, the system must attempt more arcs and change its mind more often on a passive sentence than on an active sentence. As Bever points out there is ample evidnce that passive sentences are, in fact, harder to understand than their active counterparts.

Gough (1965) reported an experiment demonstrating this effect. In this experiment subjects were first presented with a sentence and a picture and then were asked to determine whether the sentence was true or false in describing the picture. The time to make the judgment was measured. The experiment included sentences such as

(12a) The boy kicked the girl.
(12b) The girl was kicked by the boy.

Verification time was longer with passive sentences, like (12b) than for semantically equivalent active sentences like (12a). There are a variety of similar results in the literature. (For a summary of these results see Fodor, Bever, and Garrett, 1974.)

Bever's strategy also accounts for the difficulty of sentences such as

(13) The man judged the winner bowed.

over the semantically similar counterpart

(14) The man chosen the winner bowed.

In (13) the basic NVN strategy leads to the initial interpretation of the sentence as

(15) The man judged the winner.

When the final verb is encountered the sentence must be reanalyzed for the relative clause reading

(16) The man [who was] judged the winner bowed.

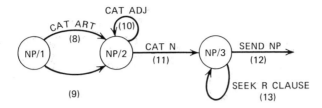

Figure 3.12
Elaborated noun-phrase network, including provision for relative clauses.

Sentences like (14) cause no such difficulty .As soon as the verb *chosen* is encountered it can be noticed that the tense is wrong for a main verb and the proper analysis of the sentence can proceed. Similarly, Bever reports the subjects find sentences like

(17) *The editor authors the newspaper* hired liked laughed.

much more difficult than sentences like

(18) The editors the authors the newspapers hired liked laughed.

Both of these sentences are, of course, difficult. Again the obvious explanation for this difference lies in the fact that the fiirst portion of (17) forms an appropriate sentence and subjects must back up and reinterpret the sentence when the verb *hired* is encountered.

The ATN account of the relative difficulties of (13) and (14) and (17) and (18) is entirely straightforward. The ATN grammar given in Figure 3.11 does not, however, accept relative clauses. We will, therefore, extend the noun phrase grammar to the point where it will accept relative clauses and then show how this addition to the grammar naturally accounts for the difference between (13) and (14) or (17) and (18).

Figure 3.12 illustrates a slightly modified version of the noun phrase network, illustrated in Figure 3.11, which accepts sentences like (13) and (18). We have modified the previous noun phrase network simply by adding an arc numbered 13 which processes relative clauses. At this point we need not elaborate as to how the relative clause subnetwork that is invoked at arc 13 operates. We will discuss its operation below when we direct our attention to the processing of relative clauses. For the moment, it is only important that our ATN model embodies Bever's strategy just so long as it tries arc 12 before it tries arc 13. If the system tries to terminate the noun phrase (i.e., traverse arc 12) prior to looking for a relative clause, we can account for the difficulty of (13) and (17) as compared to (14) and (18). In addition to this tendency

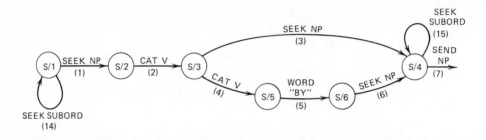

Figure 3.13
Elaborated sentence network including provision for subordinate clauses.

to prefer to interpret initial NVN sequences as *actor-action-object* sequences, Bever and Fodor, Bever, and Garrett suggest that proposed subordinate clauses are more difficult to process than trailing subordinate clauses. Thus, Weksel and Bever (1966) found that sentences like

(19a) That Mary was happy surprised Max.
(19b) When Mary left, Max was happy.
(19c) Although Mary had left, Max was happy.

are all rated more difficult to comprehend than their semantically equivalent counterparts illustrated below.

(20a) It surprised Max that Mary was happy.
(20b) Max was happy when Mary left.
(20c) Max was happy although Mary had left.

Again, Kaplan (1972) has pointed out that these differences can be readily accounted for by an ATN under the assumption that subordinate clauses are attempted only after it is determined that the first clause cannot be a main clause. This strategy is illustrated in Figure 3.13 by the addition of the two SEEK SUBORD arcs, numbered 14 and 15, to the sentence network of Figure 3.11.

Bever (1970) suggests a number of other perceptual strategies which can be represented within an ATN by assuming that arcs are attempted in a certain order. One other point raised by Kaplan which warrants discussion at this point is the relationship between arc ordering and the interpretation of syntactically ambiguous sentences. Since the processing is *depth-first*—that is, only one alternative is pursued at a time—a given ATN grammar makes strong predictions as to which of two semantically equiplausible interpretations will be made to a syntactically ambiguous sentence. Thus, in sentences like

(21) Visiting relatives can be a bore.

some subjects may interpret it first to mean

(22) Visiting relatives is a bore.

and others may interpret it first to mean

(23) Visiting relatives are a bore.

But whichever interpretation is found first, the analogous interpretation should be found in

(24) Frightening lions can be dangerous.

Similarly sentences like

(25) John felt the child trembled.

should be difficult whenever the sentence

(26) John heard the child trembled.

is difficult.
In either example the difficulty indicates that we first processed the sentences as (27a) rather than (27b).

(27a) John felt/heard the child trembled.
(27b) John felt/heard that the child trembled.

To date I know of no studies that have systematically studied differences of this sort, but their existence is clearly predicted by the ATN analysis.

Garden Path Sentences and the ATN Analysis

Sentences like (9c) The old man the boats; (14) The man judged the winner bowed; (25); and (26) are sometimes referred to as *garden path sentences*. The name refers to the fact that the analysis of these sentences leads to initial inappropriate results which must later be reanalyzed. Of course, as pointed out above, these are not only garden path sentences for humans. Our ATN model is also forced to back up during the analysis of such sentences. Suppose we ask subjects to read sentences such as these aloud. If they are behaving like ATNs they should be required to back up at that point in the sentence when they encounter the anomalous word. They should then either be forced to back up and begin reading the sentence over or at least to have a long pause at the point of the anomaly. Such an experiment was carried out in my laboratory by Mark Kramer and Al Stevens. In this experiment subjects were tape re-

corded as they read such sentences aloud and answered questions such as "Who bowed?" or "Who does what to the boats?" In addition to sentences like (9c) and (13) subjects were given sentences like
(28) The steel ships are transporting is expensive.
as well as a number of nongarden path control sentences. Later the pauses found during the reading of the sentences were measured, and the loci of all significant pauses and points where subjects started over were recorded. Our ATN model processing these sentences expects significant back up to occur at the points indicated below.

(9c) The old man △ the boats.
(13) The man judged the winner △ bowed.
(28) The steel ships are transporting △ is expensive.

Compared with each of these sentence types were sentences that were similar in form, but disambiguated either semantically or syntactically. Thus, we have

(29a) The blind sail with friends.
(29b) The merchants ship their wares.

(30a) The vegetables prepared for the dinner spoiled.
(30b) The man chosen the winner bowed.

(31a) The granite carpets are covering up is ugly.
(31b) The vegetables ships are transporting are expensive.

The first of each sentence pair is similar to its garden path model, except it is semantically anomalous. That is, it doesn't make sense to talk of a "blind sail" or of "vegetables preparing" or of "granite carpets." The second element of each pair provides syntactic cues for the correct reading. Figure 3.14 gives the percentage of sentences with pauses in each position for each sentence type. The results for each sentence type indicate that pauses occurred most frequently at the point predicted by the ATN. Moreover, a comparison of the *garden path* sentences with the *semantically disambiguated* and *syntactically disambiguated* illustrates that semantic disambiguation helped somewhat in the unusual adjective-noun pairs (i.e., "blind sail" and "granite carpets") but helped a good deal in the sentence with the embedded relative clause. The syntactic disambiguation essentially ruled out the garden path reading except in the cases of sentences like (31b) where subjects apparently miss the incompatibility in phrases like "the vegetables ships," "the wood boxes," and "the bricks houses."

To summarize, then, we have to this point discussed two aspects in which ATNs can be shown to provide good accounts of syntactic effects on sentence

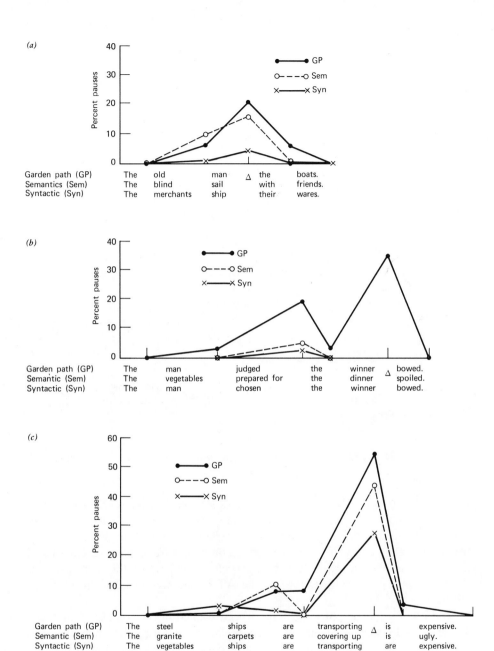

Figure 3.14
The percentage of pauses occurring at each point during the reading of three kinds of garden path sentences.

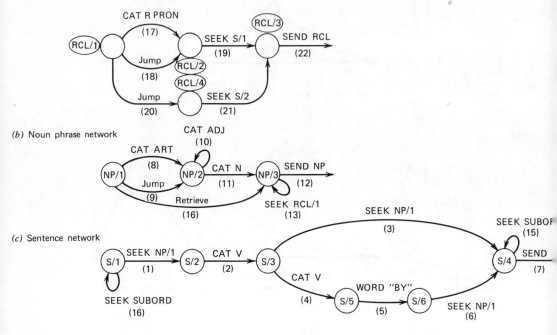

Figure 3.15
Elaborated ATN networks for relative clauses, noun phrases and sentences.

processing. First, we showed that the ordering of arcs in an ATN can account for "perceptual strategies" employed by subjects and that such strategies contribute toward the difficulty of processing certain kinds of sentences. Secondly, we showed that an ATN gives a good account of garden path sentences and the pauses that occur while processing such sentences. In this instance it is the depth-first processing strategy of the ATN that accounts for the observed effects.

Two other syntactic phenomena have been studied in the context of an ATN. These are (1) the processing of relative clauses and (2) the effects of syntactic expectations during reading. We now complete our discussion of the syntactic component with a discussion of these studies.

An ATN Model of Relative Clause Processing

We begin by extending the ATN we have thus far developed by a more explicit account of how it handles relative clauses. Figure 3.15 and Table 3.2 illustrates the relative clause subnetwork, and Figure 3.15*b* shows the augmented noun phrase network. The table lists the associated actions and conditions. The new aspects can best be illustrated by way of an example. Consider the sentence

(32) The cat that the dog chases chases mice.

As usual, the ATN begins in S/1 where it immediately encounters a SEEK NP/1 arc. The system therefore enters state NP/1 with *the* as its current word. It then parses the phrase *the cat,* assembles the noun phrase as

[DETERMINER:the, HEAD:cat]

and returns to state S/2 and looks for a verb. This fails immediately since *that* will not parse as a verb. Thus, the system returns to the noun phrase network and attempts arc 13. At this point it encounters a SEEK RCL/1. It carries out the action indicated in Table 3.2 and puts a copy of the currently constructed noun phrase on a special stack called the HOLD stack. The stack will save the noun phrase so it can be put into its proper place in the embedded relative clause. The system then shifts to state RCL/1 in the relative clause network. The word *that* is a relative pronoun so arc 17 can be immediately traversed and attention can then be shifted to the next word *the.* There is only one arc available from RCL/2, so the system must then SEEK S/1. That is the system now reenters the sentence network. The phrase *the dog* is then routinely parsed and the system finds *chases* as the main verb. At this point the system enters state S/3 and must try to find a noun phrase. The current word at this point

Table 3.2
Action and Conditions on New Arcs of Figure 3.15

Arc	Condition	Action
13	—	Push current phrase onto *Hold* stack
16	*Hold* stack contains an element pushed on when RCL network was last entered	Assign phrase on top of *Hold* stack to current noun phrase
17	—	—
18	—	—
19	—	—
20	—	Assign ACTOR to top of *Hold* stack Assign ACTION to *be*
21	—	—
22	Element pushed onto *Hold* stack at entry must have been used	Assemble Relative Clause

is the second occurrence of the word *chases*. The system then attempts arc 3 looking for a noun phrase. The system thus enters state NP/1 again. Here it fails to find a noun phrase in the usual way. However, before failing entirely it attempts arc 16. This arc is a special device associated with the HOLD list. The system can traverse the RETRIEVE and get a noun phrase from the HOLD stack just in case the noun phrase pushed onto the HOLD stack as the system traversed arc 13 still remains there. In this instance it does and the system can traverse arc 16 picking up the noun phrase from the HOLD stack and creating the following structure for the embedded sentence.

(33) [ACTOR: [DETERMINER:the, HEAD:dog],
     ACTION: chases,
     OBJECT: [DETERMINER:the, HEAD:cat]].

The system has now successfully traversed arc 19 and moves into state RCL/3. Having finished the relative clause successfully it traverses arc 22, SENDs the relative clause back to arc 13, completes the traversal of arc 13, and goes back to state NP/3. At this point arc 12 is traversed and the following representation is constructed and sent back to arc 1.

(34) [DETERMINER: the,
     HEAD: cat,
     RELCLAUSE: [ACTOR: [DETERMINER:the, HEAD:dog],
              ACTION: chases,
              OBJECT: [DETERMINER:the, HEAD:cat]]].

At this point the system, with *chases* still the current word, traverses arc 2 assigning *chases* as an action and then again traverses arc 3 picking up *mice* as the final OBJECT and thus completes the parse. The final representation of the sentence then is

(35) [ACTOR: [DETERMINER: the,
          HEAD: cat,
          RELCLAUSE: [ACTOR: [DETERMINER:the, HEAD:
                    dog],
                ACTION: chases,
                OBJECT: [DETERMINER:the, HEAD:
                cat]]]
     ACTION: chases,
     OBJECT: mice].

Kaplan (1974) and Wanner and Maratsos (1974) have suggested that the difficulty in processing relative clauses arises not so much from the number of arcs attempted, but because of the necessity to use valuable memory resources in HOLDing information on the HOLD stack. These researchers have reported a number of results supporting this view. The immediate implication of this hypothesis is that *subject relatives* such as

(36) The dog$_\triangle$that$_\triangle$chases the cat chases mice.

should be easier to process than *object relatives* like

(37) The dog$_\triangle$that the cat chases$_\triangle$chases mice.

This follows because the period of time in which something must reside on the HOLD stack is longer for object relatives than for subject relatives. [The noun phrase is pushed on the HOLD stack at the first $\triangle$ of sentences (36) and (37) and removed from the HOLD stack at the second $\triangle$.] An experiment by Wanner and Maratsos (1974) confirms this expectation by showing that object relatives disrupt memory for a list of words more severely than subject relatives.

Not only does the HOLD hypothesis predict that some sentences are more difficult overall than others, it also suggests that the processing load will vary from moment to moment during the processing of a sentence. In particular, it suggests that the processing load will reach a peak while the HOLD stack is occupied and then subside after the noun phrase is removed from the HOLD stack. Thus, consider the following two sentences:

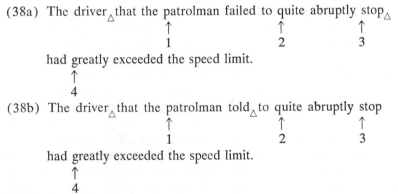

The sentences are very similar on a surface level, but the HOLD stack is emptied at different points in the two sentences. In (38a) the HOLD stack is not emptied until after the processing of the word *stop*. In (38b) it is emptied immediately after the word *told*. Thus, if processing load is partially determined by the contents of the HOLD list we should find that (38a) and (38b) are equal at point 1 on the processing of the word *patrolman* (up to that word both sentences are identical). At points 2 and 3, sentence (38a) should require more processing load than (38b) because the HOLD list in (38a) is not yet empty, but that of (38b) is. Finally, at point 4 the two sentences should

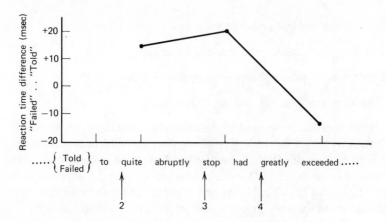

Figure 3.16
Differences of reaction times while processing sentences containing verbs like "failed minus" reaction times while processing sentences containing verbs like "told" for the three critical test points. (Data from Kaplan, 1974.)

again show no difference in processing load since the HOLD stack is empty in both cases. Kaplan (1974) attempted to test these predictions by measuring reaction times to extraneous stimuli presented at points 2, 3, and 4 in sentences like (38a) and (38b). Under the assumption that an increased processing load in the sentence comprehension task will increase reaction time to the distracting stimulus, we would expect that on points 2 and 3 the reaction time would be greater during the processing of sentences like (38a) than like (38b). At point 4 the reaction times should not differ. Figure 3.16 shows the results. At points 2 and 3 we find the expected difference between the two sentence types. However, at point 4 we find the difference reversing rather than disappearing. It is not clear what causes the difference at point 4, but the general pattern of results with sentences like (38a), showing an increased processing load while an item occupies the HOLD stack then subsiding after the HOLD stack is emptied, is certainly consistent with the hypothesis.

In a closely related series of experiments Wanner and Maratsos (1974) used a version of their memory task to measure the memory load at various points during the processing of a sentence. They presented word lists at various points during the processing of a sentence and then observed both the disruptive effect of being forced to memorize the list on the comprehensibility of the sentence. Their results were generally consistent with those of Kaplan. These researchers conclude that "the unique success of the TML [Transient Memory

Load] predictions based on the HOLD hypothesis provides substantial evidence for the ATN model."

To summarize our discussion of the ATN thus far, we have developed a concrete model for the processing of English sentences. A wide variety of evidence ranging from judgments of comprehensibility to the processing of garden path sentences to the detailed processing of relative clauses all provide credence for a model like the ATN we have been discussing. One feature of the ATN we have not discussed at any length is the account it provides for our syntactic expectations. As suggested in Chapter 2 and again in our discussion of the HEARSAY system, expectations play an important role in perception in general and language understanding in particular. Before concluding our discussion of ATNs we briefly investigate expectancy and the ATN.

Expectancy and the ATN Model

Stevens and Rumelhart (1975) used an ATN model as a tool for analysis of the role of expectancy in reading. As pointed out above, in each state of an ATN there is an ordered set of arcs that can be traversed in leaving that state. It is this ordered set which can serve as a model of a subject's expectancy while reading. Ordinarily, we expect the arcs to be ordered according to the probability of making a correct transition. Thus, the ordering of the arcs comes to reflect in some way the statistical probabilities of the English language .In their experiment Stevens and Rumelhart developed a rather general ATN grammar and then attempted, empirically, to ascertain the order of the arcs for that grammar. This was accomplished by the following method. Subjects were presented a text, three words at a time. Immediately after the third word was presented subjects were asked to "guess" the word they thought would follow. Subjects were given three guesses. If they failed to guess correctly they were then given the next three words of the text and asked to guess again. At this point we are only interested in the syntactic class of the words they guess. Suppose subjects determine what syntactic class to guess by the following manner. They process the sentence to the point where they are asked to guess. At this point they are in some state of an ATN. They guess the syntactic class of the next word by responding with a word in the class they would first look for from that state. Thus for example suppose they had just received the following partial sentence

(39) A large black dog chased the. . . .

and were asked to guess the following word. According to the grammar given in Figure 3.15 their ATN would now be in state NP/2 awaiting the next word. At this point the simple grammar allows either an adjective or a noun. If subjects choose nouns more often than adjectives we conclude that arc 11, the CAT N arc, is ordered before arc 10, the CAT ADJ arc. By following this procedure we were able to determine the appropriate arc ordering for each state in our grammar. Over all states subjects responded with a word from the most probable arc about 75% of the time. This seems to suggests that there is a reasonably fixed ordering of expectancies dependent only on the state of the network as determined by our ATN model.

Once the arc orderings had been determined, additional subjects were asked to read aloud from the passages from which the prediction data had been collected. The reading was recorded and analyzed for errors. A number of predictions follow from our ATN analysis. If subjects were in fact using the ATN to generate syntactic hypotheses about words in the string, the syntactic class of reading errors should mirror that of the predictions we had observed. This occurred. Almost 80% of the time a reading error occurred in a given state the erroneous response involved followed the most probable arc as determined from the prediction experiment. In fact, the percentage of times a particular syntactic choice was made during prediction and on errors during reading were remarkably close. Figure 3.18 illustrates the comparison for state ST/3. The data for other states are similarly close and are reported in full in Stevens and Rumelhart. We have thus demonstrated that the same mechanism that generates predictions in a prediction experiment could well be operating to help determine the nature of reading errors. Moreover, we have shown that the sorts of expectations generated from an ATN are indeed partial determiners of the errors we actually observe.

Another prediction we can make from an ATN type model is that when a subject's errors place him in a state in the grammar which makes it impossible to interpret correctly the following words we would expect him to be forced either to back up or to distort the remaining portions of the sentence he is reading. Again this prediction was confirmed in the Stevens and Rumelhart experiment. It was found that 59% of the errors which led to a wrong state were corrected by the reader. Only about 30% of errors allowing a grammatically sound completion of the sentence were corrected. The fact that errors not leading to *grammatical inconsistencies* were corrected as often as 30% of the time simply illustrates that constraints other than the simple syntactic constraints modeled by an ATN are involved in reading. In the following sections we turn our attention to the all important semantic and pragmatic constraints whose roles doubtlessly outshine the syntactic constraints we have been discussing. First, however, we reflect on the relationship between the ATN we have been discussing and the sort of comprehension system envisioned in a HEARSAY-like system.

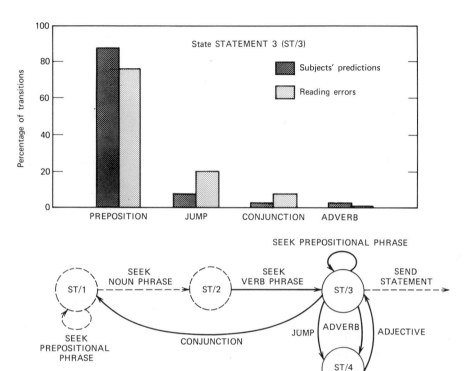

Figure 3.18

ATN AND THE HEARSAY SYSTEM

We began this chapter with a discussion of the **HEARSAY** system as a general model for language understanding. That model consisted of an interacting system of knowledge sources, each making and testing hypotheses within its own sphere of knowledge. The picture we get is of a parallel system working on many levels at once, interacting through the central message center. How do ATNs fit into the general scheme of things? How can an ATN that works serially in a depth-first word-by-word fashion interface with the highly interactive parallel **HEARSAY** system?

To see how ATNs might fit in, remember first that the ATN is only playing the role of the syntactic knowledge source. As such it plays only one small part in the overall comprehension process. Its task is merely to hypothesize possible syntactic elements and to check these hypotheses against words discovered in the input string. This is exactly the operation of the ATN we have been discussing. When the system encounters a SEEK arc it is, in effect, hypothesizing the existence of some particular syntactic element in the input signal. Moreover, when it goes to a subnetwork and begins processing it is, in effect, testing that hypothesis. Similarly, when it encounters a CAT arc, it is hypothesizing the existence of a word in that particular syntactic class.

Perhaps the primary drawback of the ATN system as we have described it is its essential *top-down* nature. That is, the ATN first hypothesizes that there will be a sentence in the input. It then attempts the first arc and tries the hypothesis that the first part of the input will form a noun phrase; next it tests the hypothesis that the first word will be a determiner, etc. All of this occurs before it looks at the first word. It would seem more reasonable, as a psychological model, if the hypotheses generated were more naturally constrained by the nature of the input. That is, it would seem more reasonable if a *bottom-up* character were added to the ATN. In fact, such an extension has been made.

Kaplan (1973) has developed a generalization of the ATN which he calls the "general syntactic processor" or GSP. A detailed discussion of GSP is beyond the scope of this chapter. Suffice it to say that Kaplan has shown how an ATN can be integrated into a general framework much like that of the HEARSAY system which allows both top-down and bottom-up sources for its hypotheses. In GSP, a hypothesis once generated, is always evaluated through an ATN subnetwork of the usual kind. For example, the occurrence of *the* in the string can initiate a SEEK NP. Once this hypothesis is generated the system uses the NP subnetwork and the ATN to test for the occurrence of the NP. The essential operating properties are thus only slightly changed.

In a recent paper, Rumelhart (in press) has attempted to put together the theory of visual feature extraction discussed in Chapter 2, the idea of the cooperating knowledge sources as in HEARSAY, and the syntactic processing of the ATN to form an account of the reading process. The following example should suffice to illustrate the operation of the model. Imagine the following experimental situation: A subject is presented with a picture (as in Figure 3.19) and allowed to view it for some time. Following this he is given a tachistoscopic presentation of a noun phrase which he knows will refer to one of the objects in the picture. His job is to read the noun phrase and determine which object in the picture was referred to. For the purposes of illustration, suppose that the actual phrase presented was "the car" referring to the Volkswagen in Figure 3.19. We now will illustrate the processes assumed to be involved in the processing of this phrase.

Figure 3.19
Context for recognition of the phrase, "The car." (Figure provided by Jean Mandler.)

As with HEARSAY, Rumelhart assumes that there is a central *message center* through which all of the relevant knowledge sources interact. Figure 3.20 illustrates the presumed state of the message center at an early point in the processing sequence. Note that six different knowledge sources are assumed in this example. Corresponding to each knowledge source is a hypothesis level in the message. Thus, at the lowest level, the *feature level,* we have the set of features assumed to have been extracted from the actual input. At the next highest level, the *letter level,* we have hypotheses about the letters presented at each position. A letter-level knowledge source is assumed to look at the feature input and postulate the most probable letter-level hypotheses. In this case, I have assumed that the two most probable letter-level hypotheses have been postulated at each position, except at the final position where the feature information is very sparse—there only the most probable hypothesis, *T,*

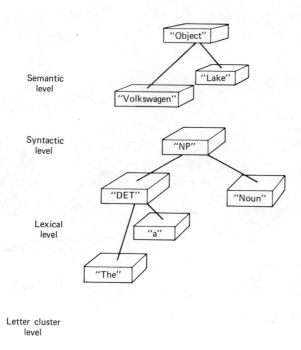

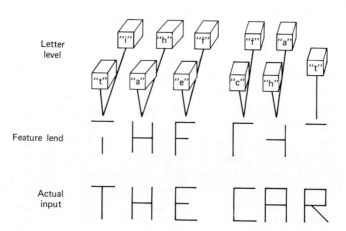

Figure 3.20
The state of the message center early in the processing of the phrase, "The car."

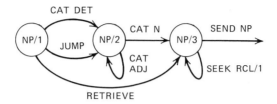

Figure 3.21
ATN noun-phrase network.

has been postulated. This mode in which higher level hypotheses are generated on the basis of the incoming lower level information is, of course, the *bottom-up* mode of processing discussed above.

At the same time this processing is taking place, expectations about the task are assumed to generate hypotheses at other levels from the *top down*. Thus, at the very top we have *semantic-level* hypotheses about what the input will refer to. Here we have the hypothesis that the phrase will refer to "an object." This expectation comes from the subject's knowledge that the phrase will refer to one of the objects in the picture. The semantic knowledge source is assumed to postulate the most salient objects in the scene as possible semantic-level hypotheses. In this case I have supposed that the Volkswagen and the lake are the most salient possibilities.

Meanwhile, the syntactic knowledge source is assumed to generate hypotheses at the *syntactic level*. In this example, I have assumed that the syntactic knowledge source is generating hypotheses based on the ATN noun phrase network illustrated in Figure 3.21. (*Note:* the syntactic knowledge source is assumed to use an NP network instead of a sentence network because the subject knows that the task involves only the presentation of noun phrases.) Thus, the syntactic knowledge source first postulates an NP and then generates, from the top down, hypotheses about the syntactic classes of the input items. Since the first arc in the NP network involves finding a DETERMINER, the system postulates that the first word is a determiner. At this point, instead of waiting to find out whether or not the first word is really a determiner as the previously discussed ATNs have done, the system moves directly to state NP/2 and postulates that the second word is a noun.

At the same time the lexical-level knowledge source is looking at the *lexical level* for information about the particular words in the input string. When the syntactic knowledge source postulates that the first word is a DETerminer, the lexical knowledge source postulates the two most probable determiners—"the" and "a."

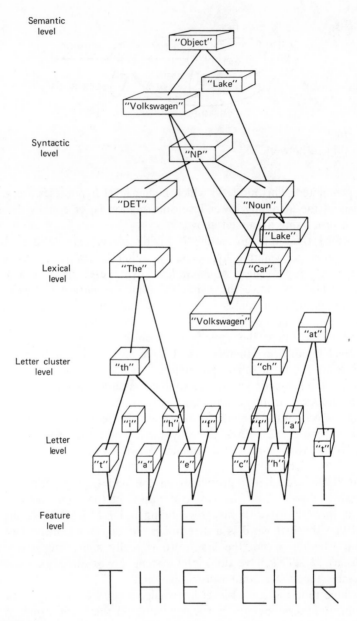

Figure 3.22
Message center later during the processing of the phrase, "The car." At this point the word "The" has already been fairly clearly determined.

Figure 3.22 illustrates the system at a later time during the processing of the same input. Note that, processing from the bottom up, the letter-cluster knowledge source has looked at the letter-level hypotheses and postulated the highly probable letter pairs at the *letter-cluster level*. In this case the clusters "th", "ch", and "at" were found. At the same time the lexical-level knowledge source looked at the letter-cluster level and at the letter level for evidence indicating that any of the postulated words are present in the input. In this case, good evidence is found for "the" and none for "a." Thus, the "the" hypothesis is strengthened and the "a" hypothesis is dropped. Simultaneously, the lexical-level knowledge source is looking at the syntactic- and semantic-level hypotheses in an attempt to form additional lexical-level hypotheses to cover the remaining portion of the input string. In this example, I have assumed that three such hypotheses have been formed—"Volkswagen" and "car" (both nouns and both possible lexical correspondents to the semantic-level "Volkswagen" hypothesis) and "lake" (a noun corresponding to the semantic-level "lake" hypothesis).

Figure 3.23 illustrates the message center at still a later point in time. All activity has now stopped on the first portion of the input and the word "the" has been accepted. However, a great deal of activity continues at the lexical level for the second part of the input. In addition to the top-down lexical hypotheses mentioned above (i.e., "Volkswagen," "car," and "lake"), the lexical-level knowledge source has found two other possible words in the letter-cluster-level and letter-level hypotheses. Thus, "cat" and "fat" have been postulated at the lexical level from the bottom up. Meanwhile, letter-level hypotheses have been generated from top down for the words "Volkswagen," "car," and "lake." At this point then, "v" and "l" have been postulated in the first position of the word, "o" in the second position, and "i", and "r" in the final position. These additional letter-level hypotheses must be checked against the feature-level input by the letter-level knowledge source.

Finally, Figure 3.24 shows the message center at a point near the end of the processing of this phrase. By this time, most of the new letter hypotheses have been rejected (except "r" in the final position) and only three lexical-level hypothesis remain: "cat," "car," and "fat." Of the three, only "car" is a plausible semantic-level hypothesis, and thus it is taken as the interpretation of the input.

In this example we have followed through, in some detail, the presumed interactions among expectations and incoming information at all of these different levels. It may appear that the processes I have outlined are too complex for the human to carry out in the half second or less that it takes to read a short phrase. In fact, this model doubtlessly errs in the opposite direction—it

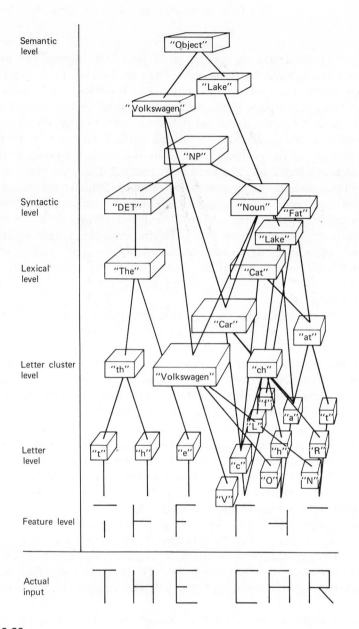

Figure 3.23
Message center at a still later point during the processing of the phrase, "The car."

144

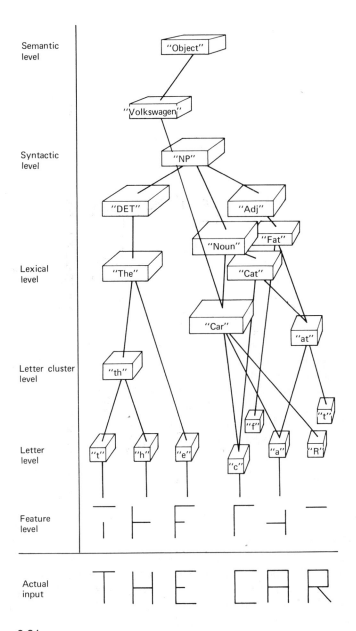

Figure 3.24
The message center fairly late in the processing of the phrase, "The car."

is much too simple to capture the complex behavior of the human reader. It is perhaps not surprising that although the serious study of reading is well over a hundred years old, we can still marvel at its complexity.

To summarize, we have given a rather lengthy development of the view that an augmented transition network can serve as an adequate model for the syntactic component of our language understanding system. We have reviewed a number of experimental results which lend credence to this general view. Finally, we have shown how the notions of an ATN can be generalized and integrated into a language comprehension system working on the principles implicit in the HEARSAY system.

THE ROLE OF SEMANTICS IN LANGUAGE UNDERSTANDING

Roughly speaking, the *semantic content* of an utterance is the *meaning* of the utterance. In spite of its obvious importance there are no well developed models of semantic processing analogous to the ATN. Nor has there been much experimentation dealing specifically with the role of semantics in language comprehension. There are, however, numerous examples of semantic effects in comprehension. There are, in addition, a variety of hypotheses about mechanisms mediating these effects.

Perhaps the most commonly observed effect is the semantic disambiguation of syntactically ambiguous sentences. Linguists have long been plagued with the problem that there are numerous syntactically valid parses of a sentence, of which often only one makes sense (i.e., is semantically meaningful). Consider the following sentences:

(40a) They are eating apples.
(40b) The children are eating apples.
(40c) The juicy red ones are eating apples.

At a syntactic level all three sentences allow for at least two readings: (1) the reading in which the first noun phrase refers to things performing the act of eating some apples; (2) the reading in which the first noun phrase refers to things said to be members of the class of "eating apples." However, at a semantic level only the first sentence remains ambiguous—and even it would be disambiguated if we had some notion as to the referent of the pronoun *they*.

Schank (1973) has given a number of similar examples. Consider, for instance,

(41a) I saw the Grand Canyon flying to New York.
(41b) I saw the Grand Canyon *while I was* flying to New York.
(41c) I saw the Grand Canyon *which was* flying to New York.

Most readers immediately interpret (41a) as meaning the same as (41b) rather than (41c) simply on the grounds that it is semantically anomalous to imagine the Grand Canyon actually flying. On the other hand, (42a) is ordinarily interpreted to mean the same as (42c) rather than (42b).

(42a) I saw the cattle grazing in the field.
(42b) I saw the cattle *while I was* grazing in the field.
(42c) I saw the cattle *which were* grazing in the field.

In (40a), (41a), and (42a) semantics plays the determining role as to which reading we get. Syntax reduces the set of possible relationships to those that are grammatically possible. Semantics reduces this set further to those that are semantically meaningful or likely.

How does our semantic knowledge interact with our syntactic knowledge in our interpretation of these sentences? The most commonly proposed mechanism uses what are sometimes called *selectional restrictions* (cf. Katz & Fodor, 1963) or *argument constraints* (cf. Rumelhart & Norman, 1973; Schank, 1973). According to this view, there is associated with each sense of each verb or adjective a set of constraints on the semantic class of the various noun phrases acceptable as arguments (subjects or objects) of the adjective or verb. Thus, for example, the verb *graze* would require of its subject that it refer to one or more of a certain class of herbivores. Similarly, the verb *fly* requires that its subject at the least be a movable object. The verb *eat* similarly would appear to require an *animate* subject. It is presumably through the use of such argument constraints that we are able to sort out the appropriate readings of (40a), (41a), and (42a). Consider, for example, how this might operate on sentences like (41a) and (42a).

Imagine that we are processing (41a) with an ATN like the one illustrated in Figure 3.15. Immediately following the word *Canyon* we look for a relative clause. We find the reduced relative (a relative clause with a deleted relative pronoun and verb *be*) given below:
(43) . . . . Grand Canyon was flying to New York.
Before allowing this reading we first check the argument constraints to see if our proposed sentence makes sense. Since *Grand Canyon* is not a movable object we can reject this possibility. On rejecting the reading we then find the subordinate clause reading of (41b). Here we have a cogent interpretation so that reading is accepted. A similar line of reasoning will show how (42c) is the

accepted interpretation of (42a). Similar reasoning will allow us to properly disambiguate the sentences of (40).

To this point we have discussed the semantic component primarily as an evaluator of hypotheses proposed by the syntactic and acoustic/visual processing. As we have already mentioned in connection with the HEARSAY system, semantics often can also *propose* hypotheses about the contents of the incoming signal. Thus, for example, a semantic process suggested that some representation of the Queen's bishop should be found in the input signal. Syntax then proposed particular phrases that might offer descriptions of the Queen's bishop, such as just *bishop* or *queen bishop,* etc., which constituted hypotheses which could be tested against the input. People are indeed capable of making semantically based predictions about what concepts to expect in an input string. In a discussion of the prediction experiment by Stevens and Rumelhart (1975) mentioned above, we concentrated primarily on subjects' ability to predict reliably the syntactic class of the next word in an incomplete sentence. However, subjects also reliably predicted the semantic character of words in context. For example, in one passage on the vocabularies specific to various trades we find the following context:

(44) Every profession or trade, every art, and every science has its technical vocabulary, the function of which is partly to designate things or processes which have no names in ordinary English. . . .
Different occupations differ in the character of their special _____.

Subjects were to fill in the blank with the word they considered most probable. We find a remarkable degree of consistency between subjects as to the semantic category into which the next word should fall. Their guesses included "jargons," "dialects," "functions," "nomenclatures," "fields," "art," "language," and "words." This is not a random collection.

Readers are just as able to develop *semantic expectations* as they are to develop *syntactic* ones. Moreover, these semantic expectations are also evident from reading errors that we observe. One example will suffice. In our free reading experiment the following phrase was misread four times.

(45a) Keynes argued that neither. . . .

The following phrases were substituted:

(45b) Keynes said that neither. . . .
(45c) Keynes proved that neither. . . .
(45d) Keynes approved that neither. . . .

Two different subjects read (45a) as (45c). It is clear that in (45b) and (45c)

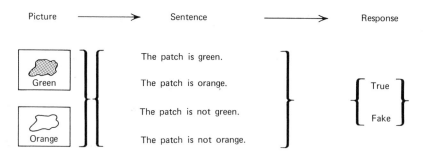

Figure 3.25
Schematic diagram of sentence verification procedure. The subject is presented with one of two pictures in this case either a green or an orange patch. This is followed by a sentence. The subjects must then respond "true" or "false" as to whether the sentence is true of the picture.

much of the sense of (45a) is maintained. The sentence (45d) is less clear. Numerous similar examples could be cited. Among them are "customer" being substituted for "consumer," "dialogues" for "dialects" (on two occasions), "interest" for "investment," etc.

It would thus seem that semantics, like syntax, plays an important role in helping us *perceive* linguistic imputs. Quite another approach to the role of semantics in sentence comprehension comes from the work of Herb Clark and his associates (cf. Clark & Chase, 1972; Just & Carpenter, 1971) and by Trabasso and his associates (cf. Trabasso, 1972; Trabasso, Rollins & Shaughnessy, 1971). In a clever series of studies these workers have demonstrated that certain concepts (those containing negation) are semantically more complex than others and are therefore more difficult to comprehend. The basic experimental paradigm can be illustrated by an experiment by Trabasso, Rollins and Shaughnessy. The procedure is illustrated in Figure 3.25. Subjects are first presented with a picture—in this case, containing either a green color patch or an orange one. They are then presented with a sentence purporting to describe the picture. Subjects must respond "true" if the sentence is true of the picture and "false" if the sentence is not true of the picture.

There are four basic sentence types in this experiment. The sentence may be either *true* or *false* of the picture and the sentence may be either *affirmative* or *negative*. Thus, suppose the green patch had been presented. Then the *true affirmative* sentence would be: *The patch is green;* the *true negative* sentence would be: *The patch isn't orange;* the *false affirmative* sentence would be: *The patch isn't green.* The basic measure in this experiment is the time needed to determine the truth or falsity of the sentence.

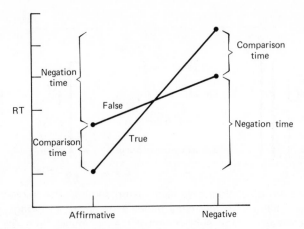

Figure 3.26
These are idealized results from a sentence comparison experiment. The figure shows reaction time as a function of whether the sentence was an affirmative or a negative sentence and whether it was true or false of the picture. (See chapter discussion for explanation.)

What is involved in determining the response? Clark (1970) and Trabasso (1970) have independently suggested that there are at least two components contributing to the difficulty of the task. (1) Subjects must compare the color term derived from the sentence with the color observed in the picture. Presumably, if the color terms match this comparison should occur faster. (2) Subjects must match the polarity of the sentence to the picture. Since the picture is presumably encoded as a positive statement about the color present in the picture, this implies that affirmative sentences should be processed faster than negative ones.

Figure 3.26 illustrates the idealized results according to such a model. The *true affirmative* sentence should be comprehended most quickly and thus elicit the fastest reaction time. This follows because both the color term and the polarity of the sentence match that of the picture. On the other hand, the *true negative* sentence should be the most difficult to comprehend and thus require the longest reaction time. This follows because it mismatches the picture representation on both polarity and color term. Its reaction time should consist of two components, one due to the time needed to process the negation and one due to the time needed to compare the mismatching color terms. The reaction times to the two kinds of *false* sentences should lie intermediate to the two *true* reaction times. For example, the time to respond to a *false affirmative* sentence involves matching the polarity of the picture and mismatching on the

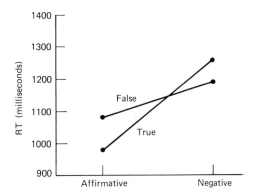

Figure 3.27
Observed reaction times for the verification of affirmative and negative sentences as a function of whether they are true or false of a previously presented picture. (Data from Trabasso et al., 1971; note the crossover of the two curves is exactly as expected from the idealized data of Figure 3.19.)

color term. It should thus exceed the *true affirmative* reaction time by only the time needed to compare the disparate color terms. Similarly, the *false negatives* should exceed the *true affirmatives* by only the time needed to process the negation.

The results of the Trabasso et al. experiment are shown in Figure 3.27. They clearly confirm the major features of the model. Similar experiments have been carried out by Chase and Clark (1972), Gough (1966), McMahon (1963), and others. In all of these studies the pattern of results illustrated in Figure 3.26 have obtained. It is tempting to conclude that the negation time effects observed in these experiments are really semantic effects rather than syntactic effects. However, these experiments used sentences with an explicit negative morpheme. It may be that the negation effects are merely a function of *syntactic complexity* and are not semantic at all. Fortunately, as Clark (1970) has pointed out, not all negation is explicitly present in the syntax of the language. Some negation is *implicit* in the meaning of certain lexical items. For example, the word *absent* means *not present* and thus contains an implicit negative. Now if our effect is truly semantic and not syntactic, we should find exactly the same pattern of results for *present/absent* as for *green/isn't green*.

Clark, Carpenter, and Just (1973) report an experiment in which they performed just this test. The general procedure is like that of Trabasso et al. Subjects were first shown a picture and then given a sentence to verify about the picture. The picture contained either a *star* or a *plus*. The sentences were

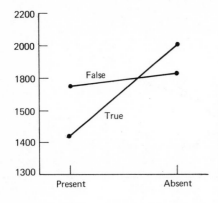

Figure 3.28
Observed reaction times in sentence verification task in which the negative element was implicit in the adjective. In this case the adjectives "present" and "absent" show the same pattern of results as sentences with explicit negative morphemes. (Data from Clark, Carpenter and Just, 1973.)

generated from the following frame:

$$\text{The} \begin{Bmatrix} \text{star} \\ \text{plus} \end{Bmatrix} \text{is} \begin{Bmatrix} \text{present} \\ \text{absent} \end{Bmatrix}$$

The results are shown in Figure 3.28. The pattern is remarkably similar to the results with explicit negation. The clear implication seems to be that the negation time is a semantic—not syntactic—effect.

A number of other experiments involving *many/few, above/below, from/to,* and a variety of other contrasting pairs have been carried out. A review of these studies is given in Clark (1970), and in Clark, Carpenter, and Just (1973). The important point for our purposes here is that these workers have developed a method for studying semantic complexity effects on comprehension and verification time. They have through clever experimentation been able to dissect the comprehension and verification process into at least two independent parts: a time for comparison between two modes of representation and a time for the analysis of polarity differences. The more of these processes that are involved in any given comprehension task, the longer it takes to process the sentence and formulate a response.

Before turning to the effects of context, let me summarize our discussion of the role of semantics in language understanding. First, it should be kept in mind that the *purpose* of language analysis is the determination of the meaning of the signal. Thus, semantics is, by definition, the central focus of language processing. Unfortunately, not much is known about the mechanisms whereby semantic knowledge interacts with other forms of knowledge to facilitate the convergence on an interpretation of an input signal. That semantics *does* in fact play a role is amply demonstrated by the numerous examples of semantic disambiguation of syntactically ambiguous sentences. In fact, this disambiguation takes place so completely and so unconsciously that most people are hardly ever aware of the degree of ambiguity of the sentences they hear until some linguistics or psychology professor points it out to them. The mechanism whereby this disambiguation occurs is not well understood. Perhaps the most plausible hypothesis is that we use argument constraints associated with the verbs and adjectives (such as the rule that the subject of *graze* must be a herbivore) to eliminate certain of the semantically improbable readings.

It would appear, however, that although such a mechanism is probably used, it is not sufficient to account for our ability to predict the semantic categories of words appearing in context. Rather, it would appear that more general mechanisms are employed to make use of general contextual information as well as these local argument constraints. To date, however, no compelling hypotheses have been suggested. Finally, in quite another vein, techniques are being developed to measure various aspects of comprehension time. The experiments by Clark and his associates have been particularly successful in isolating and measuring the actual comprehension time for the negative aspect in the meaning of sentences.

THE ROLE OF CONTEXT IN LANGUAGE UNDERSTANDING

Context effects (or as they are sometimes called *pragmatic effects*) are ubiquitous in language understanding. The degree to which context affects pattern recognition was pointed out in Chapter 2. Language understanding is, if anything, more easily affected by context. The human organism seems to be especially sensitive to the general context in which he is processing linguistic information. On the remaining section of this chapter I will first present some examples of experiments in which context effects are particularly strong. Then we will turn to a discussion of some of the mechanisms that seem to be involved in the use of contextual information.

THE BRANSFORD AND JOHNSON EXPERIMENTS

Bransford and Johnson (1973) have carried out a number of experiments designed to elucidate the role of context in the comprehension of prose passages. We will discuss three of these experiments. Each experiment consists of presenting subjects with paragraphs of prose material with or without some context, then asking the subjects to attempt to recall the material. The basic finding is that the material presented in context is more comprehensible and therefore more memorable. Consider as an example the following paragraph.

If the balloons popped the sound wouldn't be able to carry since everything would be too far away from the correct floor. A closed window would also prevent the sound from carrying, since most buildings tend to be well insulated. Since the whole operation depends on a steady flow of electricity, a break in the middle of the wire would also cause problems. Of course, the fellow could shout, but the human voice is not strong enough to carry that far. An additional problem is that a string could break on the instrument. Then there could be no accompaniment to the message. It is clear that the best situation would involve less distance. Then there would be fewer potential problems. With face to face contact, the least number of things could go wrong. [pp. 392–393.]

Some subjects were presented this passage without an accompanying picture. Others were allowed to view the picture in Figure 3.29 for 30 sec before reading the passage. Subjects without the picture found the passage nearly incomprehensible, whereas those who saw the picture before reading the passage found it completely comprehensible. Those with the context were able to recall over twice as much of the story as those who did not see the context.

One might argue that the problem here is that the scenario suggested in the picture is simply too bizarre and out of most people's experience. The reason that we ordinarily have no difficulty with passages that we read is that they usually refer to events that are less bizarre and closer to our everyday experience. Interestingly, however, having experience with the concepts discussed in a passage is not always sufficient. Consider as an example the following passage.

The procedure is actually quite simple. First you arrange things into different groups. Of course, one pile may be sufficient depending on how much there is to do. If you have to go somewhere else due to lack of facilities that is the next step, otherwise you are pretty well set. It is important not to overdo things. That is, it is better to do too few things at once than too many. In the short run this may not seem important but complications can easily arise. A mistake can be expensive as well. At first the whole procedure will seem complicated. Soon, however, it will become just another facet of life. It is difficult to foresee any end to the necessity for this task in the immediate future, but then one never can tell. After the procedure is completed one arranges the materials into different groups again. Then they can be put into their appropriate places. Eventually they will be used once more and the whole cycle will then have to be repeated. However, that is part of life. [p. 400.]

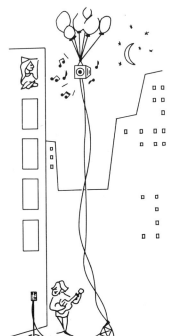

Figure 3.29
Context for interpretation of the balloon passage.
(Figure from Bransford and Johnson, 1973.)

Bransford and Johnson report that subjects find this passage just as difficult to comprehend as the *balloon passage*. However, if subjects are merely told that the topic of the passage is *washing clothes* the passage is much more understandable. Again, subjects remember nearly twice as much of the passage having been told that it is about washing clothes than when they are given the passage without a title. Thus, it is clearly not the fact that we have not had experience with the appropriate events; it is rather that there are no cues to bring the washing clothes scenario to mind. Merely knowing about it is insufficient—it must be brought to mind. Another point that should be made about this experiment is that context need not be a physical object like a picture. To merely mention a concept is sufficient to set up the appropriate contextual situation.

It thus appears that unless we can relate new inputs to some presently available knowledge framework, we fail to understand the input and on a later recall test fail to remember it. One final experiment by Bransford and Johnson illustrates that this is true not only for entire passages, but for individual sentences within a passage. Consider the following passage.

Watching a Peace March from the 40th Floor
The view was breathtaking. From the window one could see the crowd below. Everything looked extremely small from such a distance, but the colorful costumes could still be seen. Everyone semed to be moving in one direction in an orderly fashion and there seemed to be little children as well as adults. The landing was gentle, and luckily the atmosphere was such that no special suits had to be worn. At first there was a great deal of activity. Later, when the speeches started, the crowd quieted down. The man with the television camera took many shots of the setting and the crowd. Everyone was very friendly and seemed glad when the music started. [P. 412.]

In this passage the sentence beginning "The landing was gentle, . . ." is clearly out of place. In their experiment Bransford and Johnson presented half of the subjects the above paragraph as shown. The other half were presented the same paragraph under the title *A Space Trip to an Inhabited Planet*. For these subjects the entire passage forms a coherent whole. The odd sentence makes perfect sense. Now the question was what differences in memory for the critical sentence would show up between the groups.

The results showed that in a normal recall situation only 3 out of 17 subjects presented with the out-of-context sentence recalled it correctly. With the *Space Trip* title 9 out of 17 subjects recalled it correctly. There was no difference between the two groups on recall for the other sentences. On a cued recall, subjects were given the frame "The landing⎯⎯⎯⎯⎯⎯⎯⎯⎯⎯⎯⎯⎯⎯⎯ and luckily the atmosphere⎯⎯⎯⎯⎯⎯⎯⎯⎯⎯⎯⎯⎯⎯" and asked to fill in the blanks. Of the *Space Trip* subjects, 14 out of 17 correctly filled in the blanks, but only 5 of the *Peace March* subjects responded correctly.

Two points are relevant here. (1) It is clear that isolated sentences like whole passages are not understood and therefore well recalled unless they fit into the overall context. (2) It is interesting that we can have ambiguous paragraphs just as well as ambiguous sentences. It attests to our sensitivity to and dependence on the context in which we understand information that a change as small as a change in title can give two such different interpretations to the same passage.

Bransford and Johnson have thus laid out a remarkable set of data which must be accounted for. What kind of theoretical explanations can we give to these phenomena? What sort of processing mechanisms can give rise to such powerful effects? The answers to these questions are far from clear. Bransford and Johnson themselves do not attempt to explain their results. They do however point to the strong interaction between incoming information and our general knowledge of the world. No one can give a complete account for their results, but there does seem to be an emerging explanation. In the following sections I will develop some of the hypotheses that seem most promising.

THE PROBLEM OF REFERENCE

Consider the first sentence of each of the three passages presented in the preceding section.

(46a) If *the balloons* popped *the sound* wouldn't be able to carry since *everything* would be too far away from *the correct floor.*

(46b) *The procedure* is actually quite simple. First you arrange *things* into different groups.

(46c) *The view* was breathtaking. From *the window* one could see *the crowd* below.

In each sentence the italicized phrases seem to cause difficulty. When we encounter a *definite referring phrase* (such as one with the definite article, *the*), we try to discover the *referent* for the phrase. Thus, when we encounter the phrase *the balloons* we ask "What balloons?" Whenever, as in this instance, we have no good referent for the concept we go on, hoping to learn the referent later. Thus, we go on to *the sound.* Again we ask the question "What sound?" In this case we can come up with an answer, namely the sound of the balloons popping. Note, however, that although this seems the most likely referent *out of context,* in the context of Figure 3.29 a different referent would be found. In particular, it would probably be determined that *the sound* referred to the sound coming through the speaker suspended from the balloons. A similar effect occurs with *the correct floor*—"What correct floor?" No answer is apparent out of context. Thus, this phrase too becomes a loose end awaiting future input for clarification. The same problems arise in (46b). The phrase *the procedure* and the word *things* are the two critical references that are never resolved. If we could know what procedure or what things were being referred to, we would be able to comprehend the paragraph.

Perhaps (46c) provides the most interesting example. In these sentences we get the phrases *the view, the window,* and *the crowd* in the context of one of two titles:

(47a) *Watching a Peace March from the 40th Floor;*

(47b) *A Space Trip to an Inhabited Planet.*

We are able to resolve a referent for each of these phrases within either context. However, the referent we construct is different in the two cases. In the context of (47a) *the view* is clearly the view from the fortieth floor, *the windows* are the windows of the room from which we are looking out, and *the crowd* refers to the peace marchers we are watching. In the context of (47b), however, we get quite a different set of referents. *The view* refers to the view from the space ship, *the window* refers to the window of the space ship, and *the crowd* refers to the inhabitants of the planet. A careful analysis of all of these passages makes it clear that a bulk of the problem is reference. Phrases that ordinarily would be assumed to refer to something in context are instead left without any referent at all. It is clear that a good theory of the process whereby we find referents to phrases would go a long way toward solving the problems raised by the Bransford and Johnson experiments.

To understand the problem of reference it is useful to begin with the view that the purpose of language is communication. Communication is a cooperative process between a speaker (or writer) and a listener (or reader). The speaker has a set of concepts he wants to communicate. The speaker's goal is to formulate a sequence of sentences that will allow the listener to properly relate the *new* ideas in the message to the relevant concepts already known to the listener. Thus, as Clark (1973) has pointed out sentences can be broken up into two parts. One part, the *given* part, is a reference to ideas that the speaker believes are already in the listener's mind. The other part, the *new* part, is the new information that the speaker is trying to add to the listener's knowledge base. To illustrate the distinction between given and new information, consider the following examples:

(48a) I saw the man.
(48b) Given: There was a man.
(48c) New: I *saw* him.

Notice that (48a) is a perfectly ordinary sentence. However, were I to utter it seriously in a conversation I would be assuming that you already knew that there was a man (perhaps we had just discussed him), and I would be informing you that I saw him. In contrast consider the following examples:

(49a) It was I who saw John.
(49b) Given. Someone saw John.
(49c) New: *I* was the one.

(50a) It was John whom I saw.
(50b) Given: I saw someone.
(50c) New: He was *John*.

The sentences (48a), (49a), and (50a) may, in fact, all be correct descriptions of the same event. However, they differ with regard to what information the speaker is trying to communicate and what *prior* information the speaker assumes that the listeners know. Clark suggests that successful communication requires that three conditions on the nature of the *given* and *new* information be met.

1. *Appropriateness*. The Given part of the sentence ought to convey known, or knowable, information, and the New part, unknown information.
2. *Uniqueness*. The Given information provided by the speaker must enable the speaker to compute an Antecedent [referent] that is unique.
3. *Computability*. Most fundamental of all, the listener must be able to compute the intended Antecedent to the Given information based on what he knows.

Note that both the *balloon* passage and the *washing clothes* passage fail to meet all three requirements. These requirements follow from a more general principle of conversation called by Clark the *given-new contract*. Clark formulates the given-new contract as follows:

> Try to construct the Given and New information of each sentence (a) so that the listener can select or compute from memory a set of propositions corresponding to the intended unique Antecedent for the Given information, and (b) so that he will not already have the New information attached to that Antecedent.

These principles, it seems, are very general and are used by both speaker and listener in encoding and decoding input sentences. For example, it follows from the principle that a speaker will attempt to use the minimally complex description that will nevertheless allow the listener to *uniquely identify* the described concept. A very simple experiment by Olson (1970) illustrates this point nicely.

This was an experiment in communication. One subject was allowed to observe a simple event. Later, he was asked to relate one aspect of that event to another subject who had not observed the event. In one part of the experiment the event consisted of the experimenter placing a gold star under one of a set of wooden blocks on a table. The first subject was to explain to the second where the gold star was. Of particular interest was the way the subject's explanation depended on the context of the event. For example, suppose the star was placed under a white cylindrical wooden block about one inch in diameter. When the table contained a black block the same size and shape as the white one, the subject described the location of the star by saying

(51) It's under the white one.

When the table contained only the white cylindrical block and a square block, then the location was described by

(52) It's under the round one.

If the table contained four blocks, i.e., the white cylindrical one, a black square one, a black cylindrical one, and a white square one, then the location of the star was indicated by

(53) It's under the round white one.

In short, we make strong use of context in our descriptions of aspects of events. We express those and only those aspects of events that are needed to make the desired distinctions. The Bransford and Johnson stories violate these norms. They fail to give us enough information to make the needed discriminations.

Not every noun phrase communicates given information. As sentences (48)–(50) illustrate, language has developed a code whereby the speaker indicates whether or not he (the speaker) believes the information to be given or new. Examples suggested by Chafe (1972) illustrate some of these clues. Consider:

(54) Once there was a widow who owned a cow. She decided to sell the cow and buy a shop with the money.

A typical clue to given information in noun phrases is the use of pronouns and the definite article *the*. The use of the indefinite article *a* usually indicates new information. Thus, the phrases *a widow* and *a cow* are new and require no search for a referent. However, when the pronoun *she* is encountered the listener realizes that the referent is assumed to be known and a search must be initiated. In this sentence it is easily resolved that *she* refers to the *widow* just introduced. Moreover, *the cow* clearly refers to the *cow* mentioned in the preceding sentence. A particularly interesting case arises with the phrase *the money*. Here no money has been previously mentioned, but the speaker is clearly indicating that money is given information. In this example the referent can be discovered by the realization that *selling* usually involves a transfer of money and that the money under consideration could well be that received for the cow. When the referent of information clearly marked as given cannot be found, a failure in communication results.

Consider the following example:

(55) Neil Armstrong saw the crater when he landed on the moon.

Notice that *the moon* causes us no difficulty (i.e., we have no trouble answering "Which moon?"), but the reference to *the crater* makes no sense without further context. Again, it is this type of ambiguous reference that makes Bransford and Johnson's passages so difficult.

Although it is safe to say that pronouns and the definite article are normally used whenever the speaker believes that the listener can unambiguously identify the referent, very little has been said until we can specify the processes involved in actually *computing* the referent. Clark and his students (cf. Clark, 1973) have begun to develop evidence on the actual strategies employed. For example, Springston (reported by Clark, 1973) has attempted to study the process of finding pronominal referents. Springston's procedure involved presenting his subjects with a sentence like (56a) and following it with one like (56b).

(56a) Bill said that Sally nominated him.
(56b) The person nominated was Sally.

Subjects were instructed to study the first sentence until they felt they understood it and then to press a button to see the second sentence. They were then to respond *true* or *false* to the second sentence as quickly as possible. Springston took the time from the onset of the first sentence to the true-false decision as a measure of the *difficulty* of finding the pronominal referent. The following sentences illustrate Springston's analysis:

(57a) Sally said that Mary shot her.
(57b) Sally said that Mary shot herself.
(57c) John said that Mary shot herself.
(57d) John said that Mary shot him.

For each of the sentence types in (57a–d) there was a second sentence of the form:

$$(58) \quad \text{The person shot was} \left\{ \begin{array}{l} \text{Sally} \\ \text{Mary} \\ \text{John} \end{array} \right\}.$$

Springston was able to make a number of interesting conclusions from his results. First, he showed that reflexive pronouns (herself/himself) are easier than simple pronouns (her/him). This conclusion follows from the fact that (57a) takes much longer to process than (57b). Springston hypothesized that the referents of pronouns are discovered by trying each possible referent beginning with the clause containing the pronoun. When the reflexive is used we immediately find the correct referent, *Mary*, but when the simple pronoun is used we try *Mary* as a referent, reject it on syntactic grounds, and then go on to the embedding clause and try *Sally*, an acceptable referent for *her*. This hypothesis receives support from a number of other comparisons derived from the data.

Consider, for example, the implications of this hypothesis for the difference between (57b) and (57c). In both sentences an acceptable referent is found on the first attempt—thus the difference in gender of the subject of the outer clause should make no difference in processing time. On the other hand, consider the comparison between (57a) and (57d). In (57d) the subject of the embedded clause is of the wrong gender. One should therefore be able to reject *Mary* more quickly in (57d) than in (57a), leading to longer processing times for (57a) than for (57d). Indeed, the major features of this hypothesis are confirmed. Processing time for (57b) is only slightly longer than for (57c), whereas (57a) takes much longer than (57d). These and other data collected by Springston yield rather convincing evidence (1) that subjects search for referents from the current clause backwards; (2) that syntactic and semantic evidence combines to speed the rejection of unallowable alternatives.

In a similar series of experiments Haviland and Clark (1974) studied the process of finding referents to noun phrases containing the definite article. Thus, they constructed sentence pairs like:

(59a) Ed was given an alligator for his birthday.
       The alligator was his favorite present.
(59b) Ed was given lots of things for his birthday.
       The alligator was his favorite present.
(59c) Ed wanted an alligator for his birthday.
       The alligator was his favorite present.

They then attempted to measure the comprehension time for the second of each pair by the following procedure. Subjects were allowed to view the first sentence until they felt they understood it. They were then presented with the second sentence until they said they understood it. The time to understand the second sentence was recorded. The assumption, of course, was that longer comprehension times indicate more difficulty in finding a referent for the phrase *the alligator.*

On the basis of our earlier discussion, we would expect (59a) to be the easiest pair because the referent is immediately available in the first sentence. Sentences (59b) should be more difficult because the subject has to reason that indeed an alligator might well have been among the things Ed received for his birthday. On the face of it, one might expect no difference between (59a) and (59c) for, after all, the phrase *an alligator* occurs in both cases. However, a more careful analysis illustrates an interesting difference between the use of the phrase in the two sentences. In (59a) the new information that *there was an alligator* is clearly implied. But in (59c) only the *idea* of an alligator is discussed in the first sentence. No *particular alligator* is in fact introduced. Therefore, no direct referent is available in (59c), whereas one is available in (59a).

The results support all of these arguments. Comprehension is fastest in the context of sentences like (59a). It takes about one hundred eighty msec longer to find a referent in the context of sentences like (59b). Moreover, (59c) is almost as difficult. It takes about one hundred forty msec longer in the context of (59c) than of (59a). Clearly then, searching out referents to definite phrases is a real process that requires a measurable amount of time. The more subtle the reference the longer the time.

To this point we have illustrated how speakers and listeners adhere to a certain social convention—called the *given new contract*—in the encoding and decoding of linguistic messages. When encoding a message the speaker uses special syntactic markers to point to those parts of the sentence he believes the listener already to be familiar with and to which he wants to tie more information. For his part, the listener uses these same syntactic clues to direct his attention toward the intended concepts in memory, thereby allowing communication to occur. Whenever the speaker misjudges the listener, or covertly intends to mislead the listener, and thereby breaks the given-new contract, communication breaks down. The Bransford and Johnson passages illustrate the consequences of this failure.

CONVERSATIONAL POSTULATES

The given-new contract is simply one of a set of conventions used by speakers and listeners in encoding and decoding sentences. The entire set of such conventions has been called *conversational postulates* by Grice (1967). Grice's postulates derive from one basic principle called the *cooperation principle.* This can be paraphrased as: *Formulate every aspect of your utterance so as to maximally facilitate the agreed upon aims of the conversation.* Grice has divided this general principle into four categories with more specific implications: quantity, quality, relation, and manner.

Quantity

      (a) Make your contribution as informative as possible.

      (b) Do not make your contribution more informative than required.

Quality

      (a) Do not say what you believe to be false.

      (b) Do not say that for which you lack adequate evidence.

Relation

      (a) Be relevant.

Manner

      (a) Avoid obscurity of expression.

      (b) Avoid ambiguity.

      (c) Be brief.

      (d) Be orderly.

Clark (1973) suggests that the given-new contract is a subpart of Grice's maxim of manner.

It is helpful to consider some examples to see how these maxims are used to communicate information not contained in the literal use of words. Consider the following example (suggested by Gordon & Lakoff, 1971). I walk up to a friend who is clearly wearing a watch and ask

(60) Could you tell me the time?

My friend, of course, realizes that I knew that he *could* tell me the time; hence that could not be the implication of my question. Thus, he reasons, I must be asking something else. My friend could simply answer my question literally with a "Yes," but that would be decidedly uncooperative. Thus, my friend would determine that I must have been requesting that he tell me the time.

Consider the following example:

(61) Some of my children are boys.

Here the listener will ask "Why did he say *some?* It must be that some are not boys." Again, the listener is assuming that the speaker is being cooperative. Strictly speaking, of course, saying "some" is not inconsistent with "all," but listeners normally assume that the speaker has not made unnecessary qualifications (the maxim of quantity) and thus the qualification must be necessary. Numerous additional examples could be given, but the point should be clear. In ordinary conversations people assume that their partner in conversation is following the principle of cooperation. Whenever it appears that he is not, we conclude that something other than the conventional meaning of the sentence is intended.

SCHEMA THEORY OF COMPREHENSION

In our discussion of reading above we showed how the principles of knowledge interaction as postulated by the HEARSAY system could be put together with the ATN and the feature extraction theories of the previous chapter to give an account of how we can read simple phrases. A number of authors have recently suggested that the same principles can be extended to the comprehension of much larger texts (cf. Bobrow & Norman, 1975; Minsky, 1975; Schank & Abelson, 1975; Rumelhart, in press; Rumelhart & Ortony, in press). Recall, from our discussion of the reading model, that hypotheses were postulated at a variety of levels, each designed to account for some portion of the incoming information. Thus, we had letter-level, lexical-level, syntactic-level, and semantic-level hypotheses, among others. In our previous discussion semantic-level hypotheses were the highest level considered. These theorists suggest that we generate hypotheses at still higher levels and that the process of comprehending a story, like those of Bransford and Johnson discussed above, consists of finding a high level hypothesis that accounts for the story in much the same way that the hypothesis that a certain word is in the input accounts for the observed set of extracted features. Such high level hypotheses are called *schemata*.

A schema is generalized knowledge about a sequence of events. A schema, like the script of a play, has a cast of characters, a sequence of scenes, etc. An example from Schank and Abelson (1975) and Schank and the Yale AI Project (1975) will illustrate the nature of schemata and how they can be used in comprehension. Schank and Abelson describe a restaurant schema which represents the typical sequence of events encountered when going into a restaurant for a meal. Figure 3.30 shows, in schematic form, a possible restaurant schema. The schema consists of six major parts: the name of the schema, the cast of characters of the schema, and the four major scenes of the schema—entering, ordering, eating, and exiting. Imagine that we have, within our memories, schemata such as these for every more or less standardized sequence of events that we know about. In this case, then, comprehension consists of finding a schema that fits the situation (or story) we are trying to understand and discovering who, if anyone, in the story corresponds to the required characters.

Schank et al. (1975) have developed a set of computer programs which make use of schemata such as these in interpreting short stories. Consider the following simple story:

Input: John went to a restaurant. The hostess seated John. The hostess gave John a menu. John ordered lobster. He was served quickly. He left a large tip. He left the restaurant.

Upon encountering this story, the computer sets about looking for a schema that will account for the story and a map from the people mentioned in the story to the various aspects of the schema. In this case, of course, the restaurant schema can easily be found. The customer can be determined to be John, the hostess in the schema and the hostess in the story can be determined to be the same, and the meal can be determined to be lobster. On having found a satisfactory schema, the programs can either give an elaborated paraphrase of the story in which elements of the schema are added to the original story or the system can summarize the story, using the major constituents of the schema as the framework for the summary. Below is the elaborated paraphrase produced by their program:

---

schema: Restaurant.
characters: Customer, hostess, waiter, chef, cashier.
Scene 1: Entering.
    Customer goes into restaurant.
    Customer finds a place to sit.
        He may find it himself.
        He may be seated by a hostess.
            He asks the hostess for a table.
            She gives him permission to go to the table.
    Customer goes and sits at the table.
Scene 2: Ordering.
    Customer receives a menu.
    Customer reads it.
    Customer decides what to order.
    Waiter takes the order.
        Waiter sees the customer.
        Waiter goes to the customer.
        Customer orders what he wants.
    Chef cooks the meal.
Scene 3: Eating.
    After some time the waiter brings the meal from the chef.
    Customer eats the meal.
Scene 4: Exiting.
    Customer asks the waiter for the check.
    Waiter gives the check to the customer.
    Customer leaves a tip.
        The size of the tip depends on the goodness of the service.
    Customer pays the cashier.
    Customer leaves the restaurant.

Figure 3.30

Elaborated Paraphrase: John decided he was going to go to a restaurant. He went to one. He asked the hostess for a table. She told him he could go to it. He went to it. She went to it. He sat down in a chair. He got a menu from her. He read it. A waiter saw John at the table. The waiter went to it. John ordered lobster. A chef cooked it. The waiter got it from the chef. The waiter served it quickly to John. He ate it. He asked the waiter for a check. John got it from the waiter. John remembered the waiter had served him quickly. John left the waiter a large tip. John paid the check. He left the resturant.

A comparison between this and the restaurant schema will make clear how the system was able to put the input together with a stored schema to produce this elaboration. The schema theory of comprehension suggests that comprehension is, in general, a matter of finding an appropriate schema stored in memory to account for the stored input.

The ability to generate an elaboration of the story such as this is an important aspect of comprehension. If we understand something, our interpretation is always much more than the comprehension of the sum of the words of the input sentence. The Bransford and Johnson experiments demonstrate this point dramatically. The "landing of the spaceship" story and the "watching the peace march" story contain exactly the same sentences, yet our understanding of those stories is quite different. It seems clear that the primary differences here stem from a difference in the schemata used to account for the two versions of the text. Thus, although the basic sentences are the same, the "elaborated paraphrases" of the two stories are quite different.

The Schank et al. (1975) program can also generate summaries of stories by use of the schema.

Summary: John went to a restaurant and ate lobster.

Here we see the story summarized by simply referring to the restaurant schema, mentioning the major character, and the name of the meal. When we understand a sequence of inputs we can give a succinct summary of the inputs. Again, the schema plays an important role in this process. Thus, a summary can in general be given by merely mentioning the name of the schema in question and indicating the names of the various characters and objects of the schema.

One interesting implication of the schema view of comprehension involves the large number of inferences that can be made once a series of inputs is associated with a schema. Thus, our interpretation of a story contains many inferences not explicitly mentioned in the story (such as John's paying for his food and the chef's cooking it). If our interpretation of a story contains all of these parts we should expect that our recollection of the story, after some period of time, would contain many inferences that were not in the original story. We should not be able to tell the difference between information originally presented in the story and inferences made from the schema used to account for the story. An interesting experiment by Spiro (1975) illustrates this point.

In his experiment Spiro presented subjects with rather long stories about an engaged couple—Bill and Margie. In the story Bill doesn't want to have children. For a long time he doesn't bring the subject up with Margie, however, for fear that it will jeopardize their relationship. Finally, Bill decides that he must tell her. He does and (in one version of the story) Margie is very upset and they have a fight. Thus the story ends. After hearing the story the subjects are casually told that the story was true and that in fact Bill and Margie did marry and are living happily to this day.

Now, from the point of view of schema theory, the subjects must find a schema that resolves the apparent conflicts between the information presented in the story and the somewhat contrary information presented after the story. Then, six weeks later the subjects are brought back and asked to recall the story. At this point the subjects make a substantial number of errors. By far the most predominant error, however, is the importation of information indicating that Bill and Margie became reconciled. They say that Bill decided after all to have children or that Margie decided not to have children or that the couple had settled upon a compromise—adopt a child. More interesting is the fact that the subjects are as certain that the inferred events occurred in the original story as they are that the actual events of the story occurred (e.g., the fight). Here we have a good example of a schema being required to account for a sequence of inputs which demands that numerous complex inferences be made. After a period of time subjects appear unable to distinguish between those events that were actually reported and those required by the schema.

According to the view under discussion here, then, comprehension should be considered an extension of perception. We take in sensory features and attempt to account for them with low level hypotheses about, say, possible letters in a string. These hypotheses, in turn, are subsumed by others about possible words in the string. Hypotheses about words are then subsumed as constituents in hypotheses about possible sentences in the string. Then these sentences themselves are subsumed under even higher level hypotheses—or schemata. The processing is carried on both from the bottom up—that is, lower level hypotheses are "suggesting" higher level ones (the appearance of the word "restaurant" suggests the "restaurant script") and from the top down —that is, higher level hypotheses are predicting (and inferring) the existence of lower level ones. The schema theory as it is outlined here is, of course, still in its infancy. It will be some time before we are able to generate the kind of experimental evidence and theoretical sophistication needed to determine its value. Nevertheless, it does seem promising and will no doubt guide the theoretical and experimental thinking of information processing psychologists for some years to come.

SUMMARY

The process of understanding language is immensely complex, and we have as yet only a rudimentary idea of the processes involved. Nevertheless, a number of ideas have been developed which together give a broad outline of the nature of these processes. Fundamental to the view presented here is the idea that language is not a simple *bottom-up* process in which we somehow construct the meaning of input sentences out of the stimuli impinging on our eyes or ears. Rather, language understanding is an active process involving the interaction of sensory information and with our general knowledge of the world. All of these knowledge sources work together to construct the most plausible interpretation of the input signal. The details of how these systems work together is not known, but *that* they work together is clear.

Perhaps the best general model of how they work together is embodied in the HEARSAY system. In this system each knowledge source has two functions. (1) It proposes hypotheses about certain aspects of the input string. (2) It evaluates hypotheses proposed by other knowledge sources. Each knowledge source is a large topic of study in itself. Of the various possible models of the syntactic component the ATN appears to be the most promising. A simple interpretation of an ATN allows us to account for the relative comprehensibility of various syntactic types of sentences, for pauses in garden path sentences, for errors in reading, and for processing load during relative clauses. No such well formed model of the semantic and pragmatic knowledge sources have been suggested.

Again, however, it is easy to show the effects of semantics and context. It is at least clear that the argument constraints or selectional restrictions play an important role in helping us to disambiguate syntactically ambiguous inputs. Beyond that, little is known. Contextual information too plays a critical role in language understanding. Depending on the context the same sentence can be perfectly reasonable or perfect nonsense. Even less is known about how context operates within the language understanding process. At the least, it is very clear that the problem of reference is of critical importance. Linguistic inputs are designed to fit into a general framework and are dependent upon that framework to make sense. We are just now beginning to find evidence on the nature of the processes that help us tie into previous knowledge. This is a growing area of psychology—new results are generated nearly every day. These areas which were hardly touched upon by psychologists a mere ten years ago are just now beginning to take shape. Doubtless another ten years will generate a more complete picture of these important processes.

The results of all of this processing finally become available to consciousness and the focus of our active attention. At this level the information can be further processed and related to other information that we may know. Finally, the new information fades from our awareness and all that remains is a more or less passive memory trace of the input information. Eventually new related information will come in, the old information will be reactivated, and we will again become aware of the idea communicated by the original event or linguistic input. This is the process of remembering to which we now turn.

4

REMEMBERING

The human memory system receives and records for future reference the outputs of the pattern synthesizer. At any point in time, a portion of the information stored in memory is being attended to (is activated) while the rest remains passively stored outside the attentional spotlight. Activated information is readily accessible, but there are severe limitations on the amount of information than can be activated at any one time. Information that we have just received or that we have just retrieved remains for a while in the active state, but as our attention is pulled to another part of memory its activation quickly fades and it melts into the rest of memory. When inactive, information is much less accessible. We often search for such information over long periods before we find what we are looking for or give up and conclude that "we don't remember." The human memory system appears to be without limitations on capacity. The primary difficulty in remembering would appear to be more a problem of retrieval difficulty than of information loss. Often, "forgotten" information can be retrieved at a later date. Like all large scale storage systems, the human memory system appears to be highly organized, in the sense that similar units of information are stored together. It is this organization that allows us to regain access to information once we have stored it away.

In the literature on the subject, information in the temporarily activated state is said to be in *primary* or *short-term memory*. The inactive information is said to be in *secondary* or *long-term memory*. The characteristics of these two modes of storage have been extensively studied over the past fifteen or twenty years and a large body of information has been built up about each. We will thus proceed by first discussing the nature of *primary memory activation* and then turn to a discussion of the characteristics of *secondary memory storage*.

THE NATURE OF PRIMARY MEMORY ACTIVATIONS

Information to which we are presently attending or to which we have very recently attended is said to be "in primary memory" or constitute a primary memory activation. Thus, when we look up a telephone number and attempt to remember it while we dial, we are putting that number into a state of activation. As long as we hold our attention on the number, for example, by repeating it over to ourselves, we will remember it easily. But, if our attention is drawn to something else while we are dialing, the activation of that number quickly fades from memory and we are often unable to regain access to it in our memories.

Imagine that memory is like a vast array of tiny light bulbs—each light bulb representing a unit of stored information. Imagine further that we have a limited energy source so that we can cause only a few of these bulbs to be lit at any one time. These light bulbs represent that information in memory to which we are currently attending—the activated information. When we turn our attention from one thing to another in memory, new light bulbs are lit and others fade out. As new information enters memory our attention is drawn to it and a new set of light bulbs is lit. As our attention wanders again these too fade and still others are lit. Although this analogy is very rough, it does provide a useful framework for posing the various questions that have been asked about primary memory activations.

There are four characteristics of primary memory activations that have received the most attention. (1) Suppose that while still attending to our telephone number we are asked whether or not it contains a certain digit, for example, a seven. How long does it take to access this information? It is certain that we can answer very quickly, but certainly not instanteaneously. This question, in effect, asks how long does it take to access the region of memory represented by a lighted bulb, and how long does it take us to read out the contents of that region. (2) It is clear that when we try to remember a string of numbers like a phone number it is easier when the string is shorter and more difficult if it is longer. When we already know the three digit prefix and need only remember the last four digits it is much easier. When we must remember the area code as well as the seven digit number it is much harder. There are severe limitations on the amount of information that can be simultaneously active. What is the nature of this limitation? Is it due to the amount of information currently active or is it due to the aging of the memory activations? Here, in effect, we are asking whether the limit on the number of lights that can be simultaneously lit derives from the fact that there is a fixed amount of current or from the fact that once lighted a bulb remains lit only briefly. Thus, to maintain a piece of information requires that the bulb be relighted every so often. (3) Sometimes when we hold a telephone number in attention we "hear the sound" of the number or perhaps we "see the number." How do these internally generated activations of numbers relate to those generated from the actual sounds of the numbers being spoken or the actual visual image resulting from looking at the numbers? How, in general, do internally generated activations relate to those resulting from sensory stimulation? This, in effect, asks about the nature of the light bulbs themselves. How do lights lit "from memory" compare with those lit directly by the pattern synthesizer? (4) After we have looked up a telephone number enough times, we don't seem to need to look it up again. Then, even if it does slip from our attention we can usually find it again without returning to the phone book. What has happened to the number? Is this change merely a passive result of frequent reactivation or must we do something special to make the number retrievable on a later occasion? We will now consider these various characteristics in turn.

ACCESS OF INFORMATION IN PRIMARY MEMORY

How Long Does It Take?

The nature of information access from primary memory has been studied in depth in a series of experiments carried out by Sternberg (1966, 1967, 1969). The basic paradigm of these studies is straightforward. A list of digits or letters (the positive set) is presented to the subject. The size of the positive set (number of characters read) varies from one to six. Another character (the target) is then presented and subjects decide whether or not it is a member of the positive set. That is, they must check through their memory of the positive set and see if it includes the target. If it does, the subject makes a positive response;

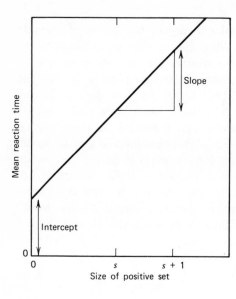

Figure 4.1
Idealized data from a memory scan experiment. The slope is a measure of the mean time taken by the comparison of the stimulus representation to the memory representation of one character. The intercept is a measure of the mean time taken by events before and/or after the series of comparisons, which include the formation of the stimulus representation. (From Sternberg, 1967.)

if not, he makes a negative response. The data of interest in these experiments are the changes in response time as a function of the size of the positive set.

Figure 4.1 shows, in idealized form, the results of Sternberg's experiments. He finds that the response time increases as a linear function of the number of items in memory. He interprets the slope of the curve as the time needed to access the stimulus representation (the output of the pattern synthesizer) and compare it with the memory representation. In his experiments the slope is on the order of 38 msec (thus, each additional item in memory adds 38 msec to the reaction time). Each access and comparison must take about 38 msec. The intercept represents the amount of time taken to form a stimulus representation and to execute the physical response. Sternberg (1967) summarizes his results as follows:

> First, mean latencies of both positive and negative responses increase linearly with the number of characters in the positive set. This has been found for positive sets of up to six characters, with digit- as well as letter-ensembles. Second, the mean increase in latency per character has the same magnitude for positive and negative responses. This equality shows that the search is exhaustive rather than being terminated when a match occurs. Reaction time increases by about 38 msec. for each member of the positive set so that the average rate of search is between 25 and 30 characters per sec. Third, although the size of the positive set affects the reaction time, the size of the full ensemble does not for ensembles that are at last twice as large as the positive set.

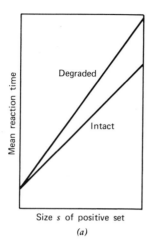 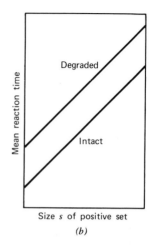

Figure 4.2
Two possibilities for the effect of test-stimulus degradation on the reaction-time function. (From Sternberg, 1967.)

From these data, Sternberg has concluded that the search through currently activated items is *serial* and *exhaustive*. That is, Sternberg believes that access of active items requires one to examine each item in turn and then, if a match is found, to respond positively. If no match is found the subject must respond negatively.

In one experiment, Sternberg (1967) used his procedure to study the nature of the synthesized pattern. This experiment followed the procedures used in the previous experiments with one exception. Sometimes the target was presented in a degraded form, whereas at other times it was intact. Sternberg reasoned that if the stimulus representation of the target is degraded when the physical stimulus is degraded, then each comparison should take longer and the slope of the line should increase (see Figure 4.2a). On the other hand, the pattern synthesizer may serve to clean up the image, so that a clear image is compared to the items in memory independent of the degraded nature of the target. In this case, it may take longer to synthesize the pattern from the degraded input, yet the comparison process should proceed as before. All of the difference should be taken up in differences in intercept and none in the slope (see Figure 4.2b). His results, shown in Figure 4.3, clearly support the latter hypothesis. We conclude from this experiment that the stimulus representation that is derived from the pattern synthesizer corresponds to what the figure is interpreted to be, not what it is. This complete representation is then

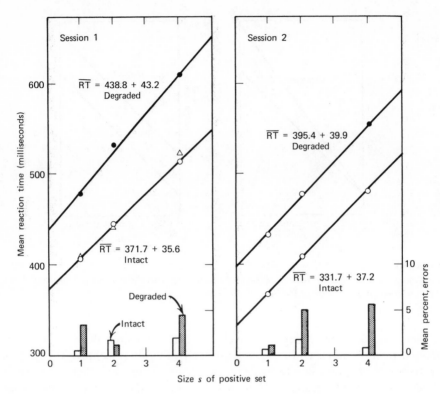

Figure 4.3
Mean reaction time and error percentages as a function of size of positive set for intact and degraded test stimuli. Left-hand and right-hand panels show data from sessions from 1 and 2, respectively. (From Sternberg, 1967.)

serially compared with the items held in memory.

Sternberg's experiments, taken as a whole, give us a pretty good idea of the way currently active information is accessed. Although access appears to be instantaneous, in fact it takes time—38 msec for each item. Furthermore, Sternberg's later experiment shows that the comparisons are made on the basis of interpreted signals, not the physical signals themselves.

STORAGE LIMITATIONS

The severe storage limitations of primary memory are well documented. These limitations seem to be of two sorts. One concerns the number of items which

Table 4.1
Ways of Recoding Sequences of Binary Digits

Binary Digits (bits)	1 0 1 0 0 0 1 0 0 1 1 1 0 0 1 1 1 0							
2:1 Chunks	10	10	00	10	01	11	00	11	10
Recoding	2	2	0	2	1	3	0	3	2
3:1 Chunks	101	000		100	111		001		110
Recoding	5	0		4	7		1		6
4:1 Chunks	1010		0010		0111		0011		10
Recoding	10		2		7		3		2
5:1 Chunks	10100		01001		11001		110		
Recoding	20		9		25		6		

can be actively held in memory at one time. People are unable to hold more than a very small number (six to ten digits, for example) of items at any one time. Attention to new inputs evidently allows old activations to fade away. There also appears to be a limitation due to temporal parameters of the activation. If one is not allowed to rehearse a list of items (repeat them to oneself either overtly or covertly), even a very short list is completely forgotten in as few as 18 sec.

The limit in storage due to the number of items in memory is called the immediate memory or attention span. This span varies between six and ten items for materials ranging from digits to letters and words. In short, we seem to be able to hold from six to ten units of information, no more. Miller (1956) has called the unit of memory information the "chunk." Miller (1956) reported one experiment, conducted by Sidney Smith, which shows how we can extend our apparent memory span by recoding the items into larger chunks at input and then reversing the process on output. Table 4.1 shows four ways of recoding a string of 0s and 1s into larger chunks. For each method of chunking there is a different number of chunks to hold in primary memory. Figure 4.4 shows the number of binary digits output as a function of the recording ratio. The dotted line in the figure represents the number of binary digits expected if the number of octal digits held in memory were a constant. These results demonstrate rather strikingly the nature of the limit on the number of chunks of information which can be held. It is the number of chunks that must be retained, not the number of input items which determines the memory span.

Although it is a general rule that the number of chunks rather than the complexity of each chunk is the determiner of the memory span there is a small range (7 ± 2) over which memory span does seem to be sensitive to the nature of the items. Cavanaugh (1972) observed that this variation had an

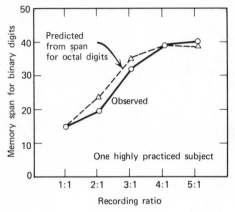

Figure 4.4
The span of immediate memory for binary digits is plotted as a function of the recoding procedure used. The predicted function is obtained by multiplying the span for octals by 2, 3, and 3.3 for recoding into base 4, 8, and 10, respectively. (From Miller, 1956.)

exact counterpart in variations of scanning rate as measured by Sternberg's paradigm. It will be recalled that digits were scanned at a rate of about 38 msec per item. The scan rate for other types of items is somewhat slower (e.g., the scan rate for nonsense syllables is about 75 msec per item). Cavanaugh found an exact linear relationship between the reciprocal of the scan rate (i.e., one over the scan rate) and the memory span for that type of item (illustrated in Figure 4.5). This complicates our picture somewhat in that it apparently takes more effort to hold some chunks than others, but it does give us some confidence that both memory span experiments and scanning rate experiments are tapping the same aspect of the memory system.

The second type of storage limitation in primary memory is illustrated clearly in an early experiment by Peterson and Peterson (1959). They presented subjects with consonant trigrams (e.g., CHJ) followed by a three-digit number. The subjects were supposed to repeat the number, and then count backwards by threes or fours from that number until a light flashed indicating that they should recall the trigram. The results from this experiment are shown in Figure 4.6. There is a clear decline in probability of correct recall as a function of the length of time after presentation. This decline is already apparent after a 3-sec delay and continues until at 18 sec almost nothing is recalled. This rapid decline in probability of a correct response with time after presentation clearly illustrates the severe temporal limitations of storage in short-term memory.

In addition to the temporal limitation and the limitation due to number of chunks, there seems to be an interaction between the two. The more chunks we are holding the faster we forget them. Murdock (1961), using the Peterson

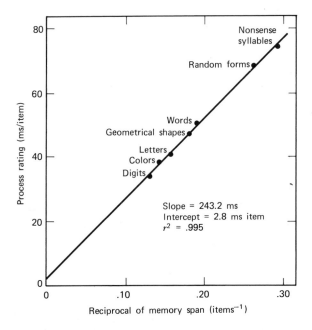

Figure 4.5
The relation between short-term memory processing rate and the reciprocal of the memory span for seven classes of stimuli. (From Cavanagh, 1972.)

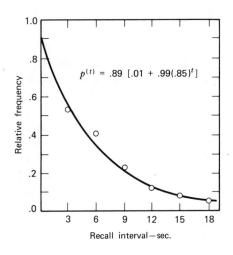

Figure 4.6
Percentage correct recalls as a function of recall delay interval. (From Peterson and Peterson, 1959.)

179

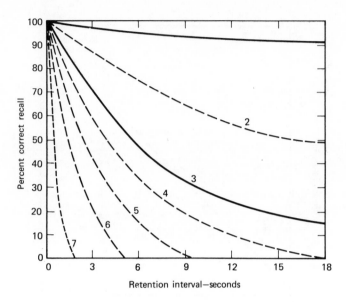

Figure 4.7
Hypothetical relationship between the number of recoded units ("chunks") in the to-be-remembered unit, the duration of the short-term retention interval, and the percentage frequency of complete correct recall, when each to-be-remembered unit is presented once. (From Melton, 1963.)

and Peterson technique, has shown that the decay curve for three unrelated words is the same as that for consonant trigrams (three chunks in either case), but that a single word decays much more slowly. After 18 sec a single word is still recalled about 80% of the time. These results and others led Melton (1963) to propose the relationship between rate of decay and number of chunks held in active memory shown in Figure 4.7. The more chunks in memory the faster forgetting seems to occur.

It is interesting to note that our interpretation of the attention literature fits very naturally with data such as these. Suppose that it takes a certain amount of processing capacity to hold an item in memory. Furthermore, suppose that it takes a certain (relatively large) amount of capacity to count backwards by threes. Thus, when a single item is being held in memory during counting there is almost enough capacity left over to maintain its activation. Hence it decays slowly. As the number of items increases, the more the remaining attentional capacity must be distributed and the more rapidly the activation dies out. A recent experiment by Anderson and Craik (1974) lends additional credence to this view. When subjects were required to carry out subsidiary tasks while learning a list of items, the items at the end of the list were forgotten much more rapidly than when no subsidiary task was required.

THE NATURE OF A PRIMARY MEMORY ACTIVATION

In our discussion of Sternberg's memory scan experiments we described evidence that a primary memory activation is a "cleaned up" version of the presented stimulus. In recent years a good deal of effort has gone into determining the nature of these memory representations and the relationship of internally generated activations to those resulting from external stimulation. There have been four different methods of inquiry into these questions using: (1) confusion errors, (2) interference effects, (3) scan rates, and (4) generation and manipulation of internal representations. Each of these methods of inquiry will be discussed in turn below.

Confusion Errors

Suppose that information decays from primary memory. Suppose further that when we attempt to retrieve a recently activated item we sometimes retrieve only a partial representation of that item. If we then try to make a response based on that partial information we will still often be correct. Sometimes, however, we will be wrong and will make an incorrect response that nevertheless shares many of the features that make up the memory representation of the correct item. By investigating the way in which errors are related to the correct responses for which they are substituted, the information processing theorist can begin to get evidence on the nature of these primary memory activations. In two well known studies Conrad (1962, 1964) used just this reasoning to conclude that the memory representation of items held in primary memory is auditory in nature. Conrad found that confusion errors in a memory span paradigm were acoustically similar to the presented items—*even when the items were originally presented visually.* Using his technique, Conrad found no evidence for visual features in the primary memory activation.

Interference Effects

In a related study, Baddeley (1966a) investigated the effects of semantic and acoustic similarity of items in the memory span test. In one condition Baddeley compared the memory for an acoustically homogeneous set of words (viz., man, cab, can, cad, cap, mad, max, mat, cat, map) with that for an acoustically more heterogeneous set (pit, few, cow, pen, sup, bar, day, hot, rig, bun) and found much poorer recall with the acoustically homogeneous list of words. When the recall of a semantically homogeneous list of words (great, large, big, huge, broad, long, tall, fat, wide, high) was compared with that for a semantically heterogeneous list (good, huge, hot, safe, thin, deep, strong, foul, old, late) very little difference was found in a test of immediate memory. However, in another experiment, Baddeley (1966b) used these same materials in a task involving only long-term memory and found just the opposite results: semantic similarity has a larger debilitating effect than acoustic similarity for long-term tasks. Thus Baddeley concludes that "It seems then that whereas STM [short-term or primary memory] relies largely on acoustic coding and is relatively unaffected by the semantic content of the message to be stored, LTM [long-term or secondary memory] uses semantic coding extensively, though not exclusively."

Scanning Experiments

A third approach to the study of primary memory activations is through the measurement of scan rates using a set of items temporarily activated in primary memory. We have already mentioned the experiment of Sternberg (1967) in which a degraded target was matched against a memory set and which lead to the conclusion that activations are "cleaned up" versions of the input stimulus.

Suppose we are searching through a set of items that are currently active in primary memory in order to get a match with some target item. Suppose further, that this particular set does not contain the target item. Now if every item in the set is very different from the target item we should be able to scan through the list very quickly. On the other hand, if each item on the list is very similar to the target item it may well take us a long time to determine that the target is not on the list. By systematically varying the ways in which the list items relate to the target we can get evidence on the nature of the primary memory activation. Pat Siple (1974), using the Sternberg paradigm, employed just this methodology. She devised lists which were acoustically but not visually similar to the target item, lists that were visually but not acoustically similar to the target, lists that were both acoustically and visually similar to the target, and lists that were neither acoustically nor visually similar to the target. Examples of the lists she used are shown in Figure 4.8. Siple varied the number of items in the memory set from one to four so that, following Sternberg's logic, she could measure the rate at which a single item could be scanned.

Figure 4.9 illustrates the expected findings under four possible hypotheses (as indicated by graphs A–D). (a) Primary memory activations are primarily auditory in nature. This hypothesis predicts that scan rate slows down when the items are auditorially similar, but that visual similarity has no effect. (b) Primary memory activations are primarily visual in nature. Scan rate should decrease only when the memory set contains visually similar items. (c) Activa

	AV	DVPG	B	JYNW	NO	
a	.492				1.143	a
v	.592	BVGC	D	FHJR	1.151	v
		JNPL	K	GTWY		
		MKHR	N	BCPT		
		BDCV	G	FKJY		
	A	SHLN	F	PRBC	V	
a	.563				1.202	a
v	1.151	SXFK	H	MWBG	.605	v
		MNSR	L	CBDG		
		TDGV	P	RFHX		
		LRJS	M	HW'VD		

Figure 4.8
Examples of lists of items that were both acoustically and visually similar to test items (AV); that were only auditorially similar (A); to the test item that were only visually similar to the test item (V); and that were neither auditorially nor visually similar to the test item (NQ). (From Siple, 1974.)

tions are multimodal—that is, both visual and auditory components are represented in the memory trace. If this assumption is correct, we would find scan rates slowed somewhat when the list contained either auditory or visually similar items and slowed about twice as much when it contained both auditorially and visually similar items. (d) Activations are abstract and not closely tied to either sensory modality. No effect on scanning rate would occur from any of the manipulations. The results are shown in Figure 4.10. Clearly, both auditory and visual features are important components of the primary memory activations. It is particularly interesting that their effects are about additive. This would seem to indicate that the activation is truly multimodal, rather than two activations, one visual and one auditory, working in parallel.

Posner and his colleagues (cf. Posner, 1973) have presented additional evidence on the multimodal nature of memory activations. In a version of Stern-

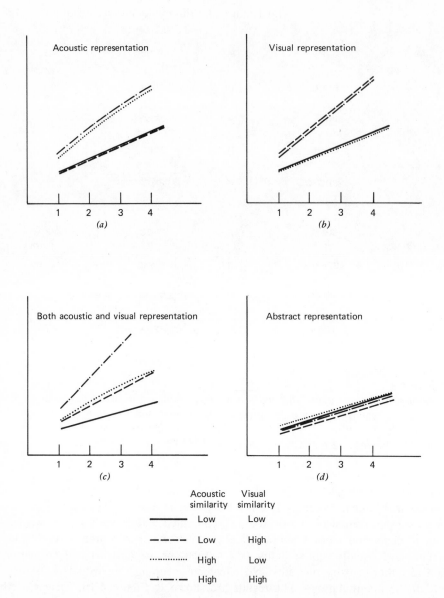

Figure 4.9

Expected findings under four possible hypotheses. *(a)* Primary memory activations are primarily auditory in nature. *(b)* Primary memory activations are primarily visual in nature. *(c)* Activations are multimodal—that is, both visual and auditory components are represented in the memory trace. *(d)* Activations are abstract and are not closely tied to either sensory modality.

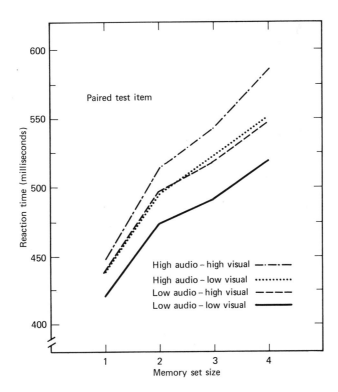

Figure 4.10
Observed reaction times for "no" responses as a function of memory set size and visual and auditory similarity of the test list to the target item. (From Siple, 1974.)

berg's paradigm Posner presented his subjects with arrays of one to four letters. The letters were either all uppercase, or all lowercase. Each array was followed by a target probe. The target matched an element of the array physically, in name only (i.e., it was an uppercase version of a lowercase letter), or it did not match. The subjects were to respond "Yes" if it matched either in name or physical identity. Otherwise they were to respond "No." The results are shown in Figure 4.11. Posner concludes:

Our results fit quite well with the view that subjects have represented both the physical form of a letter and the letter name. Suppose they had represented arrays only by letter name. In that case there is no reason that physical matches should be faster than name matches. Suppose they had only a visual representation. In that case the name level RTs [reaction times] should have reflected the time to transform each stored visual item into its name. Previous

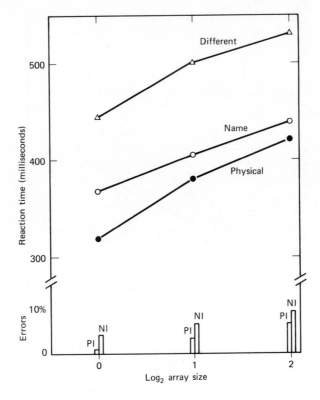

Figure 4.11
Reaction times and errors for physical and name "same" responses and for
"different" responses as a function of array size. (From Posner, 1973.)

work has shown that this process would take something like 80 msec. per item.
(Beller, 1970; Eichelman, 1970.)

To summarize our conclusions so far, we have found evidence that primary
memory activations are at least partly "sensory" in nature. This follows from
the specifically visual and specifically auditory interference observed. However,
they are not just "copies" of the original input. In memory span experiments
we find evidence implicating *auditory* coding of visually presented information.
Moreover, these activations are not even unimodal representations of some
input stimulus, but rather they appear to be multimodal and contain at least
visual, auditory, and abstract (name) attributes as well.

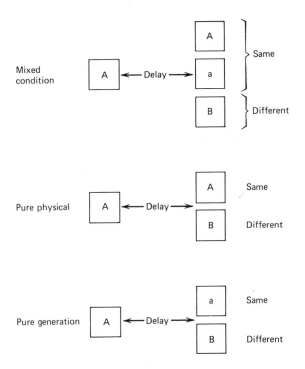

Figure 4.12
Schematic diagram of the general design of Boies' (1971) study. Three conditions are illustrated. In the mixed condition (upper panel) the second letter could be physically the same as the first letter or a lowercase version of that letter or an entirely different letter. If the second letter had the same name as the first letter, subjects were to respond "same" otherwise they were to respond "different." In the Pure Physical Condition, subjects always receive either the identical letter or an entirely different letter. In the Pure Generation Condition case, changes always occurred.

Generation and Manipulation of Memory Activations

Not only are our primary memory activations not simply copies of the stimulus giving rise to them, but sensory images can be generated and manipulated at will. A very direct example of this comes again from the work of Posner and his colleagues (cf. Posner, 1973). An experiment by one of his students (Stephen Boies, 1971) gives perhaps the clearest picture of the process of generating sensorially related memory activations.

Figure 4.12 illustrates the general design of Boies's study. In a "mixed condi-

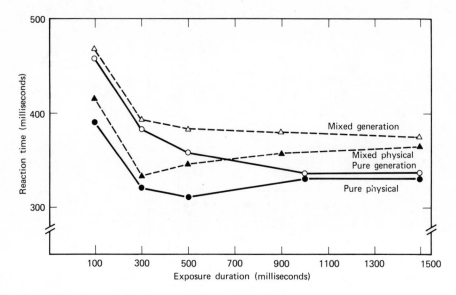

Figure 4.13
Reaction times for "same" responses as a function of condition; they indicate pure generation, pure physical, and mixed for various exposure durations for the first letter. (After Boies, 1971; from Posner, 1973.)

tion" subjects were presented with a letter of the alphabet (e.g., A). Then after a variable delay they were presented with another letter. The second letter could either be physically the same as the previous letter (e.g., A), be a lower-case version of the letter (e.g., a), or be an entirely different letter (e.g., B). If the second letter had the same name as the first letter subjects were to respond "same" otherwise "different." In "a pure physical condition," subjects always received either the identical letter or a different letter. Case changes never occurred. In "a pure generation condition" case changes always occurred. Thus subjects had to prepare themselves for a letter of the opposite case. The general logic of the experiment is that the more similar the memory activation to the test probe the faster the "same" judgment. The results are shown in Figure 4.13. Consider first a comparison of the pure physical and pure generation conditions. At delays of 1 sec or longer there is no difference in reaction times in the two conditions. This suggests that after 1 sec the memory activation that was generated as a result of the different case presentation was as similar to the probe as one resulting from the presentation of a physically identical stimulus. In the pure generation condition subjects reported that they are actually "imaging" the letter of the opposite case to help them make a match. This is, of course, completely consonant with our interpretation here.

At delays shorter than 1 sec the activation resulting from the actual stimulus presentation has an advantage. This would seem to indicate that it takes about 1 sec to generate an activation of the quality required in this match. The results of the mixed conditions again show no difference after about a 1.5-sec delay. However, this time they become asymptotic at a level about 30 msec slower than either pure condition. Boies interprets this to mean that subjects are generating two activations, one for each case, and that the additional time is that required to scan through two instead of only one at the time of match. The 30-msec difference is close to the amount of time Sternberg finds to scan one extra item in his experiments. An alternative explanation is that the match is being made at a more abstract "name" level and that the memory activation is not specific with respect to case. Either way, this experiment clearly indicates that subjects *can generate* at will memory activations which are very similar to specific expected input stimuli. They furthermore would seem to indicate that this process takes about 1 sec.

Try to answer the following question: How many windows are there in your house?

What processes did you go through trying to answer the question?

Most subjects report solving this problem by generating a spatial representation of their house and then mentally going through and counting the windows. What is the nature of the memory activation underlying the solution to this task? Lee Brooks (1968) has developed an interesting technique for measuring the character of such activations. Brooks' procedure involves inducing a conflict between the modality of the memory activation and the modality of a required response. Thus, a primarily visual task should interfere with a primarily visually guided response but leave our ability to respond verbally unaffected. A primarily auditory task should do the opposite. Subjects are asked to recall previously memorized material (e.g., sentences or line drawings) and to simultaneously respond about various aspects of the recalled material. If responding in one modality disrupts memory for one but not the other type of material, it was assumed that the memory activation underlying that recall was accomplished in a modality related to the modality of that response. Brooks describes his experimental condition as follows:

> One of the tasks in this experiment was to categorize each word in a recently presented sentence. For example, a subject listened to the sentence "a bird in the hand is not in the bush," and then successively categorized each word as a noun or a non-noun. In this instance he would produce the sequence, "no, yes, no, no, yes, no, no, no, no, yes." However, the subject was given three different

Figure 4.14
A sample output sheet for the pointing condition of Brooks' experiment. The underlined letters are those that would be pointed to in categorizing the sentence "a bird in the hand is not in the bush." The letters are staggered to force close visual monitoring of pointing. (From Brooks, 1968.)

ways of signaling this sequence: (a) saying "yes" and "no" as above, (b) tapping with the left hand for each noun, and the right hand for each non-noun, and (c) pointing to a "y" for each noun and an "n" for each non-noun as in Figure 4.14 (to produce the sequence given above, the subject would point to the top "n," the second "y," the third and fourth "n's," etc.). If the sentence is recalled in a specifically articulatory manner, then concurrently *saying* something should provide difficulties not present when the same information is signalled by a different type of response. In this case, vocal responses should take longer than either tapping or pointing.

The other task in this experiment was to categorize each corner in a line dia-

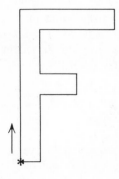

Figure 4.15
A sample of the simple block diagrams used. The asterisk and arrow show the subjects the starting point and direction they were to employ in making their responses. (From Brooks, 1968.)

Table 4.2
Mean Output Time in Seconds, Between-Subjects
Standard Deviation in Parentheses

Referent	Output		
	Pointing	Tapping	Vocal
Sentences	9.8(2.6)	7.8(2.1)	13.8(3.0)
Diagrams	28.2(12.1)	14.1(5.4)	11.3(3.5)

gram. For example, a subject looked at the block letter such as that in Figure 4.15 and then, from memory, categorized each dot [corner] as a point on the extreme top or bottom or as a point in between. In this example, starting from the asterisk and proceeding in the direction shown by the arrow, he would produce the sequence "yes, yes, yes, no, no, no, no, no, no, yes." If the "F" is recalled in a specifically visual or spatial manner, then concurrently looking at a different spatial array should lead to difficulties not present when the information is signalled in a different manner. In this case, pointing to the "y's" and "n's" should take longer than either speaking or tapping.

The results are shown in Table 4.2. It takes over 75% longer to carry out the word classification task by speaking than by tapping. Whereas it takes almost 2.5 times as long to signal information from a diagram by pointing than by speaking. The conclusion here is inescapable: we can, when called upon, generate memory activations specific to either visual or auditory sense modalities. When we do, these activations must compete with response mechanisms specific to the modality in question.

To this point we have shown that we can generate memory activations specific to either visual or auditory modalities. What kinds of manipulations can we perform on these internal representations? In the previous study Brooks demonstrated that we can mentally "move around" an image of a diagram. It turns out that we appear to have well developed mechanisms for performing rather complex transformations on these memory activations. Moreover it appears that these transformations have many of the same properties as corresponding operations on objects in the real world. Recent experiments by Roger Shepard and his colleagues illustrate this point very well.

In one of these experiments (Shepard & Metzler, 1971), subjects were shown pairs of pictures like those illustrated in Figure 4.16 and asked to determine whether the two pictures portrayed objects of the same three-dimensional shape —although in different orientations. The time required to make the judgment was measured. Subjects report that in order to make this judgment they had

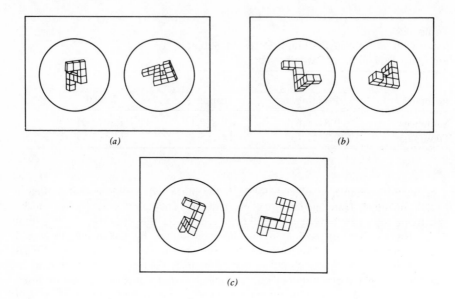

Figure 4.16
Examples of pairs of perspective line drawings presented to the subjects. *(a)* A "same" pair that differs by an 80° rotation in the picture plan. *(b)* A "same" pair that differs by an 80° rotation in depth. *(c)* A "different" pair that cannot be brought into congruence by *any* rotation. (From Shepard and Metzler, 1970.)

to imagine one of the objects rotated into the same orientation as the other and, moreover, that this "mental rotation" took time. Figure 4.17 shows the results of this experiment. The time to make the judgments increases linearly with the difference in angle between the two objects. This would seem to suggest that "rotation" is a transformation that can be applied to a memory activation. This conclusion is even more strongly supported by a later experiment by Cooper and Shepard (1973).

Presumably, in the Shepard and Metzler experiment, subjects were viewing the two objects, and then rotating their internal representation of one of the objects into congruence with the other. However, as we have previously discussed, if given enough time subjects can generate memory activations without the immediate benefit of a physical stimulus. Thus, if subjects could be informed soon enough as to the orientation of an upcoming presentation they could generate a memory activation of that stimulus configuration and make the match without further need for rotation. In this event we would expect no increase in matching time as a function of orientation differences between the

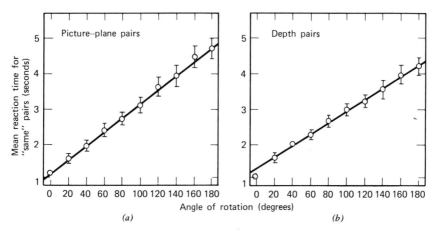

Figure 4.17
Mean reaction times for two perspective line drawings portraying objects of the same three-dimensional shape. Times are plotted as a function of angular difference in portrayed orientation; *(a)* for pairs differing by a rotation in the picture plane only, and *(b)* for pairs differing by a rotation in depth. (From Shepard and Metzler, 1970.)

first and second stimulus. In one condition of their experiment Cooper and Shepard (1973) tested this implication. In this investigation they wanted well learned stimulus configurations. So, instead of the three-dimensional objects used by Shepard and Metzler, they used letters of the alphabet. Figure 4.18 illustrates the design of this condition. Subjects were first given a 2-sec exposure to the stimulus they were to match in an upright orientation. They were then shown an arrow indicating the orientation in which they could expect to see the target stimulus. The arrow was presented for a variable period in order to give their subjects a varying amount of time to prepare for the test stimulus. Figure 4.19 shows the mean reaction time as a function of the orientation of the test stimulus for each condition of the experiment. It should be observed that (1) when given only 100 msec to prepare subjects are apparently unable to generate the proper memory activation before the onset of the test stimulus. For this situation results similar to those of Shepard and Metzler are found. On the other hand, when given a full second to prepare there is almost no effect due to orientation—indicating that when given enough time subjects can, in fact, construct an internal representation and rotate it into some predetermined position prior to the onset of the test stimulus. For intermediate preparation times we find intermediate results indicating that subjects are able

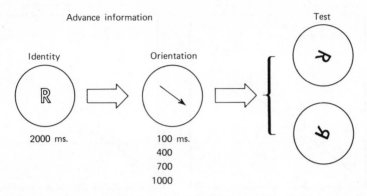

Figure 4.18
Sequence of events for the Cooper and Shepard (1973) experiment. First a character is displayed for 200-msec in normal orientation, then an arrow is presented indicating the orientation that the test character will have. The arrow is presented for either 100, 400, 700, or 1000-msec. Finally, either the rotated version of the original character or a reflected and rotation version of that character is presented. Subjects must respond as quickly as possible as to whether or not the test item is reflected. (From Cooper and Shepard, 1973.)

to make some, but not all of the necessary preparations when given only 400- or 700-msec warning.

It would seem then that there are two distinct sources of primary memory activations. One source is generated by specific kinds of sensory stimulation. The other results from an active attempt to form such an activation. In either case our memory representation appears not to be an entirely abstract concept of the object in question. Instead, it seems to be related to one or more specific input modalities. Moreover, once a memory activation is formed it can be further manipulated and transformed. Visual activations, it would seem, undergo primarily rotational transformation in a way somehow isomorphic to the transformation of similar objects in the real world. To date I know of no data on the rate of decay of the complex activations of the sort employed by Brooks, Shepard and Metzler, and Cooper and Shepard. Brooks' experiments would appear to give evidence that these memory activations can be selectively interfered with in much the same way Baddeley (1966a) shows selective interference among acoustically similar items in a standard memory span experiment. In another study Kosslyn (1973) has shown that there is a tradeoff between *size* and *degree of detail* in a visual memory activation. Kosslyn interprets this to mean that there is a limit, similar to the memory span, that applies to the amount of imaginal information that can be simultaneously active. I suspect

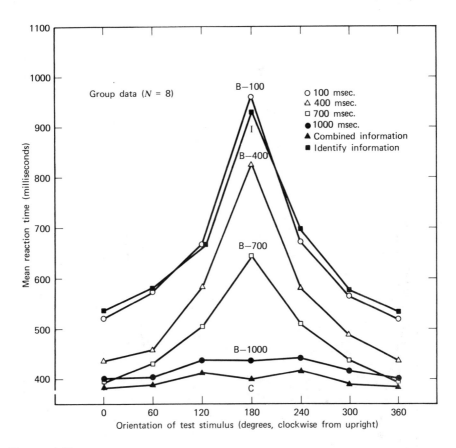

Figure 4.19
Mean reaction time as a function of orientation of the test stimulus and the duration of the presentation of the orientation information. (From Cooper and Shepard,
1973.)

that future research will find that temporary memory activations that are
primarily visual differ in no significant way from those generated by the presentation of verbal materials.

MAINTAINING PRIMARY MEMORY ACTIVATIONS

As suggested in the previous sections, without constant attention primary
memory activations soon fade and become too weak to sustain recall. Thus, in
most experiments requiring subjects to hold information for any period of

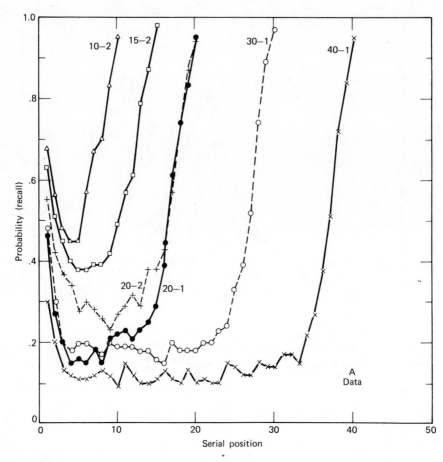

Figure 4.20
Percent recall as a function of serial position, length of presentation list, and whether the words were presented for 1- or 2- sec. intervals per word. The quickly rising portion of the curve near the end of each list is called the recency portion of the curve. The fast rising portion of the curve near the beginning of each list is called the primacy portion of the list. (From Murdock, 1961.)

time, subjects report making active attempts to maintain (e.g., rehearse) at least some of the information as primary memory activations. A number of theories of primary memory have suggested that this maintenance is the essential way that information is permanently stored (cf. Atkinson & Shiffrin, 1968; Norman & Rumelhart, 1970). The longer information is maintained in

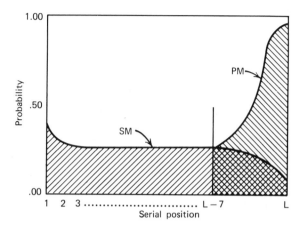

Figure 4.21
Theoretical account of serial position curve for free recall experiments. The primacy and flat portion of the serial position curve presumably depends only on secondary memory. The recency portion of the curve is presumed to depend both on primary memory and, to a lesser degree, on secondary memory. The crosshatched areas under each curve represent the amount of contribution of each memory to the probability of recall. (From Murdock, 1974.)

a primary memory activation, the stronger the memory trace finally left in secondary memory. Support for this view comes from analyses of the traditional "serial position" curve in free recall experiments.

The typical free recall experiment is much like memory span experiments, except that many more items are presented and subjects are not expected to remember the entire list perfectly. A number of different lists are presented to a number of different subjects. The serial position curve is then derived by plotting the percentage of times the first, second, third, etc., item was recalled correctly. Results typical of a wide range of such experiments are illustrated in Figure 4.20. There are three major points to notice about these curves. (1) The first few items are better remembered than all but the last few items (the so-called primacy effect). (2) The last few items are remembered best of all (the so-called recency effect). (3) There appears to be a long flat portion where recall is essentially independent of position in the input list.

The typical explanation of these results depends on the following two notions: (1) The strength of memory traces in secondary memory depends on the amount of time a representation of that item remains active in primary memory. (2) Items whose representations are active in primary memory at the time of recall are recalled with high probability—independently of their strength in secondary memory. Figure 4.21 illustrates this explanation. The curve labeled SM is intended to be roughly proportional to the amount of time information was maintained in primary memory. Early items are maintained somewhat longer because they have fewer competitors. Later items are maintained for a somewhat shorter time period because the subject must turn his attention to recall immediately after the cessation of the list. The line labeled PM is assumed to be roughly proportional to the amount of activation remaining for these items at the end of the list. The joint action of these two factors accounts very nicely for the observed results.

If these assumptions really account for the serial position curves in this situation, we should expect that if a subject were to be delayed in his recall and if during the delay period his attention were to be turned toward another task, then not only should the recency effect disappear, but in fact a "negative recency" effect should occur (that is *poorer* performance should occur on the last items of the list). This is expected because after a delay and distraction a subject must depend only on secondary memory and the hypothesis supposes that it is weaker for the last few items. Postman and Phillips (1965) and Glanzer and Cunitz (1966) both have found that an interpolated task of counting backwards by three eliminates the usual recency effect (cf. Figure 4.22). Furthermore, Craik (1970) and Darley and Murdock (1971) have shown that when the intervening task is the recall of other lists memory is poorer for the last items in the list (see Figure 4.23). Thus the expected result "negative recency" effect in fact occurs.

It would thus appear that an important by-product of holding information as a primary activation is the strengthening of the corresponding secondary memory trace. Although this may be true, a number of recent experiments have indicated that the problem is more complicated than it would appear on first sight.

Craik and Lockhart (1972) have proposed that there are at least two qualitatively different aspects to the rehearsal process. One aspect is to simply maintain information in primary memory. This kind, they suggest, has no effect on the secondary memory trace. The second aspect of rehearsal is what they refer to as the "elaborative" aspect. This involves further analysis of the *meaning* of the to-be-remembered item and the relation between its meaning and those other items which are also to be recalled. Only this aspect of rehearsal, they argue, strengthens secondary memory. In ordinary free recall experiments subjects have the explicit task of remembering the presented items over reasonably long periods of time. They therefore engage in both types of rehearsal. If, on the other hand, subjects could be induced *simply to maintain*

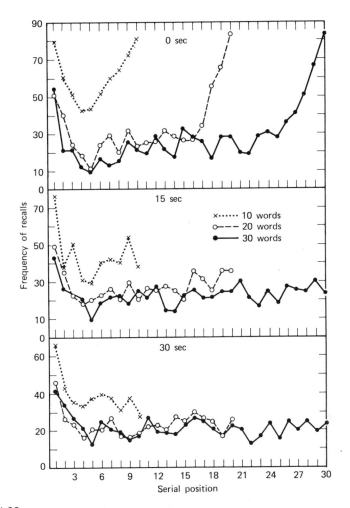

Figure 4.22
Serial position curves for 10-, 20-, and 30-item lists after 0, 15, or 30 sec. of interpolated distraction. (From Postman and Phillips, 1965.)

but not encode semantically while rehearsing we would find little or no effect of duration of the primary memory activation on later recall.

In a very clever procedure Craik and Watkins (1973) found evidence supporting this expectation. Subjects were instructed to listen to a series of word lists and then to report, at the end of the list, the last word in the list beginning with a certain "critical letter." As an example, suppose "G" is the critical

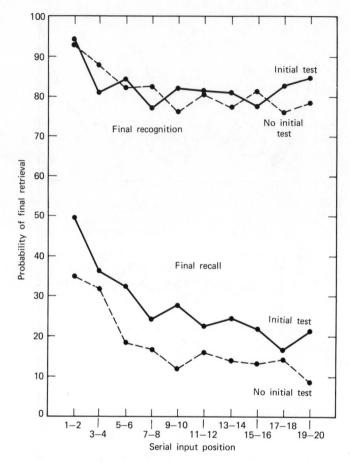

Figure 4.23
Serial position curves for final recall and final recognition of lists that were tested or were not tested immediately after presentation. Note that the final recall curve has the same shape as the "secondary memory" curve of Figure 4.21. The poor performance on the last items of the list is referred to as "negative recency." (From Darley and Murdock, 1971.)

letter and a subject received the following list: "daughter, oil, rifle, garden, grain, table, football, anchor, giraffe. . . ." The subject would first hold GARDEN, then replace it by GRAIN, then after three intervening trials replace that with GIRAFFE, etc., until the end of the list. The subject would then report the last word beginning with "G." In this way subjects were induced to hold items as temporary activations in primary memory for various amounts of time. After monitoring a number of such lists, subjects were un-expectedly asked to recall all of the items they could from any of the lists. The results showed *no effect on recall of amount of time an item was held in primary memory.* It would thus appear that maintenance alone has very little effect on retrievability from secondary memory.

However, Woodward, Bjork, and Jongeward (1973) have shown that this result doesn't necessarily mean that the secondary memory trace was not strengthened. Using a slightly different procedure Woodward et al. found re-sults exactly parallel to those mentioned above when subjects were asked to *recall* items at the end of the session. However, when subjects were shown a list of words, some of which they had seen before and some of which they had not, and asked to *recognize* which they had seen before, there was a dramatic improvement in recognition with amount of time the item was maintained in primary memory. It would thus appear that, as Craik and Lockhart have sug-gested, there are indeed two aspects to rehearsal. One of them, "the elabora-tive aspect," leads to improved recallability. The other, "the maintaining aspect," has little effect on recallability, but does have a strong effect on second-ary memory strength as measured by recognizability. As we will argue in our discussion of secondary memory, results such as these lend strong support for the notion that retrievability and recognizability of information stored in long-term memory may very well reflect different aspects of the memory system. In any case, it would appear that simply holding information as a primary memory activation does have an effect on memory strength, but little or no effect on accessibility.

SUMMARY

Before continuing with a discussion of secondary memory it will be useful to summarize the view of primary memory implicit in our discussion to this point. As the pattern synthesizer operates, representations of the input pattern are temporarily activated in memory. Without continued input from the pattern synthesizer or continued attention, they soon lose strength and disappear. More-over, only a small number of activations may be maintained at one time. It is as if a certain amount of processing capacity is required to maintain each activation—when we attempt to maintain too much at once we forget at least some of it. Although there is a strong limit on the number and duration of activations, there seems to be no limit on the complexity of any one activation. Thus by recoding into ever larger *chunks* we can maintain more and more in-formation in a single activation.

Although it seems that our access to information stored as activations in memory is instantaneous, in fact it takes time. By clever experimental manipulations we can show that it takes roughly 40 msec to access the memory activation of a single item.

Furthermore, memory activations appear to have characteristics that are specific to various sense modalities, not necessarily only to the modality of input. It may thus be appropriate to refer to these activations, at least in certain cases, as sensory images. Although a single activation may have aspects relevant to more than one sensory modality, it would appear that they most often have their primary features consonant with a single modality.

Not all of the activations are dependent on external input. We can create and use primary memory activations which have many of the same properties as those generated through the pattern synthesizer. These activations, whether they arise from internal or external sources, may be manipulated and transformed in various ways. In particular, we appear to have the ability to rotate internal representations of geometric forms. Moreover, this rotation appears to be a continuous analog of the similar operation performed on real objects.

If no interfering events occur, people seem to be able to hold primary memory activations for indefinite periods of time. It appears that the amount of time information is maintained in primary memory does have an important effect on the strength of the secondary memory trace, but it has an effect on recallability only when further processing is done on the memory activation.

Functionally, primary memory activations have been likened to an input-output buffer on a computer. The most important function of such a buffer is to hold incoming information until the central processor can analyze and further process it so that it can be properly stored in a more permanent form. The human primary memory system operates similarly. Perhaps its most important function is to hold information in a readily accessible form so that further processing and permanent storage can efficiently occur. In this role its function is analogous to that of the iconic and echoic stores mentioned in Chapter 2. These sensory stores hold information while feature analyzers process the information and the pattern synthesizer transforms it into meaningful units. Likewise, the primary memory system holds somewhat more highly refined information which can then be organized into even larger wholes and stored in the long-term memory structure.

THE NATURE OF SECONDARY MEMORY

Human long-term memory, like any large scale data storage device, is a highly organized system. A consideration of the problems of a large capacity data storage system such as a library leads to interesting insights into some of the problems that the human memory system must solve. For a data storage system like a library, storage itself poses no problem; a new book *can* be added to a library just by putting it on the shelf. If this were always done, however, the library would be useless. No one would ever know whether or not the library had a particular book. Even if one were certain that the book was there, the probability of ever finding it among the many thousands of volumes on the shelves would be very small. Therefore, libraries spend considerable effort preparing books to be put on the shelf. Each book is carefully cross listed in the card catalog. It is listed according to author, title, and any subject to which it seems pertinent. Moreover, to insure that a book can be located even when neither its exact title nor author are known, books on similar topics are located near one another on the shelves. If information is desired on a certain topic, sometimes only one book on that topic need be found in the card catalog. Once the appropriate area of the library is located, a leisurely search through the books in that vicinity will often lead to most of the books in the library on that topic.

A similar situation seems to exist within the human memory system. The storage of information itself is no problem; it is the retrieval of information once stored that causes the difficulty. If retrieval is to be assured, the information must be carefully stored according to some systematic scheme. The more topics to which the information being stored is related (i.e., the more cross referencing that is done), the greater the probability that it will eventually be retrieved. The retrieval cue, or the occasion for recalling information, is analogous to our point of entry into a card catalog in search of a book which we believe may be in the library. Whether or not we will find the desired information depends on how good the retrieval cue was, on whether or not the desired information was actually stored, and on how carefully we crossreferenced the stored information when we received it. If, for example, we simply stored a book relevant to both philosophy and psychology in the philosophy section and we want the information with reference to psychology, we will never find the book. If, on the other hand, we had noticed at storage that the book had much to say about psychological problems and cross referenced it to areas of psychology, we would have some chance of recovering the book when it was needed.

Although there are many similarities between the human memory system and a library, there is much that is different. The human memory system, unlike the library, must concurrently store information and build organizational schemes in which new data can be stored. Therefore, much of the data becomes embodied in the organizational schemes themselves. Furthermore, as new schemes replace old ones, no large scale reorganizations seem to occur.

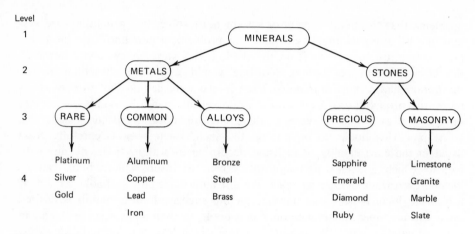

Figure 4.24
Example of spatial layout in which list items were presented in experiment by Bower, Clark, Lesgold, and Winzenz (1969). (From Bower et al., 1969.)

Thus, information stored under earlier organizational systems becomes lost or distorted when new organizational structures are developed. Finally, the quality of the information stored in libraries and that stored in human memory differs. Libraries store books which are frequently complete in themselves and thus are themselves the objects of search. Human systems appear to store more fragmentary bits of information, which are not themselves the objects of search. Thus, we seem to retrieve various bits of information which taken together may or may not be enough to answer the desired question.

SECONDARY MEMORY IS STRUCTURED

Perhaps the most straightforward lesson to be learned from our analogy of a library storage system is that the more carefully the organization is carried out the greater the chances for successful retrieval. Experiments by Bower and his associates (Bower, 1970; Bower & Clark, 1969; Bower, Clark, Lesgold & Winzenz, 1969) and Mandler and his associates (Mandler, 1967; Mandler & Pearlstone, 1966) have demonstrated this fact repeatedly. In one experiment, Bower, Clark, Lesgold, and Winzenz presented subjects lists of 28 words spatially organized as heirarchies as shown in Figure 4.24. For half of the subjects, the hierarchies presented were "natural hierarchies" (i.e., hierarchies that probably coincided with the subjects' own internal structure relating these words) such as the one in Figure 4.24. For the other half of the subjects, words were randomly placed at the various nodes of the tree. Furthermore, words from several different trees were mixed up. All subjects were presented four slides of this type (112 words in all) with 56-sec study time on each slide. Over 70 of the 112 words in the natural hierarchy were recalled, but only about 20 of the random words.

Mandler (1968) has convincingly demonstrated the value of categorization as a recall aid. In one experiment subjects were given a list of 100 words and asked to sort them into 2, 3, 4, 5, 6, or 7 categories. Subjects were allowed to sort the words until they reliably produced the same categorizations. A few days later the subjects were brought back and asked to recall as many of the words as they could remember. They were then asked to sort a new deck of 100 words into some other number of categories, and brought back again to recall as many words as they could of that list. This procedure continued until each subject had recalled a list sorted into each of the six category sizes twice. Figure 4.25 shows the number of words recalled as a function of the number of categories into which the words were sorted, for each of the subjects. The results are clear. For all but one of the subjects (No. 3), the number of words recalled was a linearly increasing function of the number of categories into which the words were sorted. Further investigation showed that this subject, when asked to sort words into n categories, put one word into each of $n-1$ categories and the rest in the remaining category. When he was later instructed to put "at least five items in each category," his performance improved dramatically and he too showed the positive correlation between category size and recall.

Interpretation of both of these experiments is easy using our library example. In the Bower et al. experiment, one would suppose that the more nearly the structure presented conformed to an already existing memorial organization, the easier it would be to find and retrieve stored information. Mandler's experiment also has a simple interpretation within this framework. The smaller the area through which one must search for stored information, the greater the probability that the desired information will in fact be found. Thus, the more categories that were used, the fewer words in each category and the higher the probability that the correct words would be found.

We mentioned in the previous section that people often can extend their apparent memory span by "chunking" incoming information and structuring it, at input, to conform with the "natural" structure of their secondary memory system. Mandler and his associates (cf. Mandler & Dean, 1969; Mandler, 1968) have developed an interesting experimental technique that allows us to observe this "chunking" process in action. The experimental paradigm, called the "one plus one task" proceeds as follows: The experimenter presents a list of words

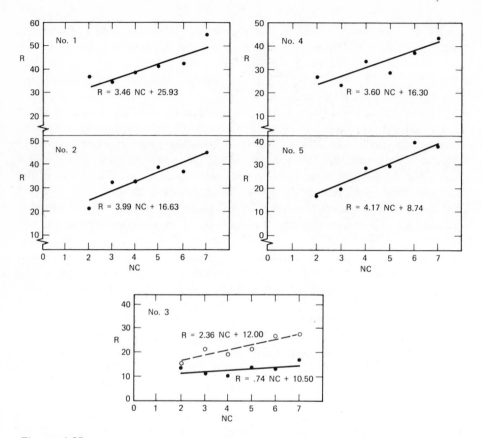

Figure 4.25
Number of words out of 100 recalled as a function of number of categories (NC) used in a prior sorting task using the same 100 items. Five curves are shown for five individual subjects. Each point represents the mean of two trials with that subject. (From Mandler, 1969.)

to the subject one word at a time. Following each presentation of a new word the subject attempts to recall, in any order, all of the words that have been presented up until that time. The experimenter never repeats an item, but the subject must repeat all of the items he remembers after each presentation. This task is particularly interesting because it gives the subject plenty of time to organize (chunk) the input items and because it gives us the opportunity to see the trial by trial results of their organizing. Table 4.3 illustrates the sequence of responses given by two subjects for the first sixteen trials of such an experiment. Notice first, that for the first few trials (until the capacity of primary memory has begun to be reached) both subjects give essentially perfect serial output. Clearly input order, rather than memory structure is the determining factor here. One of the subjects (subject No. 1) is using a first-in last-out strategy whereas the other (subject No. 7) is using a first-in first-out strategy. By the time the sixth item arrives both subjects begin to have difficulty. Subject No. 1 now begins to organize his list—skirts and pajamas are put together —momentarily losing an item in the process. Subject No. 7 simply drops an input item. On trial 7, with the presentation of "baker" subject No. 1 forms another chunk of "baker" and "engineer" thus keeping the total number of chunks down to a total of five. Subject No. 7 still has not begun to organize his list and attempts to maintain the first-in first-out order. As a result he fails to integrate "sailboat" into his output string. He is operating near the limits of primary memory capacity.

It is interesting to note that subject No. 1 forgets whole chunks at a time. Thus, on trial 10, subject No. 1 has forgotten the entire group of ships; then on trial 11 both ships are again recalled. Similarly, on trial 14 both ships are forgotten and then return again on trial 15 as a pair. Thus, by judicious use of chunking, subject No. 1 has managed to keep the number of chunks to be remembered within his capacity to hold them in primary memory. So, on trial 16 he has 5 chunks allowing him to output 15 of the 16 presented items.

Subject No. 2, however, is much more reluctant to deviate from his first-in-first-out recall strategy. Thus, on trial 10, although he is apparently retaining 6 chunks of information, he is able to output only 6 items. On trial 11 subject No. 7 first begins to deviate from the simple output strategy he has developed and places birds into a single chunk. Nevertheless, by trial 16 subject No. 7 is holding 9 chunks of information and supporting the output of only 11 items. By the end of the experiment (50 trials) subject No. 2 is categorizing his output as completely as subject No. 1 and manages to output 40 items based on 6 chunks of information. Half of the 10 items he ultimately forgot were gone by trial 15—before he had begun to make good use of his memory structure.

This experiment allows us to see, in a rather graphic way, how the structure of memory can be used to extend our basic limitation of being able to hold 7 ± 2 items of information as activations in primary memory.

The "one plus one" experiment illustrates how judicious use of memory structure can facilitate memory. It is interesting that our propensity to unify information into a single organizational system does not always help us remember better. The very process of structuring the information leads us to carefully preserve some kinds of information while destroying other kinds. Just as the

Table 4.3
One Plus One Experiment*

Subject			Trial Experimenter Subject
No. 1	1	Pajamas	Pajamas
	2	Engineer	Engineer Pajamas
	3	Skirt	Skirt Engineer Pajamas
	4	Cruiser	Cruiser Skirt Engineer Pajamas
	5	Eye	Eye Cruiser Skirt Engineer Pajamas
	6	Owl	Owl Eye Cruiser (Skirt Pajamas)
	7	Baker	(Baker Engineer) Owl Eye Cruiser (Skirt Pajamas)
	8	Lip	Lip (Baker Engineer) Owl Eye Cruiser (Skirt Pajamas)
	9	Warship	(Warship Cruiser) (Engineer Baker) Owl Eye (Skirt Pajamas)
	10	BlueJay	(BlueJay Owl) (Skirt Pajamas) (Engineer Baker)
	11	Overcoat	(Overcoat Skirt Pajamas) (Engineer Baker) Owl Eye (Cruiser Warship)
	12	Secretary	(Secretary Engineer Baker) (Warship Cruiser) (Skirt Pajamas) (Owl) (Eye Lip)
	13	Finch	(Finch Owl BlueJay) (Skirt Pajamas Overcoat) (Engineer Baker Secretary) (Lip Eye) (Warship Cruiser)
	14	Skin	(Skin Lip Eye) (Overcoat Skirt Pajamas) (Secretary Baker Engineer) (Owl Finch BlueJay)
	15	Professor	(Professor Secretary Baker Engineer) (Owl Finch BlueJay) (Skirt Overcoat Pajamas) (Warship Cruiser) (Lip Skin Eye)
	16	Shirt	(Shirt Skirt Overcoat Pajamas) (Secretary Engineer Baker) (Owl Finch BlueJay) (Cruiser Warship) (Lip Skin Eye)
No. 2	1	Pajamas	Pajamas
	2	Skin	Pajamas Skin
	3	Sloop	Pajamas Skin Sloop
	4	Leg	Pajamas Skin Sloop Leg
	5	Eagle	Pajamas Skin Sloop Leg Eagle

Table 4.3 (cont.)

6	Engineer	Pajamas Skin Sloop Eagle Engineer
7	Sailboat	Pajamas Skin Sloop Eagle Engineer
8	Skirt	Pajamas Skin Sloop Eagle Skirt Engineer
9	Lark	Pajamas Skin Sloop Eagle Engineer Lark
10	Judge	Pajamas Skin Sloop Eagle Engineer Lark
11	Face	Pajamas Skin Sloop (Eagle Lark) Engineer Face
12	Finch	Pajamas Skin Sloop Eagle Engineer Lark Face Skirt
13	Pants	Pajamas Skin Sloop Eagle Engineer Lark Face (Skirt Pants)
14	Lawyer	Pajamas Skin Sloop (Lark Eagle) (Engineer Lawyer) Face
15	Battleship	Battleship Pajamas Skin Sloop Engineer Face (Lark Eagle) (Pants Skirt) Battleship
16	Suit	Pajamas Skin Sloop Suit Battleship Engineer (Eagle Lark) Face (Skirt Pants)

*Data courtesy of George Mandler and Karolyn Patterson

library's organizational scheme preserves the information about the topic of the book, it loses information about such things as the order of acquisition or about what books were purchased together. One could imagine a library organization scheme which stored books according to their order of arrival at the library, but such a scheme would be useless for most purposes. So too, the human memory system stores information in ways that preserve the most useful aspects of the information while at the same time failing to preserve other kinds of information. Very clear demonstrations of this have been reported in a recent series of papers by Bransford and Franks (1971), Bransford, Barclay, and Franks (1972), and Barclay (1973).

In one of these experiments Barclay (1973) presented subjects with a set of ten consistent sentences from the frame given below.

$$\text{The} \begin{Bmatrix} \text{cowboy} \\ \text{artist} \\ \text{salesman} \\ \text{welder} \\ \text{fireman} \end{Bmatrix} \text{is} \begin{Bmatrix} \text{taller} \\ \\ \text{shorter} \end{Bmatrix} \text{than the} \begin{Bmatrix} \text{cowboy} \\ \text{artist} \\ \text{salesman} \\ \text{welder} \\ \text{fireman} \end{Bmatrix}.$$

An example set of 10 sentences is given in Table 4.4. It should be noted that the 10 sentences determine the following order by height of the five men:

cowboy, artist, salesman, welder, fireman

During the presentation period subjects were listening to the sentences and attempting to determine the height ordering. After the 10 sentences were presented subjects were given a list of 32 sentences and asked to judge, for each sentence, whether it was *new* (had not been among the 10 previously presented sentences) or *old* and to give on a scale 1 to 5 their degree of confidence that they were correct.

Table 4.4

Aquisition Sentences
1. The cowboy is shorter than the artist.
2. The cowboy is shorter than the welder.
3. The artist is taller than the cowboy.
4. The artist is shorter than the welder.
5. The salesman is taller than the artist.
6. The salesman is shorter than the fireman.
7. The welder is taller than the salesman.
8. The welder is shorter than the fireman.
9. The fireman is taller than the cowboy.
10. The fireman is taller than the salesman.

Table 4.4 (cont.)

	Examples of Recognition Sentences	Mean Confidence Ratings
	Old	
	1. The cowboy is shorter than the artist.	
	2. The artist is taller than the cowboy.	
	3. The salesman is shorter than the fireman.	3.28
	4. The welder is shorter than the fireman.	
	5. The fireman is taller than the salesman.	
	6. The welder is taller than the salesman.	
	Equivalent	
	1. The welder is taller than the cowboy.	
True	2. The welder is taller than the artist.	
	3. The artist is shorter than the salesman.	3.51
	4. The salesman is shorter than the welder.	
	5. The fireman is taller than the welder.	
	6. The cowboy is shorter than the fireman.	
	True New Pairs	
	1. The cowboy is shorter than the salesman.	
	2. The artist is shorter than the fireman.	2.75
	3. The salesman is taller than the cowboy.	
	4. The fireman is taller than the artist.	
	False New Pair	
	1. The cowboy is taller than the salesman.	
	2. The fireman is shorter than the artist.	4.89
	3. The artist is taller than the fireman.	
	4. The salesman is shorter than the cowboy.	
	Subject-Object Reversal (*New*)	
	1. The welder is shorter than the cowboy.	
	2. The artist is taller than the salesman.	
	3. The salesman is taller than the welder.	
False	4. The cowboy is taller than the fireman.	4.93
	5. The fireman is shorter than the cowboy.	
	6. The welder is shorter than the artist.	
	Relation-Reversal (*New*)	
	1. The cowboy is taller than the welder.	
	2. The artist is taller than the welder.	
	3. The salesman is taller than the fireman.	
	4. The welder is shorter than the salesman.	4.97
	5. The fireman is shorter than the cowboy.	
	6. The artist is shorter than the cowboy.	

The 32 test sentences consisted of 6 *old* sentences; 6 *equivalent* sentences (if an *old* sentence was "The cowboy is shorter than the welder," then the *new* sentence would be "The welder is taller than the cowboy"); 6 *subject-object reversals* (if an *old* sentence was "The salesman is taller than the artist," then the *new* sentence would be "The artist is taller than the salesman"); 6 *relation reversals* ("The artist is shorter than the fireman," becomes "The artist is taller than the fireman"); 4 *true new pairs* and 4 *false new pairs*. There were thus 16 *false* and 16 *true* sentences, 26 of which are *new* among the test sentences. Table 4.4 gives an example of a set of test sentences.

Table 4.4 gives the mean confidence ratings for each of the six categories of test sentences. A negative number indicates that subjects judged sentences in that category as being *new;* a positive number indicates that they judged sentences from that category as being *old*. The major results are very clear. Subjects are able to distinguish between *true* and *false* sentences, but not between *old* and *new* sentences. Information of the sort presented in these statements is apparently stored according to a unified (linear) organizational structure which preserves the *truth* (or meaning) of the presented sentences, but fails to preserve the details about how the information was presented. Bransford and Franks in a somewhat different experimental procedure find almost identical results. They conclude that subjects remember the *meaning* of what is presented but not the particular wording of sentences.

In another experiment Bransford, Barclay, and Franks found that subjects could not remember which of the following pair of sentences were presented:

(1a) The woman stood *on* the stool and the mouse sat on the floor beneath *it*.
(1b) The woman stood *on* the stool and the mouse sat on the floor beneath *her*.

But they had no difficulty remembering which of the following pair of sentences had been presented:

(2a) The woman stood *beside* the stool and the mouse sat on the floor beneath *it*.
(2b) The woman stood *beside* the stool and the mouse sat on the floor beneath *her*.

Again, this experiment illustrates how the memory system preserves those aspects of the input information that make a difference with respect to the system's manner of structuring the information, but fails to preserve that information that makes no difference in the *meaning* of what is said.

To summarize, secondary memory is a highly organized system. The structure plays an important role in our ordinary ability to remember. We use this structure to facilitate recall. If incoming information matches an existent memory structure we can make use of that structure to get it in the "right region of memory" and thus reduce useless search. We can use the structure in building larger chunks to allow us to hold more information as primary memory activations. Moreover, not only what we retain, but what we forget, is in large measure determined by the kinds of organizational schemes that we have built up to deal with the information we normally encounter in our daily life. Thus, in the experiment by Bransford, Barclay, and Franks we do not remember the exact pronoun used to describe the location of the mouse. Instead, we remember the spatial configuration of the woman, the mouse, and the stool. This is because spatial organization is ordinarily a more useful structure for such information than one revolving around the specific words used.

Thus, in Chapter 2 we showed that it is harder to perceive information not coinciding with our preexisting expectations. In Chapter 3 we showed that it is harder to understand something that is not consonant with our prior experiences, and now we have shown that it is harder to remember information that doesn't fit neatly into the memory structures we have already available in memory. We see increasingly that the human organism is a *positive feedback* system. That is, it perceives what it expects, it understands in terms of what it has experienced, and it remembers just what fits with what it knows.

DEPTH OF PROCESSING

Returning to our library analogy, it is clear that the more effort put into the original storage of a volume—the more places the book appears in the subject index or the more carefully it is classified—the more likely that it will be found when needed. It is also clear that not all effort that might be involved in processing a book will be of equal value for future purposes. For example, careful attention to the color of the cover or to the type font in which it is printed will rarely be of use when the book is finally needed. So it seems to be with human memory. The more attention we give to the meaning of an input —i.e., the more completely we comprehend it—the more likely that future search will prove successful. A number of recent writers have pointed out this fact (cf. Craik & Lockhart, 1972), and an increasing number of experiments have demonstrated it (cf. Hyde & Jenkins, 1973; Till & Jenkins, 1973).

In one such experiment (Bobrow & Bower, 1969) subjects were asked to recall words which they had previously disambiguated or for which they had judged the accuracy of the spelling. Substantially better recall resulted when subjects were performing the meaning oriented task (disambiguation) than when they were simply judging the accuracy of spelling.

In another experiment Treisman and Tuxworth (1974) required some subjects to listen to sentences played over a tape recorder and respond whenever they heard a word beginning with a certain phoneme (e.g., when listening for a "g" they should respond to "growing" in the following sentence: "They found a small cluster of the flowers growing in the shade of the trunk of a fallen beech tree"). Other subjects listened to similar sentences but they were to respond whenever they heard a "semantically anomalous" phrase (e.g., they should respond to "family" in the following sentence: "They found a small cluster of the flowers growing in the shade of the trunk of a fallen family tree"). Subjects were tested for their memory for these sentences either immediately following presentation or after 20 sec of counting backwards by sevens. There was almost no difference in immediate recall (which was largely due to primary memory) but the 20-sec delay caused a 15% decrement for subjects who were only listening for phonemes. The delay had very little effect on the recall of those who were listening for semantic anomalies. Here again we find that attention to meaning leads to a kind of storage that is much more efficient than attention to more superficial aspects of the sentence. The results of the delay conditions are certainly consistent with the view presented here that the organizational effects are relevant to secondary, but not primary, memory.

Another experiment (Mistler-Lachman, 1974) illustrates that even differential amounts of attention to meaning can lead to more or less useful storage. In this experiment subjects received pairs of sentences. In all cases the first sentence of the pair was a meaningful sentence. The second sentence could either (1) follow meaningfully from the first (e.g., if the first was "not all people have similar tastes," the second might be "Some women prefer housework to career life"); (2) be meaningless (e.g., if the first were "The colored telephone was a gift," the second might be "Nurses and belts have witty old brass bananas"); or (3) be meaningful but not follow from the first sentence at all (e.g., if the first were "Two new bodyguards were hired yesterday," the second might be "Textures soften a room with hard lines"). Subjects had to perform one of three tasks with these sentences. They had either to determine whether the second sentence was meaningful, to judge whether or not the second followed from the first, or to produce a third sentence that followed from the first two. Later subjects were given the subject phrase of each of the second sentences and asked to complete them. The results showed that the more deeply they had processed the sentences originally, the better their recall. Those who had simply rated meaningfulness did the poorest. Those who had to judge whether or not the sentences followed meaningfully one from another did next best, and those who had to produce a third sentence to follow meaningfully from the first two performed best of all. In short, the more deeply one processes a sentential input the better one's memory for that input.

Taken as a whole these three experiments would appear to fit very nicely into our view that access to memory, like access to a book from a library, ordinarily proceeds along semantic lines. The more carefully information is processed and the more that processing is relevant to the meaning of the input, the more likely the information can later be retrieved.

CONTEXTUAL EFFECTS IN REMEMBERING

Before abandoning our library analogy for more sophisticated theories of secondary memory, we will consider the role of context in storage and retrieval. In the previous section I suggested that the *deeper* and more semantically we processed the input the better would be our recall. However, that is not the whole story.. Even when an input is thoroughly processed and the information is carefully stored it will not be retrivable unless the *context* of retrieval matches that of storage in certain important ways. To use our library analogy again, suppose that an elderly philosophy professor donates his large and rare collection of books to the library. Suppose, in honor of such a gracious gift, the library sets up a special room named in honor of the famous donor. Moreover, since the collection is so large it receives its own card catalog, and philosophers from far and wide come to the library where, within the space of a single room, nearly every book they have ever wanted to read is kept, carefully indexed. However, let us suppose that our philosopher was more widely read than most people know. Not only does his collection include the important works in philosophy, but many valuable works in psychology not available anywhere else. We now consider the psychologist in search of one of these books. Unless, in desperation he makes a special effort to look through the famous philosopher's collection he will never find the book. He will simply look in all of the wrong places. It should be clear that the same can occur in human memory. If we learn something in one context and have not considered, in some way, its relation to a second context we will only rarely succeed in a search oriented in the second context.

An experiment by Bobrow and Light (reported in Bower, 1970) illustrates this point very well. In this experiment, subjects were presented with 44 nouns together with adjectives emphasizing one or another meaning of the nouns. Half of the subjects were presented the words with adjectives so that the nouns fell into several general classes (the "categorized list") such as BIRDS: chirping *cardinal*, homing *pigeon;* FOODS: lamb *chop*, roast *ham* etc. The adjectives in the other list were chosen so that the words were in unique categories (the "decategorized list") such as church *cardinal*, stool *pigeon*, karate *chop*, theatrical *ham*. After presentation, half of the subjects in each group were asked to

Table 4.5
Mean Words in the Free Recall or Category-Cued Recall
for the Categorized Versus Decategorized Word Lists

List	Free Recall	Cued Recall
Categorized	17	24
Decategorized	12	9

recall as many of the nouns as they could The other half were cued with the names of the general categories (e.g., FOODS, BIRDS). The results are shown in Table 4.5. In the "categorized list," the cued recall is better than free recall. This is natural, since the cues orient the searches to the appropriate area of memory. For the "decategorized list," however, the free recall is better. The cues were actually detrimental. The cues led the subjects to the wrong area of memory. The information on *ham,* for example, was stored and referenced to information about acting and the theater. Thus, telling the subject that some of the nouns were FOODS was completely misleading.

These results might lead one to suggest that information is stored in secondary memory not under particular physical stimuli like *ham,* but under word senses, as we might find them listed in a dictionary. Thus, ham as a food is different from ham as an actor. Recent experiments by Tulving and Thomson (1973), and by Barclay, Bransford, Franks, McCarrell, and Nitsch (1974) illustrate that even unambiguous terms such as *piano* are stored relative to the context in which they occur. All occurrences of *piano* are not stored in the same place.

An examination of the Barclay et al. experiment is instructive. They presented subjects with sentences such as "The man lifted the piano" or "The man tuned the piano." They then asked subjects to recall the object nouns of the presented sentences. Subjects were cued with descriptions of the object to be remembered. Thus, they received a description of the form "something heavy" or "something that sounds nice." The results showed that subjects recalled the object nouns about three times more often when given an "appropriate cue" (i.e., "something heavy" for *"the man lifted the piano"*) than when given an inappropriate cue (e.g., *"something heavy"* for *"A man tuned the piano"* or "something that sounds nice" for "The man lifted the piano"). These results and similar ones, reported by Anderson and Ortony (1975), illustrate clearly the degree of context sensitivity found in human memory. In order to find the sought after information in memory, we must have contextual guides that lead us in the right direction. Neither external stimuli nor even word senses are certain to send us in the right direction. Apparently it is just those aspects that were noticed and believed relevant at the time of storage that can serve as efficient guides back into memory.

RETRIEVING FROM SECONDARY MEMORY

The process of retrieving information from secondary memory would appear to consist of two aspects: (1) the problem of getting to the relevant location in memory—it is here that the organizational character of memory is so important; (2) the problem of constructing an appropriate output from the sketchy information found. It is not clear how either process works, but the first would appear to be analogous to the process of searching for memorial referents of definite descriptions as discussed in Chapter 3. The question initiating the retrieval process, the contextual situation in which the retrieval is done, and additional knowledge about the nature of the sought after information (such as the conceptual category in which it belongs or the events surrounding the occurrence of the to-be-remembered event, etc.) serve as joint constraints facilitating the location of one or more areas of memory.

However, the location of an appropriate area of memory does not always appear to be sufficient for recall. It is as if memories are not stored as entire units (as books are in a library) but rather the appropriate location in memory would often appear to contain only *fragments* of what is to be recalled. From this point on, the process of retrieval should best be considered *reconstructive* in the same sense that perception is considered constructive. The information stored in memory serves as constraints for memorial reconstruction just as the physical features extracted from sensory input serve as constraints for a process of perceptual construction. In addition expectations, context, and other knowledge of the world serve to constrain the final reconstruction from memory. Moreover, just as we are not always aware of the nonsensory determinants of our perceptions, so too we are not always aware of the nonmemorial constraints on our memories.

A very interesting example of the operation of such constraints was reported in a recent experiment by Loftus and Palmer (1974). In their experiment subjects first viewed a short film depicting a multicar accident. Following the presentation subjects were given a questionnaire about the accident. One of the questions concerned the speed of the autos involved in the accident. Half of the subjects were asked *"About how fast were the cars going when they smashed into each other?"* The remaining subjects received the question *"About how fast were the cars going when they hit each other?"* The questions differed only in the verb used. A week later subjects were brought back and asked another set of questions. Among this second set was the question *"Did you see any broken glass?"* (There was no broken glass in the film.) The results were very interesting. In the first place those subjects receiving the verb "smashed" in their original questionnaire gave speed estimates about 30% higher than those with the verb "hit." Moreover, about 32% of those receiving the verb "smashed" in the first questionnaire responded positively to the question about glass. Only 14% of those receiving "hit" responded positively. Loftus and Palmer suggest:

> that the subject first forms some representation of the accident he has witnessed. The experimenter then, while asking "About how fast were the cars going when they smashed into each other?" supplies a piece of external information, namely, that the cars did indeed smash into each other. When these two pieces of information are integrated, the subject has a memory of an accident more severe than in fact it was. Since broken glass is commensurate with a severe accident, the subject is more likely to think that broken glass is present. [P. 588.]

This experiment thus illustrates nicely both the integration of information from more than one source into a single memory and the use of that information to reconstruct a memory which contains aspects which were not, in fact, contained in either source.

It is difficult to find experimental techniques that give us insight into the nature of the fragments stored in memory. Perhaps the most straightforward method of doing this is to ask subjects what partial information they are using to reconstruct their final recollection. Unfortunately, this is usually not rewarding. The process operates too rapidly, and we have too little conscious awareness about the processes we use. There are situations, however, where the process seems to be slow enough that the alert information processing psychologist can run diagnostic experiments and ask the subject questions *during the process of reconstruction*. The situation I have in mind is the so-called *tip-of-the-tongue phenomenon* (TOT). We have all had the experience of being certain that we know something, knowing some things about it, but somehow not being able to think of what it is called. (Try to think of the name of "a navigational instrument used in measuring angular distances, especially the altitude of sun, moon, and stars at sea.") Brown and McNeill (1966) devised an experimental procedure which induced subjects into the TOT state and then asked them questions about the fragmentary knowledge they had available. Brown and McNeill induced the TOT state in subjects by reading them the definition of an uncommon English word (such as the one given above) and asking for the word. Often subjects would either retrieve the word immediately or conclude that they didn't know. Occasionally, the subject would be "seized" by a TOT state. While in this state subjects were asked to give a running account of the words they were considering. Some were reported to be similar in sound, but not in meaning. Others were said to be similar in meaning, but not in sound. Simultaneously, the experimenter asked questions such as "How many syllables does it have?" or "What letter does it start with?" These questions were answered with remarkable accuracy. Subjects had accurate information about both semantic and acoustic aspects of the sought after word. They often knew what letters the word started with, affixes of the word, the number of syllables, and the pattern of stress. Brown and McNeill concluded that the fragmentary information in memory can be considered like a set of features—both semantic and sensory. The list, however, is not always complete. Often it doesn't matter. We have enough to determine an output. Sometimes, however, we have some information, but not enough to determine a response completely. We then go into a TOT state. We search for more information and further constraints. If we find enough we finally get the word out. Otherwise we remain in the TOT state until we finally give up. (By the way, the navigational instrument referred to above was a sextant.)

There are other occasions in which the reconstruction process is sufficiently slowed down to observe it. This often occurs when complex events and their relationships are being retrieved. Consider the following question (from Linton, 1975). "Which came first, the death of Charles de Gaulle or the landing of the first man on the moon?" Most people living today have heard of both events. It is another matter to answer such a question. It usually requires a long sequence of reasoning and complex inference to reconstruct the actual order of these events. An experiment being carried out by Marigold Linton (1975) is investigating the process of reconstructing information about real world events. Her experiment proceeds as follows: Everyday her subject (Linton herself) writes a description, on 3 by 5 cards, of two or more events that happened to her during the day. The date is coded on the back of the cards, and the cards are randomly stored to be tested at a later time. (The testing times are designed to vary up to five years. At the time of this writing the experiment is somewhat more than half over.) On the prescribed testing date cards to be tested are pulled out. In one condition the subject attempts to determine the date on which she believes that event to have occurred. In some cases verbal protocols are recorded during recall. Below is an example taken from Linton (1975); this is for item number 6096. The description of the event is given below (p. 401):

Dedre Gentner gives her presentation in Norman's [D. A. Norman] research seminar on the semantic treatment of verbs.

[This event actually occurred on May 1, 1972, during a meeting of the LNR (Lindsay, Norman & Rumelhart) research group at the University of California,

San Diego. The various persons mentioned below were graduate students at the time. The protocol was recorded nearly two years later on February 3, 1974].

Fairly late in spring semester, 1972. Everyone was to have their papers ready for presentation sometime much earlier—perhaps April 3. I kept referring to it as the April 1 deadline although I knew it was somewhat after that. Dedre was perhaps the first person who did give her paper, or was it Steve Palmer? Could have been as late as June 1 because things were pretty well over for the summer by then? (Absolutely no recall for the event itself. I can, of course, . . . remember Dedre giving a talk. Perhaps can even recall her talking about verbs.) What might she have said? Do remember the session in which we heard the folk story and then tried to recall it. That was probably Kris's or Adele's. Of course, it might have been Dedre. But what would that have had to do with verbs? I know she was working with Steve on the project, but I don't think that they gave the presentation together. This was after the verbs of motion lecture by Fillmore. The meetings were held on Wednesday? Let's pick April 26, 1972. [*There were nine possible Wednesdays to choose among.*]
The time required to complete this protocol was seven minutes, 52 seconds. A number of major markers can be identified. First, there was the putative April 1, 1972 deadline for the paper. That dealine was violated so radically that it became a standing joke to ask people, in April, or even May, if they had finished their April 1 paper yet. So the paper could not have been before the deadline. But the quarter ended on June 1, so it could not have been after that. Frank Restle had visited for a series of colloquia and seminars around April 10 and April 12, so it could not have been then. It could not have been May 3, since I was not there that week.

These data would seem to support the view that retrieving information from memory is a two-stage process. The first stage involves the location of the relevant information in memory. This process can be characterized as a search process. It involves the use of a directing question, contextual information available at retrieval, and other related world knowledge. The second stage of retrieval involves reconstruction. In this example the stored attributes in memory play a role analogous to the input features in perception. Prior expectations, context, and knowledge about the nature of the world serve jointly to act as constraints on the final reconstruction.

In earlier sections we have referred loosely to the organizational structure of human memory. Given the complex roles that the human memory system plays and the idiosyncratic character of the organizational schemes of different people, it seems impossible to characterize the features of long-term memory in a general way. Nevertheless, we apparently have enough experiences in common and there are enough structural constraints on the way in which the organization of memory develops that some useful theoretical statements can be made about the structure of secondary memory. We now turn to such a discussion.

THE STRUCTURE OF SECONDARY MEMORY

The human secondary memory system is a vast repository of knowledge. Some of this knowledge seems to be in the form of specific memories of particular events. Other knowledge seems to be in the form of general abstractions which are no longer tied to any particular time or place. This second kind of knowledge, which might be called knowledge of the world, consists largely of generalizations we have made about the world. These generalizations consist of such information as "What a dog is," "What it means for someone to *give* something to someone else," or "What typical sequences of events occur when going to a restaurant to eat." Such generic information is presumably derived by generalization from particular experiences we have had or from things we have been told. The sum total of this conceptual knowledge constitutes what Tulving (1972) referred to as *semantic memory*. The rest of our knowledge consists of memories of specific events we have experienced or been told about. Knowledge of this second kind corresponds roughly to what Tulving referred to as *episodic memory*.

Thus, when we encounter sentences such as

(3) Abraham Lincoln was born in a log cabin.

or

(4) The man lifted the piano.

we use our *semantic memory* to assign meaning to the words and to place an interpretation on the sentences. Once an interpretation has been assigned a trace of that interpretation remains in *episodic memory,* and at a later time we might retrieve that trace and thus "remember" having been told these specific facts. Similarly, were we to actually observe a man lifting a piano, for example, we would use our semantic memories to interpret the visual information in terms of general categories such as "men" and "pianos" and "lifting" and then that interpretation would leave a trace to be retrieved at a later time as a memory of the event in question.

It should be emphasized that I am not suggesting that there are distinct parts of the memory system, say, a semantic memory and an episodic memory. All of the evidence seems to point to a single integrated secondary memory system. Rather, it turns out that different kinds of experimental techniques are useful in studying semantic memory than are useful in the study of episodic memory.

We will thus consider evidence about the structure of secondary memory in two parts corresponding to the distinction outlined above.

Structure in Semantic Memory

Semantic memory, as we are using the term, refers to that aspect of our secondary memory system which stores our knowledge about general concepts. Often these are concepts underlying the meaning of specific words, such as *dog* or *give*. Of course, there are many more of these concepts than there are words. Thus, for example, the concept for *church cardinal* is different from that for *chirping cardinal,* which is different yet from the color designated by cardinal. Moreover, there need be no single English word or even a simple phrase that corresponds directly to these concepts. Often these concepts involve knowledge about generalized sequences of events as well, such as the restaurant schema discussed in Chapter 3. It is through these general concepts that we understand linguistic inputs and generally interpret our world.

Specifying the structure of semantic memory amounts to specifying the *semantic relationships* (i.e., meaning relationships) among the concepts constituting our semantic memories. Thus, for example, the semantic relationship between *dog* and *animal* may be *subset of,* and that between *California* and *United-States* might be *part of.* All of this information is presumably stored in our memories. The problem we now set for ourselves is to determine, in a general way, the structure implicit in our semantic memories.

Consider the following problem. You are trying to induce the organizational rules of a library. However, you are not allowed to enter the library nor to ask direct questions about the organizational scheme. Instead, you can employ and question a *runner* who may enter the library to perform certain tasks for you. You may try to deduce the organizational structure by giving the runner different instructions and observing either how long it takes him to carry out your instructions or what books he brings out for you. This is roughly the situation for the information processing theorist when he attempts to answer questions about organization. A number of tasks have been tried. Some of these are analogous to those described by the following instructions and queries for our runner. Find me the book closest to this one. How far it is between these two books? Here are a bunch of books: put the ones together that are close together in the library. Are these two books on the same shelf? Is this book in such and such a set of books? The psychologist's problem is to, somehow, induce the structure from the way people have answered these kinds of questions.

We will proceed by discussing in turn a number of the major hypotheses that have been put forth about the structure of semantic memory. Most of these hypotheses have their roots outside of psychology—in linguistics, in

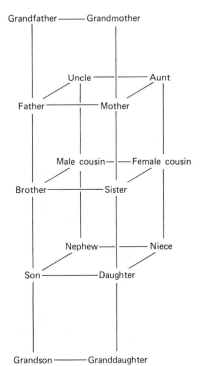

Figure 4.26
Spatial representation of kinship terms.

philosophy, and in artificial intelligence. Psychologists have adapted these hypotheses and developed experimental techniques designed to determine which, if any, of these form a reasonable basis for the human semantic memory system.

Paradigmatic Structures. Among the simplest notions about the structure of secondary memory is the view that the meaning of a given concept is defined in terms of a value on each of *n* basic *components* or *dimensions* of meaning. Thus, for example, the meaning of the concept underlying one sense of the term *man* differs from that underlying the term *woman* only by having different values on the dimension of *sex.* Such organizational systems are called *paradigmatic,* and the analysis of concepts into a set of underlying meaning components is called *componential analysis.* Perhaps *componential* analysis has been used most in the study of a set of concepts arising from the anthropological literature and the study of kinship terms (cf. Romney & D'Andrade, 1964). Figure 4.26 illustrates a structure proposed to underlie the most common English kinship terms. Under this proposal kinship terms convey three components of meaning: sex—male or female; lineage—direct or collateral; and generation —same generation, one generation removed, or two generations removed.

Suppose that our knowledge of kinship concepts was actually stored in such a paradigmatic space. How could we find out? One approach involves asking subjects to judge the similarity of pairs of these concepts (e.g., How similar in meaning are the terms "uncle" and "brother"?). Suppose that similarity is not directly stored, but instead is derived from the "psychological distance" between the concepts in memory—the "closer" two concepts are to one another in memory the more similar they are (i.e., we are asking the analog to the question: How far apart are these two books in the library?). If this assumption were correct and if our structure were correct we could predict subjects' responses to a variety of questions. For example, we would expect people to rate "brother" more similar in meaning to "sister" than to "niece," "son" closer to "father" than to "grandfather," etc. To the degree that our observed responses are consistent with our expectations we can have confidence that this structure captures important aspects of our internal representation for these concepts. We have shown how we can empirically substantiate or disconfirm some prior hypothesis we have about small portions of semantic memory. Unfortunately, not all semantic domains are as well behaved as the kinship terms. Often we have no prior expectations as to how a particular semantic domain must be organized. How then can we determine the nature of the underlying structure?

In an important paper, Shepard (1962) pointed out that we don't need to have an a priori conception about the nature of these internal structures. Rather, careful analysis of the subject's responses can allow us to "reconstruct" the space. Shepard showed that (1) if concepts in memory are stored in a multidimensional metric space and (2) if similarity judgments are made on the basis of Euclidean distance in such a space, then the space can be accurately reconstructed from a set of similarity judgments.

A number of investigators have used Shepard's method to deduce the underlying psychological space relating the various terms. In one experiment, Henley (1969) used this technique to deduce the space relating common animal terms to one another. She accomplished this in the following way. She chose thirty of the most common mammals. She then asked subjects to rate all possible pairs of the thirty mammals as to their dissimilarity on a scale between 1 and 10. A value of 1 indicated that the animals were identical and a value of 10 that they were maximally different. These data were used as input to a multidimensional scaling program, which uses the techniques devised by Shepard and others, to find the psychological space of smallest dimensionality consistent with the observed dissimilarity judgments.

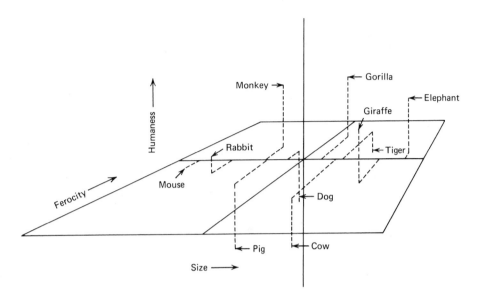

Figure 4.27
Spatial representation of selected animal terms based on data from Henley (1969). (From Rumelhart and Abrahamson, 1973.)

The results indicated that these thirty fitted well into a three-dimensional space. Figure 4.27 shows the three dimensions along with the placements of some of the animals. The three dimensions correspond roughly to size, ferocity, and what we might call humanness.

Although these *spatial representations* clearly capture some aspects of memory structure, it is just as clear that they do not capture all of it. One important kind of relationship that is not well represented by a multidimensional representational scheme is hierarchical information. Thus, although it is relatively clear where to put a new animal term—such as "panther"—it is not so clear where a term like "animal" or "mammal" would fit. We now turn to a more general representational system which allows hierarchical relationships.

Semantic Feature Model. At its most general an organizational system based on semantic features proposes that the *location* of any concept in memory can be specified by its value on any of a set of dimensions of meaning. These dimensions can either be continuous (as with *size*) or they can be discrete (as with *sex*). Thus, the paradigmatic representational systems described above are (special cases) of a general feature system. Not every concept has a value on

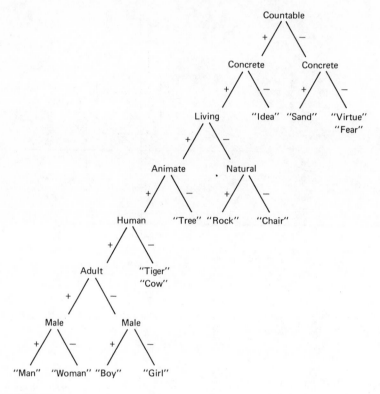

Figure 4.28
Hierarchical binary feature representation illustrating the relationships among some aspects of the meaning of various lexical items.

every dimension. Thus, for example, the distinction between male and female is usually relevant only in the case of animate (or at least living) objects. Consider the set of English words in the following matrix:

	Chair	Cow	Fear	Woman	Rock	Tiger	Tree	Virtue
Concrete	+	+	−	+	+	+	+	−
Living	−	+	−	+	−	+	+	−
Animate	−	+	−	+	−	+	−	−
Human	−	−	−	+	−	−	−	−
Male	−	−	−	−	−	−	−	−

Here each of eight words has been classified as to whether or not it is concrete, living, animate, human, or male. According to a semantic feature model

	Chair	Cow	Fear	Mother	Rock	Tiger	Tree	Virtue
Chair				3		1		
Cow				2		3	1	
Fear								3
Mother		2				2	1	
Rock	3						1	
Tiger		3		2			1	
Tree	1	1		1	1	1		
Virtue			3					

Figure 4.29
Illustration of how the classifications given by three subjects would be tabulated into matrix form for subsequent analysis. (From Miller, 1967.)

the specification of such a set of features determines the *location* of these concepts in lexical memory.

It should be noticed that there is a certain amount of redundancy in the features employed. In particular, if a concept is − CONCRETE, it determines a negative value for all of the other features listed in the matrix. Similarly, a value of − LIVING determines that the features animate, human, or male are irrelevant, etc. This hierarchical relationship among semantic features is often represented by a tree. Figure 4.28 illustrates such a tree. In this example, the highest feature is ± COUNTABLE. Thus, "ideas" and "rocks" can be counted whereas "sand" and "virtue" are *mass* nouns and cannot be counted. Concepts with the feature + COUNTABLE may be either ± LIVING. Concepts with the feature − LIVING can either be + NATURAL such as "rock" or they can be − NATURAL such as chair. The tree given in the figure is, of course, only partial, but the semantic feature hypothesis would propose that it could be expanded until virtually every concept would be specified as either a leaf or node of the tree.

Again, the ideas underlying the *semantic feature analysis* seem plausible, but how can we, as psychologists, get evidence concerning what features underlie lexical memory and how it is structured? Miller (1967, 1969) has shown how a classification procedure can be employed to get some evidence on this issue. In the classification procedure each word under consideration is written on a 3 by 5 card. Then the deck of cards is given to a subject with instructions to sort it into categories—put together those terms with the most similar meanings. Figure 4.29 illustrates the sortings of three hypothetical subjects. Subject S_1 divides the eight words into five categories, and subjects S_2 and S_3 divide them into three categories. A data matrix is the compiled. Each entry in the matrix represents a decision by a subject to put the row and column words into the

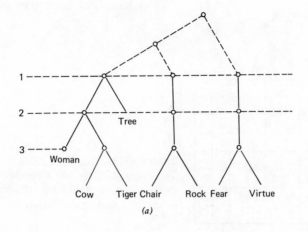

(a)

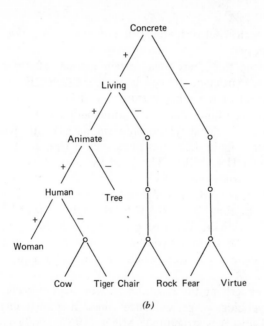

(b)

Figure 4.30
(a) Hierarchical representation of sorting data illustrated in Figure 4.30. The more times a pair of words was sorted together, the further out on the tree they branch. Since the pairs cow-tiger, chair-rock, and fear-virtue were always sorted together, they branch only at the third level of the tree. Since woman was sorted with cow and tiger two out of the three times, it branches at level two. Since tree was once sorted with the cow-tiger-woman cluster, it branches at level 1. The dotted lines at the top of the figure are hypothetical nodes relating the various clusters. (After Miller, 1967.) (b) Possible names for the various branches illustrated in (a).

228

same category. The data matrix can then be analyzed by a procedure developed by Johnson (1967) to produce a tree. The general idea of this analysis is illustrated in Figure 4.30. The more times a pair of words were clustered together the further out on the tree they branch. The pairs "cow-tiger," "chair-rock," and "fear-virtue" were always classified together (three times) so they are not separated until the very bottom of the tree. "Woman" is sorted with "cow" and "tiger" on two occasions so it splits off one level higher, etc. Johnson's hierarchical clustering program is general and will produce the best fitting tree for any data matrix. After the analysis has been run, the experimenter can look at the tree produced and compare it with some proposed system of semantic features. Figure 4.30*b* illustrates possible names for the nodes in Figure 4.30*a*.

Miller (1967, 1969) and Fillenbaum and Rapporport (1971) have applied this technique to a wide range of lexical terms. One example of the kinds of results produced is given in Figure 4.31. In many ways the results are dissappointing. Although we can see some of the features we expect (e.g., ± CONCRETE, ± LIVING, and ± HUMAN) it is less clear what to make of the rest of the structure. Notice, for example, "plant-tree" and "fear-regret" are both pairs located at extremities of the tree. Thus, as far as this tree will tell us the parts of the pairs stand in the same relation to each other. Of course, they do not. A "tree" is a kind of "plant," but "fear" and "regret" are simply both unpleasant emotional states. It would appear that a representational system which indicated the *nature* of the relationship rather than simply the closeness of the relationship would be more appropriate. We thus now turn to an organizational system designed explicitly to represent the nature of the relationships between the various concepts stored in memory.

Network Representation of Semantic Memory. In recent years perhaps the most popular representational system has been the semantic networks (cf. Anderson & Bower, 1973; Rumelhart, Lindsay, & Norman, 1972; Quillian, 1968, 1969). A semantic network consists of a set of *nodes* connected by labeled, directed pointers. The nodes represent concepts in memory, and the pointers between the nodes represent their interrelationships. Figure 4.32 illustrates a small segment of a semantic network proposed by Collins and Quillian (1969). In the figure each word or phrase represents a node and each pointer between the word represents the relationship between the nodes. Thus, for example, the relationship between "bird" and "animal" is ISA which is interpreted to mean that a bird *is a* kind of animal. One important characteristic of networks such as these is the major role the ISA relation plays. Information can be hierarchically stored. At each level we need only store the information specific to that level. Thus, the fact that an *ostrich has wings* need not be

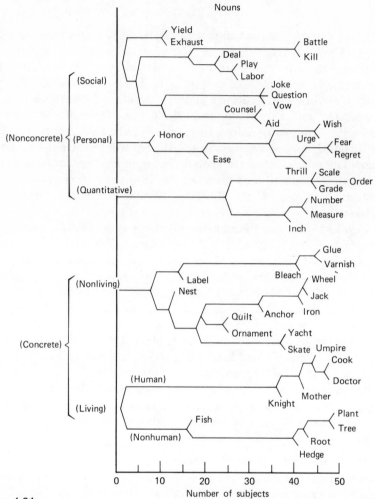

Figure 4.31
Results of the cluster analysis of 48 nouns with suggested names for the clusters indicated in parentheses. (From Miller, 1967.)

stored directly with ostrich, but can be inferred from the knowledge that an *ostrich is a bird* and a *bird has wings.* One implication of such an organizational scheme is that different information will be differentially available. Thus, the information that *a canary is yellow* is readily accessible, since that property is stored directly with canary. On the other hand, the fact that *a canary has skin* should be much less accessible, since it has to be inferred from the fact that a

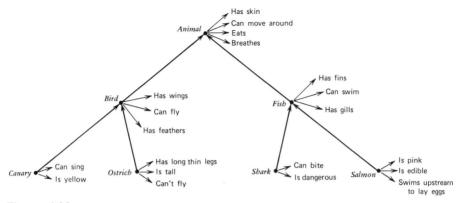

Figure 4.32
Illustration of a hypothetical memory structure for a three-level hierarchy. (From Collins and Quillian, 1969.)

canary is a bird and a *bird is an animal* and an *animal has skin.* Similarly, the fact that *a canary can fly* should be intermediately available because it can be derived solely on the basis of a canary being a bird. Collins and Quillian (1969) attempted to test this implication directly. Thus, they asked subjects questions which required differential amounts of processing to answer. Subjects were given a series of *true-false* questions and required to answer as quickly as possible. Figure 4.33 shows the reaction times required to answer questions as a function of their distance in the proposed hierarchy. The results are clearly consonant with Collins and Quillian's proposal. The more links one has to traverse to answer the question, the slower the response time. These results would seem to provide evidence in favor of the hierarchical structures proposed by Collins and Quillian. However, more recent evidence reveals a somewhat more complex picture. To begin, within this system of representation a concept is either a member of a catgory or it is not. Thus, both "canary" and "ostrich" are members of the category "bird" and it would hardly make sense to say that "canary" is more of a "bird" than "ostrich." Yet people can and do make such judgments with high reliability (cf. Rosch, 1973). Of the fifty-four best known birds, canary is rated as the fifth most "birdlike" whereas *ostrich* is rated fiftieth. Moreover, "bat" which is not a bird at all (it would seem to me) is only rated slightly worse than ostrich. This wouldn't be such a problem for the hierarchical structure if these judgments were somehow dependent on a different part of memory than the verification of simple assertions. This does not seem to be the situation. A recent paper by Smith, Shoben, and Rips (1974) illustrated clearly the relationship between verification processes and these judgments of *typicality.*

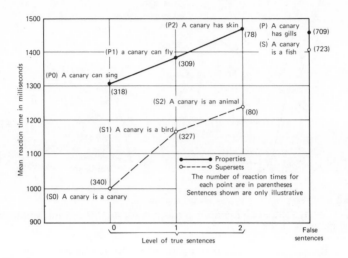

Figure 4.33
Reaction times in a sentence verification task as a function of the level of the queried property from the subject term in the hypothetical hierarchy that is illustrated in Figure 4.33. Reaction times to fault sentences are illustrated in the far right of the figure. (From Collins and Quillian, 1969.)

These researchers asked subjects to verify sentences of the form "A robin is a bird" or "A chicken is a bird." Their results showed that these questions could be answered faster for more typical instances (e.g., "robin") than for less typical instances (e.g., "chicken"). Moreover, they found that sentences such as "An ant is a bird" in which the subject noun is very dissimilar to the object noun are rejected much more quickly than sentences such as "a butterfly is a bird" in which the subject noun shares many features in common with the object noun. It is thus clear that although *logically* category membership is all or none, psychologically things can be more or less members of a conceptual category. It appears that judgment of category membership depends not so much on a fact represented directly in the structure of memory, but on a *process* which somehow determines class membership through a consideration of the similarities of the typical instance of the subject concept to the definition of the category.

The Structure of Episodic Memory
At a very general level we can characterize the process of storing and retrieving the meaning of linguistic messages as follows. As a result of the process of comprehension linguistic inputs are converted into underlying semantic repre-

sentations of the meaning of the incoming linguistic message. These representations are then stored in secondary memory forming the base for our memory of the message in question. Then, at the time of recall, the appropriate semantic representations are somehow accessed and reconstructed into sentences. Note that these sentences are not necessarily the same as those presented. They need only contain the same elements of meaning as the input sentences. Thus the structure of the memory for meaning is exactly the structure of the underlying semantic representation for the input message.

If our memory for linguistic inputs consists primarily of this meaning of the input, we should be able to distinguish sentences that have been presented from those that have not whenever the new input differs significantly in meaning from the old. This, of course, is exactly the result of experiments by Barclay (1973), and by Bransford, Barclay, and Franks (1972) mentioned above. Before we can make more detailed tests of this view we must make more assumptions about the nature of the semantic representation.

A number of workers have suggested that semantic representations consist of configurations of elementary semantic components (cf. Schank, 1973; Norman & Rumelhart, 1975). Although a detailed account of the semantic structures these and other researchers have proposed is beyond the scope of this book, a number of implications of this view can be explored here.

Suppose, for example, that whenever we hear a sentence we break the meaning of each word of the sentence into its component parts and store a configuration of these components. Suppose further that forgetting occurs at the level of these components. That is, following a presentation of a linguistic message, we store only a subset of the total set of semantic components underlying the message. The remainder are forgotten. To make this more concrete, suppose we presented the following sentence:

(5) John drove to the university.

Presumably (5) contains all of the semantic elements in the sentence

(6) John went to the university.

plus some others. Thus, we expect (5) to be recalled as (6) whenever those elements in (5) but not in (6) are forgotten. (Note that in order to recall (6) as (5) we must add components to (6). This rarely happens out of context. But, as we will see below, it can easily happen in context.) Thus, we expect an asymmetry. A more general sentence, like (6), should be recalled in place of a more specific sentence like (5) much more often that (5) is recalled in place of (6).

In an unpublished experiment carried out in our laboratory Stephen Palmer tested this prediction. Palmer presented his subjects with either general sentences like:

(7) The boy noticed the flowers in the park.

or with more specific ones like

(8) The boy noticed the tulips in the park.

Later subjects were given recognition tests with either the same sentence they were previously presented or with the other of the pair. Palmer found that subjects were much more likely to think wrongly they had seen the more general sentence than to think wrongly they had seen the more specific sentence—thus confirming the prediction.

Another implication of the general point of view developed here is that sentences that have many components in common should be more easily confused than those that do not. Gentner (1975) carried out an experiment designed to test this implication. In her experiment subjects were presented with triads of sentences like these:

(9a) Ida received the backpack.
(9b) Ida borrowed the tablecloth.
(9c) Ida ruined the drafting set.

In each triad two of the sentences contained components in common and one of the sentences was rather different from the other two. (In this example (9a) and (9b) both contain semantic elements about Ida's getting something.) Later subjects were given probes of the form:

(10a) Ida received _____.
(10b) Ida borrowed _____.
(10c) Ida ruined _____.

and were asked to fill in the blanks.

The primary prediction is that more confusions should occur between sentences like (9a) and (9b) than between either (9a) and (9c) or (9b) and (9c). The results clearly confirmed the hypothesis. Over 80% of the confusion errors were between *similar* sentences. (In this example this involved confusing "backpack" and "tablecloth.")

Gentner carried out another interesting experiment designed to give further support to the view that our memory for the meaning of strings of sentences consists of a configuration of semantic components. Suppose that the information we get from a set of sentences is not segregated in memory according to the sentence in which the information was input. Rather, a sequence of sentences simply produces a rather large configuration of interrelated semantic components. Thus, the same configuration of semantic elements can be presented in different combinations of sentences. Consider, for example, the following sequences of sentences:

(11a) Once Max needed money so Sam loaned him ten dollars. Several weeks passed and Sam thought he would never recover his money, but finally Max gave Sam the ten dollars.

(11b) Once Max needed money so Sam gave him ten dollars. Several weeks passed and Sam thought he would never recover his loan, but finally Max paid Sam the ten dollars.

In spite of the fact that slightly different words are used, (11a) and (11b) contain very much the same configuration of semantic elements. Thus, we would expect very similar recalls to result from the two presentations. Gentner attempted to test this prediction in the following way. Subjects were presented with one of two stories, each of which ended with the following sentence:

(12) Max finally gave Same the ten dollars.

In one story Max was represented as owing money to Sam. In the other, Sam merely asked Max for the money. Subjects were then asked to recall the story as accurately as possible. Those who were given the version about Max owing Sam money recalled the verb "paid" or "paid back" 47% of the time, and recalled the actually presented verb "gave" only 30% of the time. Subjects presented with the second version of the story never recalled "paid" or "paid back," but recalled "loaned" 45% of the time and the actual verb "gave" only 33% of the time.

Gentner concludes from this experiment that "subjects constructed a componential representation which encompassed not merely the immediate verb presented [gave] but also its context. When they were asked to recall the story, they had to partition their semantic structures into words, which were often different from the partition which they had originally heard." (P. 233.)

It thus appears that there is substantial evidence that the meanings of linguistic inputs can be fruitfully considered to be a configuration of elementary semantic components. However, even if we accept this conclusion we remain far from an adequate theory of the nature of these components. Some work in this area is currently underway (cf. Norman & Rumelhart, 1975), but much remains to be done.

SUMMARY

The information stored in the human secondary memory system can be categorized into two types: information specific to particular events we have experienced or been told about, and generalized information about classes of objects, events, and event sequences in the world. The sum total of information of the first sort constitutes what we have called *episodic memory*. The sum total of information of the second sort constitutes what we have called *semantic memory*. It is useful to consider how each of these types of information depends on the other. First, the generalized concepts of semantic memory are, of course, derived from our experience with specific objects, events, and event sequences through a process of abstraction or generalization. So, in this sense, semantic memory is a simple derivative of episodic memories. On the other hand, the nature of semantic memory determines what is stored in episodic memory in the first place. That is, we comprehend the world in terms of the categories, concepts, and the interrelationships among these evident in semantic memory. It is then our *interpretation* of the event we have observed that remains in episodic memory. In this sense, what appears in episodic memory is determined by the categories and concepts already available in semantic memory. Of course, new concepts can emerge—our old categories are not always sufficient to deal with all of the incoming information. But even then our new categories are usually built out of new configurations of our old ones.

We now turn to a discussion of the processes whereby we reason, think, and solve problems. To reason is to somehow go beyond the particular facts stored in memory, to generate new facts and ideas to deal with new situations and questions. As we shall see, it is the *structure* of secondary memory that often allows us to go beyond our memories and solve novel problems.

5
REASONING

Psychological literature supplies no established technical meaning for the term *reasoning*. We are, therefore, suggesting a meaning for the term which coincides with the perspective developed in the previous sections. We use the term reasoning to denote those processes of information retrieval that rely for success on the *structure,* as opposed to the *content,* of organized memory. Thus, one might answer the question "Who was the father of your country?" in at least two different ways. In one case, the specific information that George Washington was the "father of our country" might be stored and used to answer the question. On the other hand, when specific information is not available one can consult the meanings of the words in question and one's knowledge of history to derive a reasonable answer. The first of these methods might be called remembering, since retrieval depends for the most part on the specific information stored. The second method may be identified with reasoning, since in this case it was the *form* of the relationship among the words that determined the response. The same act of reasoning could have been applied to the question "Who was the father of your state?" or "Who was the mother of your country?" It was not the specific content of the question but the form of the relationships among the words that determined the response.

If one accepts this definition of reasoning, then the task of the theorist becomes clear. To understand the reasoning process, the theorist must (1) specify the form of the memory structure in question and (2) determine the algorithm that is to be applied in the reasoning process in question.

By our definition, then, we have already discussed many reasoning tasks. As a simple example, recall our discussion of similarity judgments. In that case our memory representation was a simple paradigmatic space and our algorithm was to measure the distance between the two concepts. More complex reasoning tasks require more complex memory structures and more complex algorithms. In the following sections we illustrate how even simple memory structures and relatively simple algorithms can nevertheless give remarkable accounts of complex reasoning tasks.

ANALOGICAL REASONING

Despite psychologists' considerable confidence that analogical reasoning plays an important role in intelligent behavior, analogy formation has received little systematic attention. One exception is the work of Rumelhart and Abrahamson (1973). They proposed a theory of analogy formation which predicts subjects' responses to problems of the form: A is to B as C is to which of the following: $X_1, X_2, X_3,$ or X_4 [denoted $A : B : : C : (X_1, X_2, X_3, X_4)$]. Thus, for example, given the problem "apple" is to "tree" as "grape" is to which of the following: "flower," "vine," "stalk," or "orange," we would like a theory which would predict that subjects would choose "vine."

Analogy formation apparently involves two steps. First, it involves the extraction of a relationship between the A and B elements of the analogy and, second, the search for similar relationships between the C element and one of the X_i. The problem for the theorist is to define, in a general way, the set of relationships between two elements. Rumelhart and Abrahamson solve this problem in the following way. They assume that all elements in an analogy are imbedded in an m-dimensional similarity space (of the type discussed in the preceding chapter) in which dissimilarity is represented by the Euclidean distance between the items. Thus, the set of relationships between any two elements is represented by the directed distance between them. A more formal statement of the hypothesis involved makes the implications clearer.

Consider an analogy of the form $A : B : : C : (X_1, X_2, \ldots, X_n)$. We make the following three assumptions:

1. Each of the $n + 3$ words in the problem can be represented as a point in an m-dimensional similarity space. Hence, corresponding to each word, X_i, is a vector $X_i = (x_{i1}, x_{i2}, \ldots x_{im})$ where the x_{ij} represent the coordinate values of element X_i for dimension j.[1]
2. For any three words, A, B, C, there is an ideal analogy, denoted I, such that $A : B : : C : I$, whose coordinates are given by the vector $I = B + C - A$.
3. The probability that any given alternative, X_i, is chosen from among the set $X_1, \ldots, X$ is assumed to be a monotonically decreasing function of its relative distance from the ideal analogy point.

That is, we assume that each word in an analogy can be represented as a point in an m-dimensional similarity space. The ideal analogy is given by that point in the space that lies the same directed distance from C as B lies from A. Finally, the closer a given alternative is to the ideal analogy point, the higher the probability that it will be chosen—over alternatives that are further from the ideal analogy point—as the best analogy.

Predictions from these assumptions can be illustrated with reference to the eight faces shown in Figure 5.1. Each face corresponds to a corner in the three-dimensional similarity space shown in the figure. The coordinates of each face are shown beside the face. Consider, for example, Analogy 1 in the figure $A : E : : D : (B, C, F, G, H)$. For simplicity, assume that the space shown in Figure 5.1 satisfies assumption 1 above. Then, from assumption 2 we find the ideal analogy 1 by first finding the distance and direction from A to E. In this case A is at the lower left and E at the lower right, so the vector connecting them passes from left to right across the face of the cube. Next we must find point D and move from D across the cube from left to right. This takes us to H. From assumption 3 we thus predict that face H will be chosen most often to be the correct analogy.

Analogy 2 is a similar example: $H : B : : G : (A, C, D, E, F)$. First we locate H and find that the directed distance from H to B passes diagonally from right to left and from back to front across the cube. Next we locate G and diagonally across the cube from G. When we do this we find that A is the ideal analogy. Thus, face A is the best solution here. Numerous similar analogies can be found from this set of objects simply by following assumptions 1, 2, and 3. We now turn to a more serious test of these assumptions.

Recall that the first requirement of the hypothesis is a set of elements located in a Euclidean similarity space. Rumelhart and Abrahamson used the set of animal names scaled by Henley (1969) and discussed in the previous chapter

[1]A vector in a multidimensional space can be thought of as an arrow in that space of specified length pointing in a specified direction.

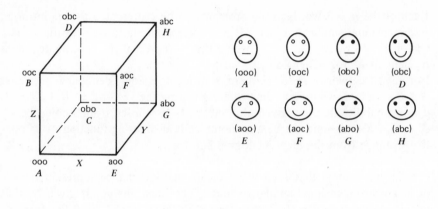

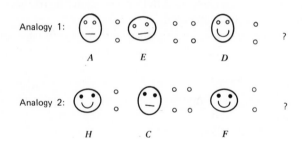

Figure 5.1

(a) Hypothetical space illustrating the similarity relations among faces illustrated in (b). (c) Sample analogies. (See chapter discussion for explanation.)

(see Figure 4.27). These authors chose animal names at random from the set of 30 scaled by Henley and found 30 different analogies. Sets of alternatives were constructed again at random with the constraint that none of the alternative names appeared in the problem and that the alternatives were spaced at four distinct distances from the ideal analogy point. Table 5.1 shows several of the analogies actually constructed. Subjects were asked to rank the alternatives from best to worst. These ranks were then compared with predictions made using assumptions 1–3. Table 5.2 gives the proportion of responses, averaged over subjects and analogy problems, for which any given rank was given to the jth closest response alternative. Thus, the upper left-hand entry of the table implies that 70.9 percent of the Rank 1 responses were given to the response alternative closest to the ideal point. Only 4.3% of the Rank 1 responses were given to the most distant response alternative.

Table 5.1
Example Analogies and Solutions

RAT:PIG::GOAT: _____
A. CHIMPANZEE
B. COW
C. RABBIT
D. SHEEP

RANKS
1. B
2. D
3. C
4. A

CAMEL:DONKEY::RABBIT: _____
A. ANTELOPE
B. BEAVER
C. CAT
D. TIGER

RANKS
1. B
2. C
3. A
4. D

FOX:HORSE::GORILLA: _____
A. ANTELOPE
B. DONKEY
C. ELEPHANT
D. WOLF

RANKS
1. C
2. A
3. B
4. D

LION:WOLF::GOAT: _____
A. CAT
B. CHIMPANZEE
C. GORILLA
D. PIG

RANKS
1. D
2. A
3. B
4. C

Table 5.2
Subjects' Rankings as a Function of Alternative Distance

		Subject Assigned Ranks			
		1	2	3	4
Rank Distance	1	.709	.180	.069	.046
of the	2	.177	.546	.137	.129
Alternative	3	.086	.160	.526	.226
from I	4	.043	.111	.243	.600

These results are in clear support of the theory outlined above. In addition to leading to some insight into the solution of analogies, this theory shows how answers to reasoning problems can frequently be considered the results of the application of simple algorithms, or rules, to a more or less complex memory structure.

At a very general level, the theory outlined above suggests that the solutions of analogies of the sort A : B : : C : ? are found by (1) finding the transformation that converts A into B, (2) applying that transformation to C to produce an ideal analogy, and (3) comparing the ideal to each of the alternatives and choosing the closest. If our memory structure consists merely of a multidimensional space, as illustrated above, the transformations involved are simply vector translations. However, when more complex means are required to represent the memory structure, the transformations are not so straightforward. Consider as an example geometric analogy problems. Two such problems are illustrated in Figure 5.2. In cases such as these, multidimensional representations are not adequate. We will illustrate the application of this general theory to a *relational* memory structure.

The outline to be given here is based on the work of Thomas Evans (1968) who devised a computer program to solve geometrical analogies. Although the examples I will discuss differ in several ways from his original work, his system employed essentially the algorithm outlined below.

Figure 5.3 is a representation of the three terms of the analogy problem illustrated in Figure 5.2a. First we have to designate the five objects contained in these figures. We denote these with D for the dot, R for the rectangle, T for the triangle, C for the conical segment of a circle, and Z for the letter Z. Then each item of the analogy is represented by a list of the objects in that item coupled with the set of relationships that hold among those items. Thus, the first term, A, is represented by its list of elements (D, R, and T) followed by the set of relations holding among the elements. Thus, the dot, D, is above the triangle, T, so we have ABOVE (D, T). Similarly, the rectangle, R is inside

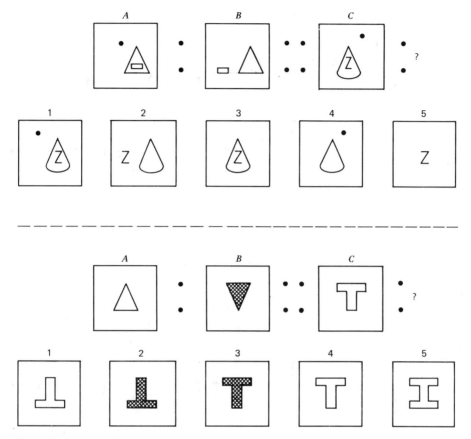

Figure 5.2
Examples of geometric analogy problems.

the triangle, hence INSIDE (R, T). In similar fashion, the internal representation is given for all three terms of the problem.

The next step is to specify the transformation that converts term A into term B. This step can be characterized as finding a *set* of transformations which maps each object in term A onto an object in term B (or, in the case of deletion, onto the null object $\emptyset$) and which maps every relationship between every pair of objects in A onto a relationship between a pair of objects in B (or, in the case that one of the objects has been deleted, onto $\emptyset$). The problem is to find that set of transformations which, in some sense, involves the fewest changes. Figure 5.4 illustrates the minimum transformations required to map

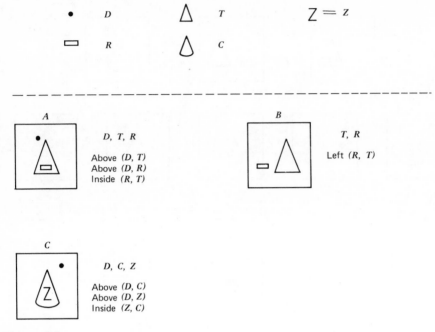

Figure 5.3
Evans' representation of various geometric figures.

A into *B* and to map *A* into *C*. The best fitting transformation from *A* to *B* requires four changes; the best from *A* to *C* requires two. The next problem is to apply one of the transformations (say the one from *A* to *B*) to the third term (*C*) to derive the *ideal analogy* solution for the problem. Thus, we delete the first object (the dot), leave the other two intact (the conical segment and the *Z*), convert the relation INSIDE to the relation LEFT, and we have derived the *ideal solution*. Figure 5.5 illustrates this application. Now, since the ideal solution is among the alternative set, we choose this ideal. Most people agree with this choice.

The example in Figure 5.2*b* illustrates that we can get transformations on the objects themselves as well as on relations between objects. Thus, whenever two objects are related by a known transformation, it is represented not as a change in the relations of objects of the scene, but as a change in the properties of the objects. (In Evans's program such transformations as size changes, rotations, and reflections about the vertical or horizontal axis were recognized.) Then, in the transformation rules, properties of objects are treated analogously

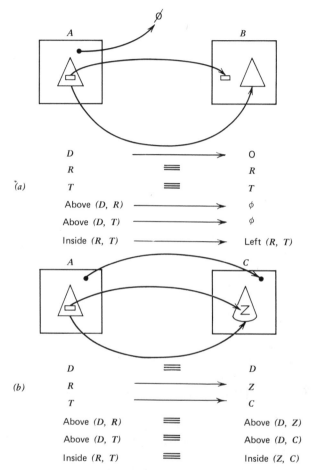

Figure 5.4
Examples of Evans' program transforming one figure into another. (See chapter discussion for explanation.)

to relations between objects. Figure 5.6 illustrates the representations associated with the individual terms of the analogy along with the transformations required to construct the ideal analogy term. In this example there are only two basic objects, a triangle, *TRI*, and a block, *T*. In addition, there are two properties that the objects may have. They may be a SHADEd or ROTATEd version of the basic forms. Again our procedure produces the proper ideal analogy point.

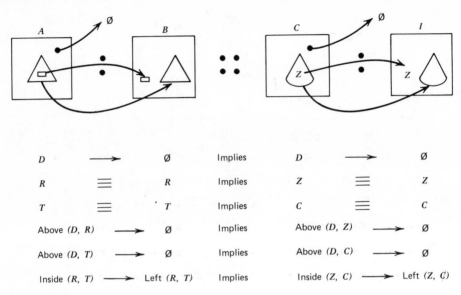

D	$\longrightarrow$	Ø	Implies	D	$\longrightarrow$	Ø
R	$\equiv$	R	Implies	Z	$\equiv$	Z
T	$\equiv$	' T	Implies	C	$\equiv$	C
Above *(D, R)*	$\longrightarrow$	Ø	Implies	Above *(D, Z)*	$\longrightarrow$	Ø
Above *(D, T)*	$\longrightarrow$	Ø	Implies	Above *(D, C)*	$\longrightarrow$	Ø
Inside *(R, T)*	$\longrightarrow$ Left *(R, T)*		Implies	Inside *(Z, C)*	$\longrightarrow$ Left *(Z, C)*	

Figure 5.5
(See chapter discussion for explanation.)

Although this procedure appears to work reasonably well, there are two points that should be mentioned. First, there is not always a unique "best" transformation between the various terms of the analogy. In this example several ideal analogy points may exist. Secondly, our original description can make a difference in the final result we arrive at. Thus, in our last example, we could have described the relationship between the triangle in *A* and the one in *B* as being REFLECTed about the horizontal axis rather than ROTATEd 180°. In our example it didn't matter since the block *T* was symmetric about the vertical axis. But had term *B* contained a block *R* rather than a *T* we would have gotten a different answer. Thus, in general we have to construct an ideal analogy point for every description of each term.

To date, no formal experiments have been done comparing Evans' program with data taken from human subjects. Evans did, however give a rough idea of how his program would perform on geometric analogy problems actually included on "intelligence tests." Evans reports that his program will score correctly on between 15 and 20 out of the 30 problems on one of these tests. This compares to an average of about 17 out of 30 for ninth graders, 18 out of 30 for tenth graders, 19 out of 30 for eleventh graders, and 20 out of 30 for twelfth graders. It is thus clear that the level of competence using

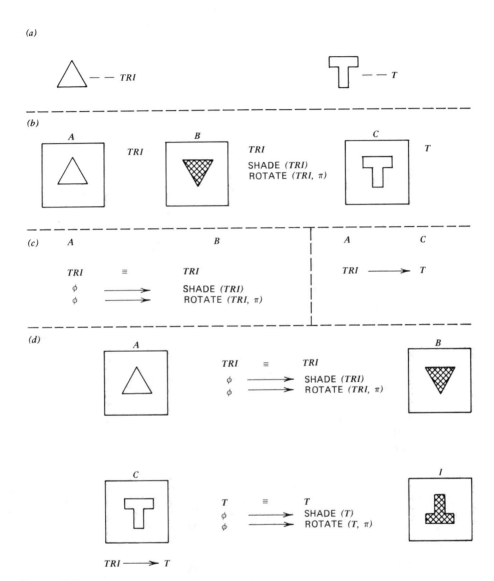

Figure 5.6
(See chapter discussion for explanation.)

Evans's system is clearly on a par with that for high school students taking the same tests.

We have thus illustrated how one fairly general notion of what analogical reasoning is could be applied to two different kinds of memory structures to lead to models which compare very favorably with the way people perform on similar problems. It might be argued that the account given here works very well for the contrived set of problems given in testing situations, but that it has very little to do with the way people actually use analogical relationships in ordinary thinking. Allan Collins has studied how people reason in relatively unconstrained conversational situations. We now turn to a discussion of his work on *functional reasoning*.

FUNCTIONAL REASONING

Collins and his associates (cf. Collins, Warnock, Aiello & Miller, 1975) have been studying the processes people use to answer questions when they don't know the answers. Their standard technique involve a tutorial situation in which the tutor asks a series of questions on some topic (usually geography) and the student must devise and rationalize answers. The students ordinarily have some knowledge about the subject matter and must use the specific information they have, along with whatever general knowledge they might deem applicable to generate an answer. One process that they frequently observe in their tutorial sessions is what they call *functional reasoning*. Roughly speaking, functional reasoning involves taking a fact, determining plausible reasons why that fact is true (i.e., the functional determinants of the fact), generalizing the reasons into a rule, and applying the rule in a new situation. Table 5.3 gives a number of examples collected by Collins et al. from their tutorial sessions.

The first example illustrates the basic features of functional reasoning very clearly. The student uses one fact he knows (i.e., that there are 3 or 4 piano tuners in New Haven), hypothesizes a functional determiner of the fact (i.e., population), forms a general rule (i.e., cities have about 1 piano tuner per 100,000 people), and applies the rule to the new situation (New York should have about 70 piano tuners), and then modifies the result to account for other variables (e.g., number of piano tuners may not be linearly related to population, or New Haven may have an especially large number of pianos) to determine the final answer.

It should be noted that this process is much like the analogical reasoning theory described above. The subject essentially set up for himself the following analogy:

New Haven: 3 piano tunners:: New York: ? piano tuners.

Table 5.3
Tutor-Student Dialogue Excerpts Illustrating Functional Reasoning

1.	(T)	How many piano tuners do you think there are in New York City?
	(S)	Well there are 3 or 4 in New Haven, which has about 300,000 people. That's about 1 per 100,000. New York has 7-million people, so that would make 70. I'll say 50 or 60.
2.	(T)	Where in North America do you think rice might be grown?
	(S)	Louisiana.
	(T)	Why there?
	(S)	Places where there is a lot of water. I think rice requires the ability to selectively flood fields. . . .
	(T)	O.K. Do you think there's a lot of rice in say, Washington and Oregon?
	(S)	Aha, I don't think so.
	(T)	Why?
	(S)	There's a lot of water up there too, but there's two reasons. First the climate isn't conducive, and second I don't think the land is flat enough. You've got to have flat land so you can flood a lot of it, unless you terrace it.
3.	(T)	What kind of grains do you think they grow in Africa, and where, then? (Pause.) Well where would they grow rice if they grew it anywhere?
	(S)	If they grew it anywhere, I suppose they'd grow it in the Nile region, and they'd grow it in the tropics where there was an adequate terrain for it.

He determined that population was the relevant dimension and derived his answer.

The second example illustrates a similar reasoning process. This student has presumably extracted a general relationship between climatic conditions and the growing of rice. He apparently believes that it has to be warm, there has to be plenty of water, and the land has to be flat. When asked to name specific places where rice might grow, he simply asks himself where these conditions hold, and answers the questions on that basis. If asked whether or not rice will grow in a certain place, he simply asks whether or not it seems to meet these general conditions. This example differs from the previous one in that the relationship between rice growing and climatic conditions had already been (at least somewhat) worked out. In the first example we were able to see the subject perform the abstraction. Nevertheless, the fundamental reasoning process seems to be the same.

Collins et al. have given many other examples of such functional reasoning processes. Although it is very difficult to propose and test adequate theories in such unstructured situations, Collins and his colleagues have been trying to describe this process. They have observed in their tutorial sessions enough to implement similar processes within a computer simulation model. Memory, in their model, is structured in a semantic network of the sort suggested by Quillian (1968) and discussed above. The specific processes they have implemented are too complex to go into here, but they are beginning to have some success in specifying these functional reasoning processes within the context of a semantic network.

Perhaps the area of reasoning that has undergone the most systematic study over the longest period of time is that of problem solving. In this area a subject is given a problem (a starting state) and a set of criteria to specify when a solution (goal state) has been reached. The primary variable of interest is the process whereby one moves from the starting state to the goal state. We now turn to a discussion of some of the work in this area.

SOLVING PROBLEMS

Problem solving can be considered a highly complex form of reasoning which requires the generation and assimilation of new memory structures in order to answer a query. Since the pioneering work of Newell, Shaw, and Simon (1958) with the *general problem solver* (GPS, a computer program designed to prove theorems and solve other logical and mathematical problems), problem solving has been of interest to information processing theorists. The approach of the information processing theorist to problem solving has been to attempt to chart the sequence of events from the statement of the problem to its final solution; that is, to attempt to understand the *process* involved in deriving the solution. Perhaps the most extensive recent effort to chart problem solving behavior is illustrated in the book by Newell and Simon (1972). In this book they give in-depth analysis of problem solving in three different contexts: in deriving solutions for crypt-arithmetic problems, solving theorems in logic, and playing chess. In order to give the flavor of the kind of analysis they carried out we will consider one of their examples, crypt-arithmetic.

In their study Newell and Simon gave subjects a crypt-arithmetic problem to solve and observed their behavior during solution. That is, they gave subjects the problem:

$$
\begin{array}{r}
\mathrm{DONALD} \\
+\ \mathrm{GERALD} \\
\hline
\mathrm{ROBERT}
\end{array}
$$

where $<D = 5>$

in which each letter of the problem stands for a digit. No digit has more than one letter assigned to it, and no letter is assigned to more than one digit. The task of the subject is to find the unique assignment of digits to letters that solves this addition problem. Newell and Simon observed subjects' behavior by asking them to write down any tentative solutions they reached and to "think out loud" as they solved the problem. Their speech was recorded and later analyzed.

In their analysis of problem solving, Newell and Simon introduce the notion of the *problem space*. The problem space consists of a set of possible *states of knowledge* about the problem and a set of *operators* which apply to these states to produce new states of knowledge. A problem is posed by giving an *initial state* of knowledge and asking the subject to find a path to a *final state* of knowledge which includes the answer to the problem. Thus, the problem solving process is characterized by the sequence of states of knowledge through which a subject passes on his way from the initial to the final state and by the set of operators which moved him from one state to another.

Newell and Simon developed the *problem behavior graph* on which they attempted to represent a subject's sequence of states of knowledge (as indicated by his verbalizations) during a problem solving session.

Figure 5.7 is a portion of a problem behavior graph representing the sequence of states of knowledge for one subject during his initial attempts to solve the crypt-arithmetic problem posed above. In this figure each box represents a state of knowledge. The functions written on the horizontal lines represent the operators which were applied to get from one state of knowledge to another. Table 5.4 defines the operators used in the figure.

The initial state of knowledge in the problem behavior graph is indicated by the box in the upper left-hand corner of the figure; in addition to the general rules of solution, it includes the specific information that $D = 5$. The operator, PC(c1) (i.e., process column 1), indicates that the subject added $D + D$ (i.e., $5 + 5$) and concluded that $T = 0$. The subject then set a goal: GET R. That is, he established the subgoal of finding the value of R. Time in the figure goes to the right and then down, so the next state of knowledge is immediately to the right of the former state. Here the operator PC(c2) is applied to deduce that R is odd. The subject then backtracked and applied PC(c2) again, checking his previous conclusion (a recalculation of this sort is indicated by a double line in the figure). Finding again that R is odd, the subject applied the operator GN(R). That is, he generated possible values of R and came up with the values 1, 3, 5, 7, and 9. He then tested those values with the operator TEST and concluded that R must not be 5. He then backtracked again and changed his attention to column 6. He applied operator PC(c6) and concluded

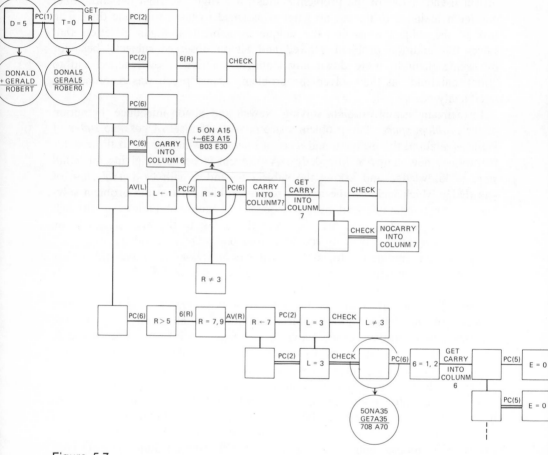

Figure 5.7
An example of part of a problem behavior graph for the solution to the crypt arithmetic problem DONALD plus GERALD equals ROBERT. (Redrawn from Newell and Simon, 1972.) (See chapter discussion for explanation.)

that G was even. He then backtracked again and checked his conclusion. On checking, he discovered that he didn't know the value of the carry into column 6, denoted t6, and therefore his previous conclusion was in doubt. He then returned again to column 2 and temporarily assigned the value 1 to L, that is, he applied the operator AV(L) (assign value to L) and used the value I. He then applied PC(c2) again, concluding R = 3. Returning to column 6 he again

Table 5.4

GN(v)	*Generate v.* The input to GN is a variable with whatever information is known about it. The output is the set of admissible values, *not* taking into account whether or not the values are assigned to other letters.

	Examples	Output
	L (nothing known)	0,1,2, . . .
	R odd	1,3,5,7,9
	R odd, R>5	7,9

AV(v)	*Assign value to v.* The input to AV is a variable with whatever information is known about it. The output is an assignment of a digit to that variable. If the digit to be assigned is determined prior to performing AV, we can write AV(v,d).

	Examples	Output
	AV(L)	L←1
	AV(R)	R←9

TD(l,d)	*Test if d is admissible for l.* The input to TD is a letter with whatever is known about it and a digit. The output is a statement either that the digit is admissible or that it is not. TD takes into account (1) whether d is used for another l, or (2) whether d is outside the known restrictions for the given l.

PC(c)	*Process column c.* The input to PC is all the information in the state about the three letters and two carries associated with a column. The output is an expression, e, about some of the variables (l and t) of the column. The specification of what variable to get information about may or may not be determined prior to performing PC; if so we can write PC(c,v).

Examples:	t_i	$r1 + r2 = r3$			t_{i+1}	Output
c1	0	D=5	D=5	T	?	T=0, t2=1
c2	1	L	L	R	?	R odd
c6	?	D=5	G	R←7	0	G=1,2; t6?

performed PC(c6) and discovered he needed to know the value of the carry into column 7. Since it was not given in the problem proper, he asked the experimenter; the experimenter answered that there was no carry; still not satisfied, the subject asked again and then concluded that $t7=0$. He thus decided that $R \neq 3$. The subject then performed the operation PC(c6) again and concluded that R was greater than 5. Applying GN(R) under these new restrictions led to the conclusion that R=7,9. The subject assigned the value of 7 to R and then performing PC(c2) again, concluded that L=3. Testing this led him to believe that he was wrong and $L \neq 3$. Backtracking, he performed PC(c2) again, concluded that L=3 and found no reason to question his conclusion this time. Then performing PC($c6$), he concluded that $G = 1$ or 2. He then set another goal, to get $t6$ (the carry into column 6). Performing the operation PC($c5$) led to the conclusion that $E = 0$; checking that conclusion led to the same conclusion. The subject continued in this fashion, checking and rechecking various conclusions, until he eventually solved the problem. The section given here is only about one-sixth of the total number of "states of knowledge" that Newell and Simon charted in their analysis of this subject's behavior.

It should be emphasized that the problem behavior graph presented here is simply a translation of the subject's verbal behavior during solution. As such, it is not a theory of problem solving. It should be considered as a transformation of the data (i.e., the subject's verbalizations) which helps make the algorithms and strategies employed by the subject more obvious. Newell and Simon conclude that the successful encoding of their subject's behavior into the problem graph implies:

1. The subject's problem solving proceeds through the states of knowledge given in the figure. That is, evidence exists that S3 [the subject represented in our Figure 5.7] had these various states of knowledge and proceeded on a path through them from the initial state to the solution.
2. The operators PC, GN, AV, and TD account for *all* his transitions to new states of knowledge. (Returns to prior states are governed by other processes.)
3. The operators, along with a set of processes for selecting operators, evaluating states of knowledge for termination, and selecting prior nodes to which to return, constitute a sufficient set of processes for explaining the subject's behavior. [PP. 185–186.]

The point of this presentation has been simply to illustrate one possible means by which problem solving behavior might be understood. In a later part of their book Newell and Simon attempt to generate a set of rules which would underlie the choice of operators at any given point in time. We will not discuss those rules here. Instead we will turn to a discussion of a simpler theory, but one which gives a good insight into many of the processes central to problem solving behavior.

THE GENERAL PROBLEM SOLVER

Problem solving is certainly one of the most complex activities the human being engages in. It calls, in one way or another, on all of the information processing facilities we have mentioned in the previous chapters of the book. It would therefore be very surprising to find a complete and widely accepted theory of problem solving. Nevertheless, Allen Newell and Herb Simon and their colleagues (cf. Newell, Shaw & Simon, 1958, 1962; Newell & Simon, 1963, 1972; and Ernst & Newell, 1969) have made a major contribution to our understanding of "higher mental processes." The most important of their theoretical ideas have been embodied in the *general problem solver*. We will proceed by first giving a general description of GPS, illustrating its use in certain problem solving domains, and then showing how the basic ideas of GPS can be applied to the analysis of human problem solving behavior. The basic problem solving strategy built into GPS is what is called *means-ends analysis*. Newell and Simon (1972) illustrate the intuitive reasoning underlying the means-ends analysis as follows:

> I want to take my son to nursery school. What's the difference between what I have and what I want? One of distance. What changes distance? My automobile. My automobile won't work. What is needed to make it work? A new battery. What has new batteries? An auto repair shop. I want the repair shop to put in a new battery; but the shop doesn't know I need one. What is the difficulty? One of communication. What allows communication? A telephone . . . and so on. [P. 416.]

Thus means-ends analysis involves setting a high level goal (e.g., son at nursery school), looking for an important difference between the current state of the world and the goal state (e.g., distance), looking for a method that could reduce or eliminate the difference (e.g., use of the automobile), setting as a subgoal the application of that method, and then recursively applying means-ends analysis to the attainment of this subgoal.

GPS contains three different goal types.

1. *Transform Current State Goal Type.* Find a way to transform the current state of the world into a goal state.
2. *Reduce Difference Goal Type.* Reduce the difference between the current state of the world and some goal state by modifying the current state.
3. *Apply Operator Goal Type.* Apply an operator to the current state of the world to produce a new state.

The methods used by GPS to achieve each of these three goal types is illustrated in Figure 5.8. The *transform method* consists of three steps: (1) Match the current state of the world to the goal state and find a difference. (2) Reduce the difference found by creating a new state of the world. (3) Transform that new state of the world into the goal state.

The *method employed for reducing a difference* also consists of three steps. (1) Search memory for an operator relevant to reducing the difference. (2)

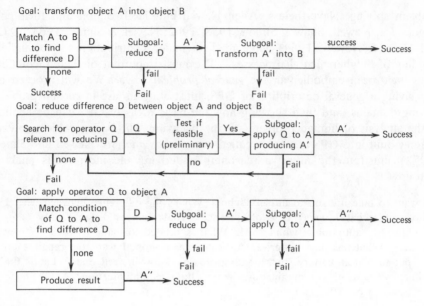

Figure 5.8
Flow diagram illustrating the operation of CPS. (From Newell and Simon, 1972.)

Check to see if the operator is feasible. (3) Apply the operator to the current state of the world producing a new state. If the operator fails to produce a new state then try to find a new operator.

Finally, the *method of application* consists of three parts. (1) Match the conditions for the operator to the current state of the world. (2) If there is a difference try to reduce it, producing a new state of the world. (3) Try to apply the operator to the new state of the world.

In addition to this general methodology which GPS uses to solve any problem, each problem given to GPS must be complete with the following additional information: (1) A starting state of the world. (2) A goal configuration of the world. (3) A set of allowable operators along with their preconditions and results. An example will serve to clarify the operation of GPS and the specification of problems within GPS.

The Hobbits and the Orcs Problem

Three Hobbits and three Orcs are traveling together when they come to a river. They must get across the river. At the river's edge they find a boat.

Unfortunately, the boat will only hold two creatures at once. The problem arises because of the nature of the Orcs. Orcs are peaceable enough as long as they do not outnumber the Hobbits they accompany. If at any time, however, the Orcs outnumber the Hobbits they are with, they will gang up and devour the Hobbits. The problem, then, is to find a method of transporting all six creatures across the river without the Hobbits ever being outnumbered.

This problem (also known as the missionaries and cannibals problem) has been studied extensively in the laboratory (cf. Greeno, 1974; Thomas, 1974) and has been solved by several versions of GPS (cf. Ernst & Newell, 1969; Newell & Simon, 1963). It will thus make a good example with which to illustrate GPS's operation. Due to the number of steps in the problem as outlined above, we will begin with a slightly simpler version—namely, one in which there are only two Hobbits and two Orcs.

The specification of a problem for GPS requires a statement of (1) The general form of states of the world in the problem, (2) the initial state of the world, (3) the goal state, and (4) the operators, along with their preconditions, that are allowed in converting one state of the world into another. Below we specify each of these for our simplified version of the problem.

General Form of States of the World. A complete description of the state of the world consists of the specification of: (1) the number of Hobbits on each bank of the river, (2) the number of Orcs on each bank of the river, and (3) the side of the river that has the boat.

Initial State of the World. At the start we have: two Hobbits on the left bank of the river, two Orcs on the left bank of the river, and the boat on the left side of the river.

Desired Goal State of the World. The goal state consists of the state of the world in which we have: two Hobbits on the right bank of the river, two Orcs on the right bank of the river, and the boat on the right side of the river.

Operators. There is but a single operator called *MOVE*. It has the form *MOVE* x Hobbits and y Orcs to the Z bank of the river. It succeeds if (1) $1 \leq x + y \leq 2$ and if (2) at both banks, either the number of Hobbits is zero or the number of Hobbits is no less than the number of Orcs.

Condition. Things can only be moved from bank Z when the boat is at bank Z.

Figure 5.9 shows the operation of GPS on this problem. The box labeled S_0 illustrates the initial state with the Hobbits (labeled H) and the Orcs (labeled O) on the left bank of the river (the left side of the box) and the boat (B) on the left side of the river. The box labeled S_f illustrates the desired goal state with all on the right side. We begin by setting up a *transform goal*—we

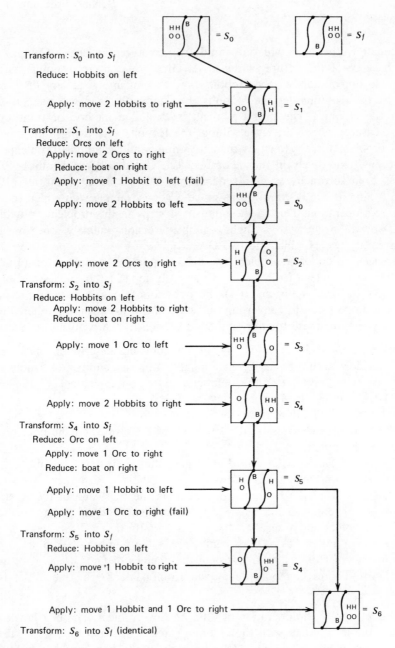

Figure 5.9
Sequence of subgoals involved in the solution of the Hobbits and Orcs' problem.
(See chapter discussion for explanation.)

258

want to try to *transform* the initial state S_0 into the final state S_f. According
to the *transform* method (Figure 5.8) GPS first tries to find a difference between S_0 and S_f and then tries to *reduce* the difference. It compares the two
states and decides that there are too many Hobbits on the left bank. It then
tries to reduce this difference. It determined that moving two Hobbits to the
right would help reduce the difference. It thus *applies* the *MOVE* operator and
produces the new state S_1. It has now succeeded in reducing the difference, so
it attempts the final step of the *transform* method which is to recursively invoke
the transform method on the newly produced state, S_1. This time GPS notices
that there are too many Orcs on the left side of the river. It thus decides to
try to move two Orcs to the right side of the river. However, when GPS tries
to invoke the MOVE operator it discovers that the boat is on the right, and
it cannot move the Orcs until it can get the boat on the left side. Now, since
the boat must have at least one creature in it GPS decides to try to have the
minimum number, namely one, Hobbit bring the boat back. However, it notices
that that would result in one Hobbit and two Orcs on the left bank of the
river, so that attempt fails. GPS then looks for another method to get the boat
back across the river. This time it decides to bring both Hobbits back (returning to the initial state). At this point the boat is back on the left bank and
GPS can carry out its goal of *moving* the two Orcs to the right bank, thus
producing S_2. The system has now succeeded in reducing the number of Orcs
on the left and has produced a new state. It thus proceeds to try to *transform*
S_2 into S_f. GPS continues in this fashion until it reaches state S_5 (a Hobbit
and Orc on each side, the boat on the left side). Here it makes a false start
and returns to state S_4. Realizing that it has already produced this state, GPS
backs up to state S_5 again and finally produces the *goal state, S_f.* It took GPS
27 steps to solve this problem and it only really backed up once. When
GPS solved the version with three Hobbits and three Orcs it took just twice
as many, 54 steps (Ernst & Newell, 1969).

In addition to the Hobbits and Orcs problem GPS has solved the Tower of
Hanoi, the Bridges of Königsberg, the waterjug task, numerous proofs in sym-
bolic logic, and many other problems, proofs, and puzzles. Although GPS is
one of the few well developed theories of problem solving, its solution of the
Hobbits and Orcs problem does not coincide, in close detail, with the way
people solve this problem. Greeno has pointed out that the kind of error illustrated in the move from S_5 to S_6 in Figure 5.9 almost never occurs with human
subjects. Humans never fail to notice that they should bring *both* the Hobbit
and the Orc back—even though their *goal* in bringing the Hobbit back (like
GPS's) is just to get in position to bring the last Orc over. Greeno and Thomas
(1974) both suggest that humans use operators larger than a single *move*.

For example, a human problem solver would probably conceptualize our problem as (1) get an Orc on the right bank and the boat on the left $(S_2 \wedge S_3)$, (2) get the Hobbits across (S_4), and (3) go get the last Orc $(S_5 \wedge S_6)$. Although humans may well use a GPS-like *means-ends* analysis, the level of analysis used by the human appears to be of a coarser grain than that of GPS.

GPS, however, does appear to provide nice accounts of certain other kinds of problem solving tasks. For example, Newell and Simon (1972) have demonstrated that GPS's methods and level of analysis correspond very closely to that used by people carrying out simple proofs in logic. Moreover, it should be clear from our discussion of the previvous section that people employ a GPS-like means-ends analysis in their solution of crypt-arithmetic problems. GPS, just like human subjects, passes through a sequence of states of knowledge; GPS sets up goals, tries, fails, returns to earlier states, and proceeds again. Thus, even though GPS is not a model of the detailed processing people carry out in such tasks, the basic GPS framework is very powerful and gives us perhaps our best view of how a person can organize and process complex problems from start to finish.

There are in human problem solving, however, a number of aspects that are not present in GPS. One of these is the development of new specific strategies and expectations to deal more effectively with problems of the same type. We now turn to a discussion of these *context effects*.

THE ROLE OF EXPECTATIONS ON PROBLEM SOLVING

Consider the matrix of nine dots illustrated in Figure 5.10a; starting wherever you wish, draw four *straight* lines that will pass through every point while not lifting your pencil from the paper.

You are given nine match sticks organized into three rows and three columns of three match sticks each (as illustrated in Figure 5.10b). In addition, you are given three additional matchsticks to work with. Your task is to place the three additional match sticks so that there are four match sticks in each row and each column.

Take six of the original match sticks in Figure 5.10b. Now rearrange the *six* so they form four equilateral triangles.

Consider the picture illustrated in Figure 5.11; it contains a candle and several other household objects (matches and box full of tacks). Your task is to think of a way of getting the candle on the wall so that it would burn properly using only the objects illustrated in the figure. Note: if your solution seems as if it might not work, it is probably wrong, so try again.

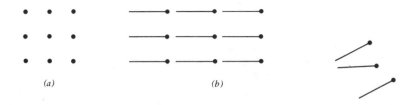

(a)   (b)

Figure 5.10

(a) The nine-dot problem. The problem is to draw four straight lines through the nine dots that passes through every point while not lifting your pencil from the paper. (b) The problem here is to place the three additional matchsticks shown on the right-hand side of the figure so that there are four matchsticks in each row and in each column. (c) This problem can be carried out using six of the matchsticks illustrated in (b). In this case the problem is to rearrange the six so that they form four equilateral triangles.

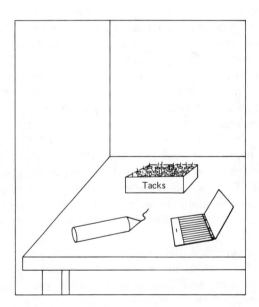

Figure 5.11

The candle problem. The figure contains a candle, matches, and a box full of tacks. Your task is to think of a way of getting the candle on the wall so that it would burn properly, using only the objects illustrated in the figure.

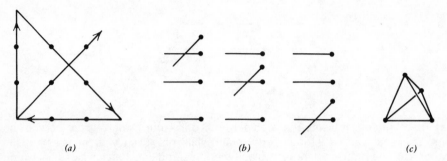

Figure 5.12
(a) Solution to the nine dot problem. *(b)* Solution to the first matchstick problem.
(c) Solution to the second matchstick problem.

All of these problems have something in common. They are all very easy problems that are made difficult by one thing only—our prior expectations about the allowable solutions to these problems. The solution to the first problem, the nine dot problem, is illustrated in Figure 5.12*a*. Here the problem comes from the fact that the configuration forms a natural square and we tend to impose the constraint that our lines may not go outside the square. The solution to the second problem is illustrated in Figure 5.12*b*. Here again, we tend to expect that the matches shouldn't cross, but rather should lie in a line with the matches already there. The third problem causes difficulty because we fail to consider the third dimension (see Figure 5.12*c*) and we tend to look only at two dimensions.

The solution to the fourth problem is illustrated in Figure 5.13. This is presumably difficult because of what Duncker (1945) has called *functional fixity* —the tendency to see things in terms of their *current function* rather than their *potential function*. Thus, we tend to see the box as a container for the tacks rather than as a possible platform for the candle. When given an initial picture like that of Figure 5.14 subjects find the illustrated solution over twice as often (cf. Adamson, 1952).

We shouldn't be surprised that problem solving, like perceiving, understanding sentences, and remembering, is strongly influenced by our expectations. Building up expectations and then making efficient use of these seems to be a primary mechanism of the human information processing system. However, as we have illustrated in these other domains, strong expectations can occasionally get an experienced problem solver into trouble where a novice would solve the problem with ease. Perhaps the most famous example of this arises in Luchins' waterjug problems (Luchins, 1942).

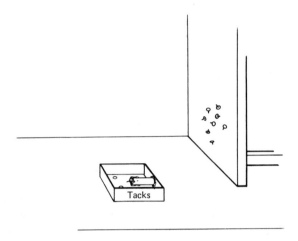

Figure 5.13
Solution to the candle problem.

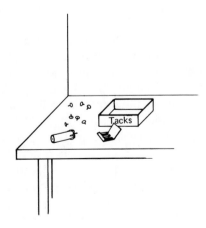

Figure 5.14
An alternative presentation of the candle problem that leads to an easier solution.

Table 5.5

Problem	Capacity of Each Jar, in Quarts			Number of Quarts of Water to be Obtained
1	29	3	—	20
2	21	127	3	100
3	14	163	25	99
4	18	43	10	5
5	9	42	6	21
6	20	59	4	31
7	23	49	3	20
8	15	39	3	18

Consider the following problem: You are given a waterjug which holds 29 quarts and another which holds 3 quarts, how can you get exactly 20 quarts in the 29-quart container? Assume that there is a sink available so that either jug can be filled and any excess water not wanted can be poured down the sink.

A typical solution to this problem involves first filling the 29-quart jug, then filling the 3-quart jug by pouring water from the 29-quart jug. The 3-quart jug is emptied down the sink. It is filled again from the larger jug (leaving 23 quarts of water in the 29-quart jug). The 3-quart jug is emptied again. Finally, the 3-quart jug is once more filled from the larger jug, leaving the desired 20 quarts in the 29-quart jug.

Luchins gave his subjects a series of problems of this sort, most of them involving three jugs. Eight of the problems are given in Table 5.5. Subjects were given these problems one at a time and had to come up with a solution for each. All of the problems can be solved by first filling the largest container, filling the next largest container from the first, and then filling the smaller container twice. However, problems 7 and 8 can also be solved by more direct methods. Problem 7 can be solved by first filling the middle container and then pouring 3 quarts into the smallest container. Problem 8 has a similarly direct solution. In Luchins's experiment some of the subjects were given the problems in the order 1 through 8, as shown in Table 5.5. The remainder went directly from problem 1 to problems 7 and 8. The results showed that whereas all subjects going directly from problem 1 to 7 and 8 solved the problems by the direct method, only 22% of those who solved problems 2 through 6 solved problems 7 and 8 directly.

This is just a very blatant example of what is very common in human thought processes. The human being is constantly adapting to its environment, constantly building up expectancies to help it deal with the world as it has been experienced. However, to just the degree that our expectations help us deal with the constancies of the world, so too do they leave us at a disadvantage when the world changes.

SUMMARY

The processes whereby people reason are many and varied. This chapter should be considered just a small sample of the enormous number of strategies available to people. It should be noted here that these strategies, by and large, are knowledge, stored in memory, searched for, activated, evaluated, and modified. The process of reasoning can be considered a continuation at a slower pace of the same processes that have already become automated in language comprehension, which in turn are extensions of our perceptual processing apparatus. We have touched on a few of the most important of these strategies. Analogical and functional reasoning are perhaps the most basic reasoning processes we use. Whenever we enter a "new" situation we can consider it "just a slight extension of an old situation" and thus draw from our knowledge store just those strategies that were useful in the old situation. Then, we become very sensitive to local context; our strategies are modified and honed until we find one that works very well in our particular situation. Then, when again we enter a new situation we draw upon our analogical reasoning ability once more and attempt the new problem. Finally, means-ends analysis is one of the most pervasive strategies we find in human problem solving. People are goal directed —behavior is seldom (if ever) random. Their behavior is well understood by asking "what are they trying to do?" The information processing theorist asks not only "what" but "how."

REFERENCES

Adamson, R. E. Functional fixedness as related to problem solving: A repetition of three experiments. *Journal of Experimental Psychology,* 1952, *44,* 288–291.

Anderson, C. M. B., & Craik, F. I. M. The effect of a concurrent task on recall from primary memory. *Journal of Verbal Learning and Verbal Behavior,* 1974, *13,* 107–113.

Anderson, J. R., & Bower, G. H. *Human associative memory.* Washington, D.C.: Winston, 1973.

Anderson, R C., & Ortony, A. On putting apples into bottles—A problem of Polysemy. *Cognitive Psycholoy,* 1975, *7,* 167–180.

Atkinson, R. C., & Shiffrin, R. M. Human memory: A proposed system and its control processes. In K. W. Spence & J. T. Spence (Eds.), *The psychology of learning and motivation* (Vol. 2). New York: Academic Press, 1968.

Averbach, E., & Coriell, A. S. Short-term memory in vision. *Bell System Technical Journal,* 1961, *40,* 309–328.

Baddeley, A. D. Short-term memory for word sequences as a function of acoustic, semantic, and formal similarity. *Quarterly Journal of Experimental Psychology,* 1966a, *18,* 362–365.

Baddeley, A. D. The influence of acoustic and semantic similarity on long-term memory for word sequences. *Quarterly Journal of Experimental Psychology,* 1966b, *18,* 302–309.

Barclay, J. R. The role of comprehension in remembering sentences. *Cognitive Psychology,* 1973, *4,* 229–254.

Barclay, J. R., Bransford, J. D., Franks, J. J., McCarrell, N. S., & Nitsch, K. Comprehension and semantic flexibility, *Journal of Verbal Learning and Verbal Behavior,* 1974, *13,* 471–481.

Barlow, H. B., Levick, W. R. & Yoon, M. Responses to single quanta of light in retinal ganglion cells in the cat. *Vision Research,* 1971 Supplement No. 3, 87–101.

Beller, H., K. Parallel and serial stages in matching. *Journal of Experimental Psychology,* 1970, *84,* 213–219.

Bever, T. G. The cognitive basis for linguistic structures. In J. R. Hayes (Ed.), *Cognition and the development of language.* New York: Wiley, 1970.

266

Biederman, I. Perceiving real-world scenes. *Science,* 1972, *177,* 77–80.

Bobrow, D., & Fraser, B. An augmented state transition network analysis procedure. In D. Walker & L. Norton (Eds.), *Proceedings of the International Joint Conference on Artificial Intelligence.* Washington, D.C., 1969.

Bobrow, D. G., & Norman, D. A. Some principles of memory schemata. In D. G. Bobrow & A. M. Collins (Eds.), *Representation and Understanding: Studies in Cognitive Science* New York: Academic Press, 1975.

Bobrow, S. A., & Bower, G. H. Comprehension and recall of sentences. *Journal of Experimental Psychology,* 1969, *80,* 455–461.

Boies, S. J. Memory codes in a speeded classification task. Unpublished Doctoral Dissertation. University of Oregon, 1971.

Boring, E. G. A new ambiguous figure. *American Journal of Psychology,* 1930, *42,* 444–445.

Bower, G. H. Organizational factors in memory. *Cognitive Psychology,* 1970, *1,* 18–46.

Bower, G. H., & Clark, M. C. Narrative stories as mediators for serial learning. *Psychonomic Science,* 1969, *14,* 181–182.

Bower, G. H., Clark, M. C., Lesgold, A. M., & Winzenz, D. Hierarchical retrieval schemes in recall of categorized word lists. *Journal of Verbal Learning and Verbal Behavior,* 1969, *8,* 323–343.

Boynton, R. M. Color vision. In J. W. Kling & L. Riggs (Eds.) *Eperimental Psychology,* New York: Holt, Rinehart & Winston, 1971.

Bransford, J. D., Barclay, J. R., & Franks, J. J. Sentence memory: A constructive versus interpretive approach. *Cognitive Psychology,* 1972, *3,* 193–209.

Bransford, J. D., & Franks, J. J. The abstraction of linguistic ideas. *Cognitive Psychology,* 1971, *2,* 331–350.

Bransford, J. D., & Johnson, M. K. Considerations of some problems of comprehension. In W. G. Chase (Ed.), *Visual information processing,* New York: Academic Press, 1973.

Broadbent, D. E. *Perception and communication.* Pergamon Press: New York, 1958.

Broadbent, D. E. Word-frequency effect and response bias. *Psychological Review,* 1967, *74,* 1–15.

Brooks, L. R. Spatial and verbal components of the fact of recall. *Canadian Journal of Psychology,* 1968, *22,* 349–368.

Brown, R., & McNeill, D. The "tip of the tongue" phenomenon. *Journal of Verbal Learning and Verbal Behavior,* 1966, *5,* 325–337.

Brugge, J. F., Anderson, D. J., Hind, J. E., & Rose, J. E. Time structure of discharges in single auditory nerve fibers of the squirrel monkey in response to complex periodic sounds. *Journal of Neurophysiology,* 1969, *32,* 386–401.

Bruner, J. S., & Potter, M. Inference in visual recognition, *Science,* 1964, *144,* 424–425.

Cavanaugh, J. P. Relation between the immediate memory span and the memory search rate. *Psychological Review,* 1972, *79,* 525–530.

Chafe, W. L. Discourse structure and human knowledge. In R.O. Freedle & J. B. Carroll (Eds.), *Language comprehension and the acquisition of knowledge,* Washington, D.C.: Winston, 1972.

Chase, W. G. & Clark, H. A. Mental operations in the comparison of sentences and pictures. In L. W. Gregg (Ed.) *Cognition in Learning and Memory.* New York: Wiley, 1972.

Cherry, E. C. Some experiments on the recognition of speech with one and with two ears. *Journal of the Acoustical Society of America,* 1953, *25,* 975–979.

Clark, H. H. How we understand negation. Paper presented at Workshop on Cognitive Organization and Psychological Processes, University of California, Irvine, August 1970.

Clark, H. H. Comprehension and the Given-New contract. Paper presented for conference on "The role of grammar in interdisciplinary linguistic research," University of Bielfeld, Bielfeld, Germany, December 1973.

Clark, H. H., Carpenter, P. A., & Just, M. A. On the meeting of semantics and perception. In W. G. Chase (Ed.), *Visual information processing.* New York: Academic Press, 1973.

Clark, H. H., & Chase, W. G. On the process of comparing sentences against pictures. *Cognitive Psychology,* 1972, *3,* 472–515.

Collins, A. M., & Quillian, M. R. Retrieval time from semantic memory. *Journal of Verbal Learning and Verbal Behavior,* 1969, *8,* 240–247.

Collins, A., Warnock, E. H., Aiello, N., & Miller, M. L. Reasoning from incomplete knowledge. In D. G. Bobrow & A. Collins (Eds.), *Representation and understanding: studies in cognitive science.* New York: Academic Press, 1975.

Conrad, R. An association between memory errors and errors due to acoustic masking of speech. *Nature,* 1962, *196,* 1314–1315(a).

Conrad, R. Acoustic confusions in immediate memory. *British Journal of Psychology,* 1964, *55,* 75–84.

Cooper, L. A., & Shepard, R. N. Chronometric studies of the rotation of mental images. In W. G. Chase (Ed.), *Visual information processing.* New York: Academic Press, 1973.

Cornsweet, T. *Visual perception.* New York: Academic Press, 1970.

Craik, F. I. M. The fate of primary memory items in free recall. *Journal of Verbal Learning and Verbal Behavior,* 1970, *9,* 143–148.

Craik, F. I. M., & Lockhart, R. S. Levels of processing: A framework for memory research. *Journal of Verbal Learning and Verbal Behavior,* 1972, *11,* 671–684.

Craik, F. I. M., & Watkins, M. J. The role of rehearsal in short-term memory. *Journal of Verbal Learning and Verbal Behavior,* 1973, *12,* 599–607.

Crowder, R. G., & Morton, J. Precategorical acoustic storage. *Perception & Psychophysics,* 1969, *5,* 365–373.

Darley, C. F., & Murdock, B. B., Jr. Effects of prior free recall testing on final recall and recognition. *Journal of Experimental Psychology,* 1971, *91,* 66–73.

Darwin, C. J., Turvey, M. T., & Crowder, R. G. An auditory analogue of the Sperling partial report procedure: Evidence for brief auditory storage. *Cognitive Psychology,* 1972, *3,* 255–267.

Duncker, K. On problem solving. *Psychological Monographs,* 1945, *58,* Whole No: 270.

Eichelman, W. H. Stimulus and response repetition effects for naming letters. *Perception and Psychophysics,* 1970, *7,* 94–96.

Eriksen, C. W., & Collins, J. F. Some temporal characteristics of visual perception. *Journal of Experimental Psychology,* 1967, *74,* 476–484.

Ernst, G. W., & Newell, A. *GPS: A case study in generality and problem solving.* New York: Academic Press, 1969.

Estes, W. K. The locus of inferential and perceptual processes in letter identification. *Journal of Experimental Psychology: General,* 1975, *1,* 122–145.

Evans, T. G. A program for the solution of geometric-analogy intelligence test questions. In M. L. Minsky (Ed.), *Semantic information processing,* Cambridge, Mass.: MIT Press, 1968.

Fillenbaum, S. & Rapporport, A. *Structures in the subjective lexicon.* New York: Academic Press, 1971.

Fodor, J. A., Bever, T. G., & Garrett, M. F. *The psychology of language.* New York: McGraw-Hill, 1974.

Fraisse, P., Visual perceptive simultaneity and masking of letters successively presented. *Perception and Psychophysics,* 1966, *1,* 285–287.

Frederiksen, J. R. Paper presented at summer conference on Mathematical Theories of Memory at the Massachusetts Institute of Technology, July 1969.

Gentner, D. Evidence for the psychological reality of semantic components: the verbs of possession. In D. A. Norman, D. E. Rumelhart & LNR, *Explorations in Cognition.* San Francisco: Freeman, 1975.

Glanzer, M., & Cunitz, A. R. Two storage mechanisms in free recall. *Journal of Verbal Learning and Verbal Behavior,* 1966, *5,* 351–360.

Gordon, D., & Lakoff, G. *Conversational postulates.* Papers from the Seventh Regional Meeting, Chicago Linguistic Society, April 1971.

Gough, P. B. Grammatical transformations and speed of understanding. *Journal of Verbal Learning and Verbal Behavior,* 1965, *4,* 107–111.

Gough, P. B. The verification of sentences: The effects of delay of evidence and sentence length. *Journal of Verbal Learning and Verbal Behavior,* 1966, *5,* 429–496.

Graboi, D. Physical shape, practice and meaning in visual search. Unpublished doctoral dissertation, University of California, San Diego, 1974.

Green, D. M., & Luce, R. D. Counting and timing mechanisms in auditory discrimination and reaction time. In D. H. Krantz, R. C. Atkinson, R. D. Luce, & P. Suppes (Eds.), *Contemporary developments in mathematical psychology, II.* San Francisco: Freeman, 1974.

Greeno, J. G. Hobits and Orcs: Acquisition of a sequential concept. *Cognitive Psychology,* 1974, *6,* 270–293.

Grice, H. P. *Logic and conversation.* The William James Lectures, Harvard University, 1967.

Haviland, S. E., & Clark, H. H. Acquiring new information as a process in comprehension. *Journal of Verbal Learning and Verbal Behavior,* 1974, 13, 512–521.

Hecht, S., Schlaer, S., & Pirenne, M. H. Energy, quanta, and vision. *Journal of General Psychology,* 1942, *25,* 819–840.

Henley, N. M. A psychological study of the semantics of animal terms. *Journal of Verbal Learning and Verbal Behavior,* 1969, *8,* 176–184.

Hind, J. E., Anderson, D. J., Brugge, J. F., & Rose, J. E. Coding of information pertaining to paired low-frequency tones in single auditory nerve fibers of the squirrel monkey. *Journal of Neurophysiology,* 1967, *30,* 794–816.

Hubel, D. H. Integrative processes in central visual pathways of the cat. *Journal of the Optical Society of America,* 1963, *53,* 58–66.

Hubel, D. H., & Wiesel, T. N. Receptive fields of single neurones in the cat's striate cortex. *Journal of Physiology,* 1959, *148,* 574–591.

Hubel, D. H., & Wiesel, T. N. Receptive fields, binocular intearction, and functional architecture in the cat's visual cortex. *Journal of Physiology,* 1962, *160,* 106–154.

Hubel, D. H., & Wiesel, T. N. Receptive fields and functional architecture in two nonstriate visual areas (18 & 19) of the cat. *Journal of Neurophysiology,* 1965, *28,* 229–289.

Hubel, D. H., & Wiesel, T. N. Receptive fields and functional architecture of monkey striate cortex. *Journal of Physiology,* 1968, *195,* 215–243.

Huey, E. B. The psychology and pedagogy of reading. Cambridge: MIT Press, 1968. (Originally published by Macmillan, 1908.)

Hyde, T. S., & Jenkins, J. J. Recall for words as a function of semantic, graphic and syntactic orienting tasks. *Journal of Verbal Learning and Verbal Behavior,* 1973, *12,* 471–480.

Johnson, S. C. Hierarchical clustering schemes. *Psychometrika,* 1967, *32,* 241–254.

Johnston, J. C. *The role of contextual constraint in the perception of letters in words.* Unpublished doctoral dissertation, University of Pennsylvania, 1974.

Johnston, J. C., & McClelland, J. L. Visual factors in word perception. *Perception and Psychophysics,* 1973, *14,* 365–370.

Just, M., & Carpenter, P. Comprehension of negation with quantification. *Journal of Verbal Learning and Verbal Behavior,* 1971, *10,* 244–253.

Kaplan, R. M. Augmented transition networks as psychological models of sentence comprehension. *Artificial Intelligence,* 1972, *3,* 77–100.

Kaplan, R. M. A general syntactic processor. In R. Rustin (Ed.), *Natural language processing.* New York: Algorithmics Press, 1973.

Kaplan, R. M. *Transient processing load in relative clauses.* Unpublished dissertation, Harvard University, 1974.

Katz, J. J., & Fodor, J. A. The structure of semantic theory. *Language,* 1963, *39,* 170–210.

Keele, S. W., & Chase, W. G. Short-term visual storage. *Perception and Psychophysics,* 1967, *2,* 383–386.

Kosslyn, S. M. Scanning visual images: Some structural implications. *Perception and Psychophysics,* 1973, *14,* 90–94.

Kuffler, S. W. Discharge patterns and functional organization of mammalian retina. *Journal of Neurophysiology,* 1953, *16,* 37–68.

Leeper, R. A study of a neglected portion of the field of learning—the development of sensory organization. *Journal of Genetic Psychology,* 1935, *46,* 41–75.

Lesser, V. R., Fennell, R. D., Erman, L. D., & Reddy, D. R. *Organization of the HEARSAY II speech understanding system.* (Working Papers in Speech Recognition III.) Carnegie-Mellon University, 1974, 11–21.

Linton, M. Memory for real-world events. In D. A. Norman, D. E. Rumelhart, & the LNR Research Group, *Explorations in cognition.* San Francisco: Freeman, 1975.

Lindgren, N. Machine recognition of human language. Part III—cursive script recognition. *IEEE spectrum,* May, 1965, 104–116.

Mandler, G. Organization and memory, In. K. W. Spence & J. T. Spence (Eds.) Psychology of Learning and Motivation, Vol. 1. New York: Academic Press, 1967.

Mandler, G. Organized recall: Individual functions. *Psychonomic Science,* 1968, *13,* 235–236.

Mandler, G. & Dean, P. J. Seriation: development of serial order in free recall. *Journal of Experimental Psychology,* 1969, *81,* 207–215.

Mandler, G., & Pearlstone, Z. Free and constrained concept learning and subsequent recall. *Journal of Verbal Learning and Verbal Behavior,* 1966, *5,* 126–131.

McClelland, J. L. *The role of preliminary letter identification in the perception of words and non-words.* Unpublished doctoral dissertation, University of Pennsylvania, 1975.

McMahon, L. E. Grammatical analysis as part of understanding a sentence. Unpublished doctoral dissertation, Harvard University, 1963.

Melton, A. W. Implications of short-term memory for a general theory of memory. *Journal of Verbal Learning and Verbal Behavior*, 1963, *2*, 1–21.

Meyer, D. E., & Schvaneveldt, R. W. Facilitation in recognizing pairs of words: Evidence of a dependence between retrieval operations. *Journal of Experimental Psychology*, 1971, *90*, 227–234.

Meyer, D. E., Schvaneveldt, R. W., & Ruddy, M. G. Activation of lexical memory. Paper presented at the meeting of the Psychonomic Society, St. Louis, November, 1972.

Meyer, D. E., Schvaneveldt, R. W., & Ruddy, M. G. Functions of phonemic and graphic codes in visual word recognition. *Memory and Cognitiion*, 1974, *2*, 309–321.

Miller, G. A. The magical number seven, plus or minus two: Some limits on our capacity for processing information. *Psychological Review*, 1956, *63*, 81–97.

Miller, G. A. Empirical methods in the study of semantics. In D. L. Arm (Ed.), *Journeys in Science: Small steps—great strides*. Albuquerque: University of New Mexico Press, 1967.

Miller, G. A. A psychological method to investigate verbal concepts. *Journal of Mathematical Psychology*, 1969, *6*, 169–191.

Miller, G. A., Bruner, J. S., & Postman, L. Familiarity of letter sequences and tachistoscopic identification. *Journal of Genetic Psychology*, 1954, *50*, 129–139.

Miller, G. A., & Isard, S. Some perceptual consequences of linguistic rules. *Journal of Verbal Learning and Verbal Behavior*, 1963, *2*, 217–228.

Minsky, M. A framework for representing knowledge. In P. H. Winston (Ed.) *The Psychology of Computer Vision*, New York: McGraw-Hill, 1975.

Mistler-Lachman, J. L. Depth of comprehension and sentence memory. *Journal of Verbal Learning and Verbal Behavior*, 1974, *13*, 98–106.

Moray, N. Attention in dichotic listening: Affective cues and the effect of instructions. *Quarterly Journal of Experimental Psychology*, 1959, *11*, 56–60.

Murdock, B. B., Jr. The retention of individual items. *Journal of Experimental Psychology*, 1961, *62*, 618–625.

Murdock, B. B., Jr. The serial position effect in free recall. *Journal of Experimental Psychology*, 1962, *64*, 482–488.

Murdock, B. B., Jr. *Human memory: Theory and data*. Potomac, Md.: Erlbaum Associates, 1974.

Neisser, U. Decision time without reaction time: Experiments in visual scanning. *American Journal of Psychology*, 1963, *76*, 376–385.

Neisser, U. *Cognitive psychology*. New York: Appleton-Century-Crofts, 1967.

Neisser, U., & Beller, H. K. Searching through word lists. *British Journal of Psychology*, 1965, *56*, 349–358.

Neisser, U., & Lazar, R. Searching for ten targets simultaneously. *Perceptual and Motor Skills*, 1964, *17*, 955–961.

Newell, A., Shaw, J. C., & Simon, H. A. Elements of a theory of human problem solving. *Psychological Review*, 1958, *65*, 151–166.

Newell, A., Shaw, J. C., & Simon, H. A. Elements of a theory of human problem solving. G. Terrell, & M. Wertheimer (Eds), *Contemporary approaches to creative thinking*. New York: Atherton Press, 1962.

Newell, A., & Simon, H. A. GPS, a program that simulates human thought. In E. A.

Feigenbaum & J. Feldman (Eds.), *Computers and thought*. New York: McGraw-Hill, 1963.

Newell, A., & Simon, H. A. *Human problem solving*. Englewood Cliffs, N.J.: Prentice-Hall, 1972.

Norman, D. A., & Bobrow, D. G. On data-limited and resource-limited processes. *Cognitive Psychology*, 1975, *7*, 44–64.

Norman, D. A., & Rumelhart, D. E. A system for perception and memory. In D. A. Norman (Ed.), *Models of human memory*. New York: Academic Press, 1970.

Norman, D. A., Rumelhart, D. E., & the LNR Research Group. *Explorations in cognition*. San Francisco: Freeman, 1975.

Olson, D. R. Language and thought: Aspects of a cognitive theory of semantics. *Psychological Review*, 1970, *77*, 257–273.

Palmer, S. E. The effects of contextual scenes on the identification of objects. *Memory and Cognition*, 1975a, *3*, 519–526.

Palmer, S. E. Visual perception and world knowledge: Notes on a model of sensory cognitive interaction. In Norman, D. A., Rumelhart, D. E., and the LNR Research Group, *Explorations in cognition*. San Francisco, Freeman, 1975b.

Penrose, L. & Penrose, R. Impossible objects: A special type of illusion. *British Journal of Psychology*, 1958, *49*, 31–33.

Peterson, L. R., & Peterson, M. J. Short-term retention of individual verbal items. *Journal of Experimental Psychology*, 1959, *58*, 193–198.

Pillsbury, W. B. A study in apperception. *American Journal of Psychology*, 1897, *8*, 315–393.

Pirenne, M. H. *Vision and the eye*. New York: Barnes and Noble, 1967.

Posner, M. I. Abstraction and the process of recognition. In G. H. Bower & J. T. Spence (Eds.), *Psychology of learning and motivation* (Vol. 3). New York: Academic Press, 1969.

Posner, M. I. Coordination of codes. In W. G. Chase (Ed.), *Visual information processing*. New York: Academic Press, 1973.

Posner, M. I., Boies, S. J., Eichelman, W. H., & Taylor, R. L. Retention of visual and name codes of single letters. *Journal of Experimental Psychology Monograph*, 1969, *79*, No. 1, Part 2.

Posner, M. I., & Keele, S. W. Decay of information from a single letter. *Science*, 1967, *158*, 137–139.

Posner, M. I., & Mitchell, R. F. Chronometric analysis of classification. *Psychological Review*, 1967, *74*, 392–409.

Postman, L., & Phillips, L. W. Short-term temporal changes in free recall. *Quarterly Journal of Experimental Psychology*, 1965, *17*, 132–138.

Potter, R. K., Kopp, G. A., & Green, H. C. *Visible speech*. New York: Van Nostrand, 1947.

Quillian, M. R. Semantic memory. In M. L. Minsky (Ed.), *Semantic information processing*. Cambridge, Mass.: MIT Press, 1968.

Quillian, M. R. The teachable language comprehender. *Communications of the Association for Computing Machinery*, 1969, *12*, 459–475.

Raab, D. H. Backward masking. *Psychological Bulletin*, 1963, *60*, 118–139.

Reddy, D. R., Erman, L. D., Fennell, R. D., & Neely, R. B The HEARSAY speech understanding system: An example of the recognition process. *Proceedings of the Third International Joint Conference on Artificial Intelligence*, Stanford, California, 1973.

Reicher, G. M. Perceptual recognition as a function of meaningfulness of stimulus material. *Journal of Experimental Psychology*, 1969, *81*, 274–280.

Riesz, R. R. Differential intensity sensitivity of the ear for pure tones, *Physiological Review*, 1928, *31*, 867–875.

Romney, A. K., & D'Andrade, R. G. Cognitive aspects of English kin terms. In A. K. Romney & R. G. D'Andrade (Eds.), *Transactional Studies in Cognition, American Anthropolgist*, 1964, *66*, No. 3, Part 2.

Rosch, E. H. On the internal structure of perceptual and semantic categories. In T. Moore (Ed.), *Cognitive development and the acquisition of language*. New York: Academic Press, 1973.

Rose, J. E., Brugge, J. F., Anderson, D. J., & Hind, J. E. Phase-locked response to low-frequency tones in single auditory nerve fibers of the squirrel monkey. *Journal of Neurophysiology*, 1967, *30*, 769–793.

Rose, J. E., Brugge, J. F., Anderson, D. J., & Hind, J. E. Some possible neural correlates of combination tones. *Journal of Neurophysiology*, 1969, *32*, 402–423.

Rubin, E. *Synoplevede Figurer*. Copenhagen: Gyldendalske, 1915.

Ruddy, M. G., Meyer, D. E., & Schvaneveldt, R. W. Context effects on phonemic encoding in visual word recognition. Paper read at the meeting of the Midwestern Psychological Association, Chicago, May 1973.

Rumelhart, D. E. A multicomponent theory of the perception of briefly exposed visual displays. *Journal of Mathematical Psychology*, 1970, *7*, 191–218.

Rumelhart, D. E. A multicomponent theory of the confusion among briefly alphabetic characters. Center for Human Information Processing (Tech. Rpt. No. 22). University of California, San Diego, November 1971.

Rumelhart, D. E. Toward an interactive model of reading. In S. Dornic (Ed.), *Attention and performance VI*. Hillsdale, N.J.: Laurence Erlbaum, in press.

Rumelhart, D. E., & Abrahamson, A. A. A model for analogical reasoning. *Cognitive Psychology*, 1973, *5*, 1–28.

Rumelhart, D. E., Lindsay, P. H., & Norman, D. A. A process model for long-term memory. In E. Tulving & W. Donaldson (Eds.), *Organization of memory*. New York: Academic Press, 1972.

Rumelhart, D. E., & Norman, D. A. Active semantic networks as a model of human memory. *Proceedings of the Third International Joint Conference on Artificial Intelligence*, Stanford, California, 1973.

Rumelhart, D. E., Ortony, A. The representation of knowledge in memory. In R. C. Anderson, R. J. Spiro, & W. E. Montague (Eds.), *Schooling and the Acquisition of Knowledge*. Hillsdale, N.J.: Laurence Erlbaum, in press.

Rumelhart, D. E., & Siple, P. Process of recognizing tachistoscopically presented words. *Psychological Review*, 1974, *81*, 99–118.

Sakitt, B. Counting every quantum. *Journal of Psyiology*, 1972, *223*, 131–150.

Schank, R. C. Identification of conceptualizations underlying natural language. In R. C. Schank & K. M. Colby (Eds.), *Computer models of thought and language*. San Francisco: Freeman, 1973.

Schank, R. C., & Abelson, R. P. Scripts, plans, and knowledge. *Proceedings of the Fourth International Joint Conference on Artificial Intelligence*, Stanford, California, 1975.

Schank, R. C., & the Yale AI Project. SAM—A story understander. Research Report No. 43. Yale University, Committee on Computer Science, August 1975.

Schvaneveldt, R. W., & Meyer, D. E. Retrieval and comparison processes in semantic memory. In S. Kornblum (Ed.), *Attention and performance IV*. New York: Academic Press, 1973.

Selfridge, O. G. Pattern recognition and modern computers. *Proceedings of the Western Joint Computer Conference*, Los Angeles, 1955.

Selfridge, O. G. Pandemonium: A paradigm for learning. In *Symposium on the mechanisation of thought processes*. London: H. M. Stationery Office, 1959.

Selfridge, O. G., & Neisser, U. Pattern recognition by machine. *Scientific American*, 1960, *203*, 60–68.

Shepard, R. N. The analysis of proximities: Multidimensional scaling with an unknown distance function: I. *Psychometrika*, 1962, *27*, 125–140.

Shepard, R. N., & Metzler, J. Mental rotation of three-dimensional objects. *Science*, 1971. *171*, 701–703.

Shiffrin, R. M., Pisoni, D. B., & Casteneda-Mendez, K. Is attention shared between the ears? *Cognitive Psychology*, 1974, *6*, 190–216.

Siebert, W. M. Stimulus transformations in the peripheral auditory system. In P. A. Kolers & M. Eden (Eds.), *Recognizing patterns*. Cambridge, Mass.: MIT Press. 1968.

Siple, P. A. Encoding in short-term memory: Implications from reaction-time studies. Unpublished doctoral dissertation, University of California, San Diego, 1974.

Smith, E. E., Shoben, E. J., & Rips, L. J. Structure and process in semantic memory: A featural model for semantic decisions. *Psychological Review*, 1974, *81*, 214–241.

Sorkin, R. D., & Pohlman, L. D. Some models of observer behavior in two-channel auditory signal detection. *Perception and Psychophysics*, 1973, *14*, 101–109.

Sperling, G. The information available in brief visual presentations. *Psychological Monographs*, 1960, *74*, 1–29.

Sperling, G. A model for visual memory tasks. *Human Factors*, 1963, *5*, 19–31.

Spiro, R. J. Inferential reconstruction in memory for connected discourse. Laboratory for Cognitive Studies in Education (Tech. Rpt. No. 2). University of Illinois at Urbana-Champaign, October 1975.

Springer, R. M. Neural factors in visual anisotropy. Unpublished doctoral dissertation, University of California, San Diego, 1973.

Sternberg, S. High-speed scanning in human memory. *Science*, 1966, *153*, 652–654.

Sternberg, S. Two operations in character recognition: Some evidence from reaction time measurements. *Perception and Psychophysics*, 1967, *2*, 45–53.

Sternberg, S. Memory scanning: Mental processes revealed by reaction-time experiments. *American Scientist*, 1969, *57*, 421–457.

Stevens, A. L., & Rumelhart, D. E. Errors in reading: Analysis using an augmented network model of grammar. In D. A. Norman, D. E. Rumelhart, & the LNR Research Group, *Explorations in cognition*. San Francisco: Freeman, 1975.

Sutherland, N. S. Stimulus analyzing mechanisms. In *Symposium on the mechanisation of thought processes*. London: H. M. Stationery Office, 1959.

Swensson, R. G. The elusive tradeoff: Speed versus accuracy in visual discrimination tasks. *Perception and Psychology*, 1972, *12*, 16–32.

Swensson, R. G., & Edwards, W. Response strategies in a two-choice reaction task with a continuous cost for time. *Journal of Experimental Psychology*, 1971, *88*, 67–81.

Thomas, J. C., Jr. An analysis of behavior in the Hobbits-Orcs problem. *Cognitive Psychology*, 1974, *6*, 257–270.

Thompson, J. H. What happens to the stimulus in backward masking? *Journal of Experimental Psychology*, 1966, *71*, 580–586.

Thomson, L. C. & Wright, W. D. The convergence of the tritanopic confusion loci and the derivation of the fundamental response functions. *Journal of the Optical Society of America*, 1953, *43*, 890–894.

Thorne, J., Bratley, P., & Dewar, H. The syntactic analysis of English by machine. In D. Michie (Ed.), *Machine intelligence, 3*. New York: American Elsevier, 1968.

Till, R. E., & Jenkins, J. J. The effects of cued orienting tasks on the free recall of words. *Journal of Verbal Learning and Verbal Behavior*, 1973, *12*, 489–498.

Trabasso, T. Reasoning and the processing of negative information. Invited Address, Division 3, 78th Annual Convention, American Psychological Association, Miami Beach, September 1970.

Trabasso, T. Mental operations in language comprehension. In R. O. Freedle & J. B. Carroll (Eds.), *Language comprehension and the acquisition of knowledge*. Washington, D.C.: Winston, 1972.

Trabasso, T., Rollins, H., & Shaughnessy, E. Storage and verification stages in processing concepts. *Cognitive Psychology*, 1971, *2*, 239–289.

Treisman, A. M. Contextual cues in selective listening. *Quarterly Journal of Experimental Psychology*, 1960, *12*, 242–248.

Treisman, A. M., & Geffen, G. Selective attention: Perception or response? *Quarterly Journal of Experimental Psychology*, 1967, *19*, 1–17.

Treisman, A. M., & Tuxworth, J. Immediate and delayed recall of sentences after perceptual processing at different levels. *Journal of Verbal Learning and Verbal Behavior*, 1974, *13*, 38–44.

Tulving, E., Episodic and semantic memory. In E. Tulving and W. Donaldson (Eds.), *Organization of Memory*, New York: Academic Press, 1972.

Tulving, E., Mandler, G., & Baumal, R. Interaction of two sources of information in tachistoscopic word recognition. *Canadian Journal of Psychology*, 1964, *18*, 62–71.

Tulving, E., & Thomson, D. M. Encoding specificity and retrieval processes in episodic memory. *Psychological Review*, 1973, *80*, 352–373.

van den Brink, G., & Bouman, M. A. Visual thresholds for moving point sources. *Journal of the Optical Society of America*, 1957, *47*, 612–618.

Wagner, H. G., MacNicol, E. F. Jr., & Wolbarscht, M. L. Functional basis for 'on'-center and 'off'-center receptive fields in the retina. *Journal of the Optical Society of America*, 1963, *53*, 66–70.

Walsh, D. A., & Jenkins, J. J. Effects of orienting tasks of free recall in incidental learning: "Difficulty," "effort" and "process" explanations. *Journal of Verbal Learning and Verbal Behavior*, 1973, *12*, 481–488.

Wanner, E., & Maratsos, M. M. On understanding relative clauses. Unpublished manuscript. Harvard University, Department of Psychology and Social Relations, 1974.

Weksel, W., & Bever, T. G. Harvard Cognitive Studies Progress Report, 1966. (Reported in J. A. Fodor, T. G. Bever & M .F. Garrett, *The Psychology of Language*, New York: McGraw-Hill, 1974.)

Wiesel, T. N. Recording inhibition and excitation in the cat's retinal ganglion cells with intracellular electrodes. *Nature*, 1959, *183*, 264–265.

Woods, W. A. Transitional network grammars for natural language analysis. *Communications of the ACM*, 1970, *13*, 591–606.

Woods, W. A., Kaplan, R. M. The lunar sciences natural language information system. BBN report No. 2265, Bolt, Beranek and Newman Inc. Cambridge, Mass. 1971.

Woodward, A. E., Jr., Bjork, R. A., & Jongeward, R. H., Jr. Recall and recognition as a function of primary rehearsal. *Journal of Verbal Learning and Verbal Behavior*, 1973, *12*, 608–617.

GLOSSARY

Accessing memory
  Retrieving information from memory.

Acoustic features
  Characteristics we abstract from the acoustic signal. See also feature.

Action
  In the context of an ATN, an action is a particular structure, structure-building, or modifying operation associated with a particular arc in an ATN.

Analogical reasoning
  The use or discovery of a similarity of relationships between two pairs of concepts. Thus, for example, the determination that the relationship between two concepts, A and B, is the same as that between two other concepts, C and D, constitutes a classical case of analogical reasoning.

Anomalous sentences
  Sentences that are syntactically correct but that do not seem to make semantic sense. "Colorless green ideas sleep furiously" is a classic example of an anomalous sentence.

Arc
  An arc is an arrow connecting two nodes in a network. In an ATN, an arc is represented by an arrow connecting two circles representing the two states of the ATN. Normally, in an ATN, an arc is labeled by the class of lexical items which, if encountered, allows a transition from one state to the next. See also network and augmented transition network.

Argument constraints
> Those constraints associated with the argument of verbs, adjectives, adverbs, and the like, which must be satisfied by the concept filling that argument slot. Thus, for example, the verb "sleep" requires an animate subject, the adjective "green" requires its argument to be a physical object, and the adverb "furiously" requires that the sentence it modifies describe an activity that can be done actively. It is presumably the violation of these constraints that causes anomalies such as, "Green ideas sleep furiously."

ATN
> See augmented transition network.

Attention
> The concept of attention refers to situations involving the allotment of processing resources to one or another processing activity. We are said to attend to something when we allot our resources to the processing of that thing.

Attention span
> The number of things of a certain sort to which one can attend at a given time.

Attenuator
> A device that reduces the intensity of inputs that pass through it. An attenuation model of attention holds that information from unattended channels is not entirely shut out of the system; the rate of information flow over these channels is merely reduced somewhat.

Auditory nerve
> The eighth nerve that carries auditory information from the cochlea of the ear to higher centers of the brain.

Augmented transition network (ATN)
> A notation for expressing an algorithm for natural language parsing. The notation involves the specification of states, represented by circles, and the allowable transitions between states, represented by arcs connecting the various states.

Backward masking
> The detrimental effect of one stimulus (auditory or visual) on the perception of another that preceded it in time. See forward masking and masking.

Basilar membrane
> An inner ear membrane that plays a central role in the transduction of acoustic information into neural information.

Bipolar cells
>Cells in the retina between the receptors and the retinal ganglion cells. These cells appear to play a role in the funneling of numerous receptors to a single retinal ganglion cell.

Bottom-up processing
>Stimulus driven processing. Whenever the particular pattern of processing is determined primarily by the stimulus, the processing is said to be bottom-up or data driven. Whenever it is primarily determined by hypotheses about the nature of the input, it is said to be top-down or conceptually driven processing. See top-down processing.

Buffer
>A memory used to hold information data while data can be further processed. Buffer memories are normally used when the length of time that the data are available from the input device is shorter than the amount of time it takes to process the information.

Chunks
>Memory units. A letter, a word, or a sentence can be a single unit of memory. Miller (1956) has suggested that we can hold 7 $\pm$ 2 chunks of information in primary memory at one time, independent of the complexity of the chunk. See primary memory.

Cochlea
>The major organ of the inner ear. The cochlea houses the organ of Corti, which includes the basilar membrane and the hair cells—the primary devices in the transduction of acoustic into neural information.

Cognitive demon
>A device in Selfridge's (1959) Pandemonium model of pattern recognition that recognizes conceptual units, such as words or letters. See pandemonium.

Complex cell
>A type of cell occurring in the visual cortex that responds to lines and edges of a fixed orientation independently of the precise location of the line on the retina. See simple cell.

Componential analysis
>The analysis of word meanings to determine their elementary semantic components. For example, the word "boy" might be analyzed as containing three components, + male, + human, and − adult. Thus, according to this analysis, the meaning of "boy" would be nonadult male human.

Computational demon

In Selfridge's (1959) Pandemonium model of pattern recognition, a computational demon is a device that recognizes particular features of the input and feeds that information into other computational demons or to cognitive demons. See pandemonium.

Cones

The receptors in the retina that operate at higher levels of illumination and that carry information about color.

Confusion errors

In the context of pattern recognition, the confusion of one character for another. Such errors can lead to insight as to the features extracted from the stimulus.

Context

The general situation surrounding the occurrence of some event. In general, any events occurring in the spatial and/or temporal vicinity of a given event can be considered as part of the context of that event.

Conversational postulates

Rules of conversation. Thus, for example, "Be sincere" might be a conversational postulate that demands participants in a conversation not lie.

Cornea

The transparent outside covering of the front of the eye.

Cortex

The outer layer of the brain.

Dark light

That which causes our visual receptors to fire in the absence of actual light stimulation.

Data limited processing

A task is said to be data limited when our ability to perform well is determined by the quality of the information with which we have to work rather than with the amount of effort we put into the task. See also resource limited processing.

Decision demon

In Selfridge's (1959) Pandemonium model of pattern recognition, the decision demon is the device that must finally determine which of the various alternative possible patterns has been encountered. The decision demon gets inputs from the cognitive demons. See pandemonium.

Degraded stimulus
  A stimulus that has been made more difficult to perceive by the reduction of the signal-to-noise ratio. See signal-to-noise ratio.

Depth of processing
  A stimulus can be said to be processed at various levels. Consider, for example, a situation in which a person is shown a word and asked to determine whether or not it is written in capital letters, whether or not it rhymes with some other word, or whether it is in the same semantic category as some other word. In the first case, only very peripheral processing is required; in the second, somewhat deeper analysis is required; and in the last case, rather deep analysis is presumably involved. These various depths of processing lead to progressively more easily retrieved memory traces.

Determiners
  Articles like the, a, an, this, etc.

Disambiguation
  The determination of the meaning of an ambiguous word or sentence.

Dynes
  A measure of the intensity of the pressure wave, especially as involved in an acoustic stimulus.

Echoic memory
  A faithful memory representation of acoustic stimuli. This is the acoustic counterpart of the iconic memory in vision. See iconic memory and precategorical acoustic store.

Electrode
  A device used to sense changes in electrical potential. Electrodes are sometimes implanted in particular neurons to monitor their activity.

Embedded
  One thing is said to be embedded in another when it appears as a constituent of the other. Thus the sentence, "John went home" is embedded in the sentence, "Mary said that John went home."

Encoding
  The process of assigning an interpretation to an input and the storage, in memory, of a representation of that interpretation.

Episodic memory
> The memory for particular events in which we have been involved. See semantic memory.

Euclidean proximity space
> A possibly multidimensional representation of item similarity in which the dissimilarity between items is represented by the distance between them in the space. Distance is measured according to the euclidean metric in which the distance between two points is given by the square root of the sum of the squares of the differences on each dimension.

Exhaustive search
> A search that requires the checking of each of the possible alternatives. See also serial search.

Exposure duration
> The amount of time that a visual stimulus is presented.

False alarm rate
> The probability, in a signal detection task, that a subject responds that a particular signal is present when in fact it was not present. See signal detection task, hit rate, and ROC curve.

Feature
> A characteristic of a sensory input that is computed as part of the primary analysis process. Featural information is presumed to serve as the basis for all more complex pattern analysis.

Feature extraction
> The process whereby the sensory system constructs a featural representation of a sensory input.

Fixation point
> A dot displayed on a screen at which one is supposed to look. A fixation point is often used in experiments involving brief visual presentations to show the subject where to look to see the to-be-presented stimulus.

Forced choice
> An experimental procedure analogous to a multiple choice test in which the subject is presented with a limited set of response alternatives and must choose one of them.

Forward masking
> The detrimental effect that one stimulus (auditory or visual) has on our perception of a stimulus presented slightly later in time. See masking and backward masking.

Free recall

The procedure in memory experiments where a subject is given a list of items to remember and then, at some later point, is asked to remember them in any order he wishes. See primacy effect, recency effect, and serial position curve.

Frequency of a tone

The rate, usually measured in hertz or cycles per second, at which the sound pressure occilates. The pitch of a tone is primarily determined by its frequency.

Fricative

A class of phonemes or elementary speech sounds that includes the phonemes /f/ and /v/. See also phoneme.

Functional fixity

The tendency, evidenced in problem-solving situations, to view an object as having only one function and not realizing that it can be used for something else. Thus, for example, when looking for something to hammer in a nail with, we might overlook a shoe. Duncker (1945) is noted for describing this phenomenon.

Functional reasoning

A kind of reasoning in which we attempt to deduce characteristics of a situation about which we have no direct knowledge through the use of the knowledge of how what we don't know depends on what we do know. Thus, although we may never have been told that rice is not a major product of Alaska, this fact can be surmised through our knowledge of the growing conditions of rice and our knowledge of the geography of Alaska.

Garden path sentences

Sentences in which we are initially led to interpret wrongly and only late in our reading of the sentence is there the clue that allows us to properly interpret the sentence given. Thus, "The plastic red boxes are made of is soft" and "The old man the boats" are garden path sentences.

General problem solver (GPS)

A computer program developed by Newall and Simon (c.f. Newall & Simon, 1972) to solve a large class of problems. See also means-ends analysis.

General syntactic processor (GSP)
>A computer program designed by Kaplan (1975) or the parsing of natural language inputs. The program is a generalization of the ATN parser.

Given-new distinction
>Sentences communicate new information by relating a new fact to some previously given information. For example, the sentence "It was John who broke the window" presupposes that the listener already knows that some-one broke the window (the given information) and communicates that John was that someone (the new information). See also presupposition.

Grammar of a language
>The rules that determine the variety of forms in which sentences in the language can be put. See also syntactic knowledge.

Hair cells
>The cells in the cochlea that sense movement of the basilar membrane and convert this motion into a train of neural impulses in the auditory nerve.

HEARSAY system
>A computer system developed by Raj Reddy and his colleagues for the automatic interpretation of continuously spoken speech.

Hertz
>The unit of measurement of frequency equal to 1 cycle per second. Thus, a 1000-Hz pure tone is a tone that passes through 1000 cycles per second.

Hit rate
>In a signal detection situation, the hit rate is the probability that the subject will say "yes" the signal is present when, in fact, it was present. See also false alarm rate and ROC curve.

HOLD stack
>A stack used by an ATN in the processing of relative clauses.

Hypothesis
>An hypothesis is a possible interpretation of a situation.

Iconic memory
>Peripheral visual information store that maintains a faithful representation of visual inputs for roughly 1 sec after offset of the stimulus. Recent evidence seems to suggest that the icon is the result of retinal persistence of the image. See echoic memory.

Image demon
 In Selfridge's (1959) Pandemonium model of pattern recognition, the
 image demons were the most peripheral inputs to the system.

Immediate memory
 See primary memory.

Increment threshold procedure
 The psychophysical procedure whereby a subject is asked to detect a
 small increment in the intensity of I against a background signal. The in-
 tensity needed to make the increment detectable 75% of the time is called
 ΔI. The ratio of ΔI to I gives the Weber fraction for that stimulus situation.
 See also Weber fraction.

Inference
 The process of drawing new conclusions from old knowledge.

Information accrual process
 The process of gathering information from a sensory source. See also
 feature extraction.

Inhibitory effect
 One neuron is said to have an inhibitory effect on another whenever an
 increase in activity of the first causes a decrease in the activity of the
 second.

Inter-spike interval
 The time between successive firings of a given neuron.

j.n.d.
 A just noticeable difference. Two stimuli are said to differ by a j.n.d. when
 they can be distinguished just 75% of the time.

Knowledge sources
 In the context of HEARSAY, a knowledge source is an independent
 module of knowledge that provides information for the interpretation of
 the speech input. HEARSAY employs acoustic, syntactic, semantic, and
 pragmatic knowledge sources.

Lexical information
 Knowledge about words. This knowledge includes information about the
 syntax, semantics, rules of pronunciation, and the spelling of each word.

Long-term memory
 See secondary memory.

Masking

A situation in which one stimulus, the masker, when presented closely in time and space to a second stimulus, the target, causes difficulty in the perception of the target. See also backward masking and forward masking.

Means-ends analysis

The problem-solving algorithm used by the general problem solver. The means-ends analysis involves solving a problem by the following procedure:
1. The solution state of the problem is the current goal.
2. If the current goal is immediately obtainable, it is obtained and the next subgoal (if there are any) becomes the current goal.
3. If the current goal is not immediately obtainable, it is broken into subgoals and the first subgoal becomes the current goal.
4. This process is repeated from (2) until either all goals and subgoals have been accomplished and the problem is solved, or until a subgoal can neither be broken down nor immediately obtained. In this latter case, failure has occurred. See also general problem solver.

Memory trace

Any change in the contents of memory due to the processing of an input can be considered to constitute a trace of that input.

Message center

In the context of HEARSAY, the message center is a central data store that can be accessed by all of the knowledge sources and through which the various knowledge sources communicate. See also HEARSAY.

Morpheme

A meaningful linguistic unit that contains no smaller meaningful parts. Thus, for example, a word would constitute a morpheme unless it contained a meaningful suffix or prefix. Moreover, meaningful suffixes and prefixes such as /un-/ and /-ed/ also constitute morphemes.

Multimodel

In the context of the nature of memory representations, a memory representation is said to be multimodal if it contains within it elements of more than one sensory modality. Thus, for example, an image may contain both auditory and visual components and thus be multimodal.

Network

A network is a kind of graph that consists of a set of nodes and a set of arcs interrelating them. The arcs may be directed so that an arc from node A to node B does not necessarily imply that there is an arc from B to A. Arcs may also be labeled so that an arc from A to B labeled $R1$ can represent a different relationship than an arc from A to B labeled $R2$, etc. Networks are useful for representing the semantic relations among concepts in memory. See also node and arc.

Node

One of the elements of a network. In a semantic network the nodes represent concepts and the arcs connecting them represent relationships between concepts. See also network and arc.

Noun phrase

A constituent of a sentence that consists of a noun and its modifiers. Thus, the sentence "Sam saw the man who robbed the bank" has the following noun phrases: "Sam," "the bank," and "the man who robbed the bank."

Ossicles

The three tiny bones of the middle ear which carry the vibrations from the tympanic membrane (eardrum) to the inner ear.

Oval window

A small membrane in the cochlea to which the ossicles are attached. It is the movement of this membrane that disturbs the fluid in the inner ear and eventually leads to the stimulation of the auditory nerve fibers.

Pandemonium

The name of the pattern recognition system proposed by Selfridge (1959). The Pandemonium system consists of the parallel operation of many "demons", each searching the input for evidence of themselves and each informing the other demons whenever evidence relevant to them is found. See also cognitive demon, image demon, decision demon, and computational demon.

Paradigm

An experimental paradigm is a particular experimental methodology that is in general use for studying a variety of problems.

Paradigmatic

A paradigmatic representation is a kind of multidimensional representation in which each to-be-represented item has a value on each of the dimensions on which the items differ.

Parallel processing

A kind of processing system in which several operations may be carried out at one time.

Parallel search
> A search that is carried out by investigating all alternatives at once. See also serial search.

Parsing
> The process of determining the constituent structure of a sentence, that is, the process of determining the grammatical relationships among the various parts of a sentence.

Pattern synthesizer
> The device that takes as inputs sensory features and other extrasensory knowledge sources (as in HEARSAY), and produces as output a "most probable interpretation" of the inputs.

Phoneme
> The minimal unit of speech that distinguishes one morpheme from another. Thus, for example, the word pairs "bit" and "pit" differ in their first phoneme: the first has the phoneme /b/ and the second the phoneme /p/. Similarly, the pairs "bit" and "bat" and "bit" and "bid" differ in their second and third phonemes, respectively. It should be emphasized that phonemes represent sounds and not letters. Hence, the same letter can represent different phonemes at different times (e.g., the "c" in cite and in cub represent the phonemes /s/ and /k/ respectively) and different letters can represent the same phoneme (e.g., /f/ and /ph/ often represent the same phoneme).

Photon
> An elementary particle of light. It is the absorption of photons by the receptors of the eye that leads ultimately to our experience of seeing light.

Poisson distribution
> The probability distribution of the number of events occurring randomly in time to occur during any given period of time.

Positive feedback system
> A processing system in which the processing of signals of a certain sort facilitates the future processing of signals of the same sort.

Positive set
> See target set.

Pragmatic knowledge
> Knowledge about the situation in which a particular utterance occurs that is used in the interpretation of that utterance.

Precategorical acoustic store

A peripheral acoustic information store that is presumed to maintain a relatively faithful acoustic representation of an auditory signal while further processing is being done on the input. This is assumed to be analogous to iconic memory. See echoic memory and iconic memory.

Presupposition

An assumption that the speaker assumes the hearer shares and without which the utterance of the speaker does not make sense. Thus, for example, the statement "The king of France is bald" is odd inasmuch as it presupposes that there is a king of France. See also given-new distinction.

Primacy effect

The phenomenon in a free recall situation in which the first words in a list are better recalled than those in the middle of the list. See recency effect, serial position curve, and free recall.

Primary memory

Our immediate memory for what has just occurred. The classic example of information held in primary memory is the telephone number that we hold temporarily while we dial the phone number but forget immediately thereafter. See also secondary memory.

Problem behavior graph

A graph representing the sequences of states of knowledge through which a person has passed while solving a problem. Problem behavior graphs were developed by Newall and Simon (c.f. Newall & Simon, 1972).

Quanta of light

See photon.

Reaction time

The time required for one to make a judgement about a stimulus. In simple reaction time experiments the judgement is simply whether or not a stimulus has yet been presented. In choice reaction time experiments the judgement is about which of two or more stimuli have been presented. In still more complex experiments the judgement is whether or not the presented stimulus has some specified characteristic.

Recall test

A test in which a subject is asked to retrieve some previously presented information. See free recall.

Recency effect
> The advantage in a free recall situation of words near the end of the list over words in the middle of the list. See also free recall, primacy effect, and serial position curve.

Receptive field of a neuron
> The region of the retina over which variation in stimulation effects the responding of that neuron.

Recognition memory test
> A memory testing procedure in which subjects are presented with a set of items, some of which were previously presented and some of which were not. For each item the subject must decide whether or not he believes that item was previously presented.

Refractory period of a neuron
> The period following the firing of a neuron during which it cannot be stimulated (absolute refractory period) or during which it requires much more stimulation to cause it to fire (relative refractory period).

Relative clause
> A clause that modifies a noun. Thus, in the noun phrase "the man who robbed the bank," the clause "who robbed the bank" is a relative clause.

Resource limited processing
> A processing situation in which the limit on the quality of performance is determined by the amount of effort applied to the task rather than to other factors. See also data limited processing.

Retina
> The portion of the eye that contains the light sensitive receptors of the eye: the rods and the cones. See rods and cones.

Retinal ganglion cells
> The cells that receive and cumulate inputs from the receptors (via the bipolar cells) and relay information about intensity patterns to the higher centers of the brain.

ROC (or receiver operating characteristic) curve
> In a signal detection situation the ROC curve is the plot of the hit rate as a function of the false alarm rate for a fixed level of discriminability. See also hit rate and false alarm rate.

Rods
> Light sensitive receptors in the retina. The rods are the most sensitive of our photo receptors and do not communicate color information. Night vision is primarily mediated by the rods. See also cones, the other major category of light sensitive receptors in the eye.

Saturate
> A neuron is said to saturate when it is firing at its maximum rate. The maximum rate is determined by the refractory period of the neuron. At its fastest, a neuron can fire once whenever it recovers from its refractory state. A reasonable maximum rate of firing for most neurons is between 100 and 1000 times per second.

Schedular
> In the HEARSAY system the schedular is that device which allocates processing resources to the various knowledge sources. In general, in a parallel processing environment with limited resources, a scheduler is needed to allocate resources.

Schema
> An abstract cognitive representation of a generalized concept or situation. A schema contains, as part of its specification, the network of interrelations that characterize the major constituents of the situation or concept in question.

Secondary memory
> Our relatively large and relatively permanent mass storage memory device. Whenever we remember something after more than a few seconds without conscious attention, we are assumed to retrieve the information from secondary memory. Secondary memory is also called long-term memory. See also primary memory.

SEEK
> In the context of an ATN, an arc labeled SEEK X is a call for the system to activate the X sub-network of the ATN and search for an X at that point in the input string.

Selectional restrictions
> See argument constraints.

Semantic knowledge
> Knowledge about the meaning of words and the rules whereby the meanings of words are put together to construct the meanings of higher units such as sentences, paragraphs, stories, and the like.

Semantic memory
: The repository of semantic knowledge.

Semantic network
: A network representation of semantic memory. See also network and semantic memory.

Sensory registers
: Sensory memories that hold a relatively faithful representation of sensory input for a brief period of time. Examples of sensory registers are the iconic and echoic memory systems. See also precategorical acoustic store, iconic memory, and echoic memory.

Serial position curve
: In a free recall situation, the serial position curve is a plot of the probability that an item was recalled as a function of the position of the item in the input list. Classically, the serial position curve is a bow-shaped curve in which items presented early and late in the list are better recalled than those presented in the middle of the list. See also free recall, recency effect, and primacy effect.

Serial search
: Search procedure that involves the sequential examination of the various possible alternatives among which we are searching. A self-terminating serial search involves a termination of the search procedure on discovery of the target item. An exhaustive serial search requires that all alternatives be considered in turn before a final decision can be made.

Shadowing
: A procedure for studying selective attention in which a subject must listen to two different auditory messages—one presented to each ear. The subject is asked to repeat aloud the input to one of the ears while signals to be detected are played to the other "unattended" ear. The typical finding is that shadowing (repeating aloud) the information to one ear makes it almost impossible to monitor sophisticated inputs to the other ear.

Short-term memory
: See primary memory.

Signal-detection task
: A task in which a subject must decide which of a small set of possible stimuli has been presented. See also hit rate, false alarm rate, and ROC curve.

Signal-to-noise ratio
    The ratio of the intensity of a signal to be detected to the intensity of a noise background against which the signal must be detected. Naturally, the higher the signal-to-noise ratio the easier it is to detect the signal.

Simple cell
    A type of cell in the visual cortex that responds to lines and edges in a particular location and orientation on the retina. See also complex cell.

Sine wave tone
    A pure tone. It is called a sine wave because the pressure wave set up by the signal generator in this case varies according to the sine function.

Spatial representations
    A means of representation of information in which the information is represented in some sort of geometric space. See also Euclidean proximity space.

Spectoral absorption curves
    The plot of the probability that a given kind of visual receptor will absorb a photon of a particular wavelength as a function of wavelength. Different spectoral absorption curves of different kinds of cones allow us to see color. See also cones.

Speech spectorgrams
    A representation of a speech waveform in which the frequency components of the waveform are plotted against time. In such a plot the intensity of a frequency component is indicated by the darkness of the line associated with that component.

Speed-accuracy tradeoff
    In most situations in which reaction times are measured, a subject has a choice of responding more quickly but less accurately, or more accurately but less quickly. This trade-off between speed and accuracy often makes reaction time results difficult to interpret.

Syntactic knowledge
    Knowledge about the form, as opposed to the meaning, of legitimate linguistic utterances. Syntactic knowledge is knowledge of the grammar of the language. See grammar.

Tachistoscopic stimulus
    A visual stimulus presented for less than about 250 msec is said to have been tachistoscopically presented. This value is chosen because voluntary

eye movements require about 250 msec to occur. Thus a tachistoscopic presentation involves a presentation without eye movements.

Target set

In a search experiment, in which a subject is searching through a list of one or more items for instances of one or more targets, the set of items for which one is searching is called the target set.

Template matching model

A model of character recognition in which one is assumed to match on each of a set of internal templates against the image of the presented character and measure the deviation of the presented character from each template. The character whose template best matches is assumed to have been presented.

Threshold

The threshold of a stimulus is the level of intensity of that stimulus at which it can just be detected.

Tip-of-the-tongue phenomenon (TOT)

The phenomenon in which a one can remember the meaning of a concept and can also remember some characteristics of the name of the concept, but can't quite remember the correct name.

Top-down processing

A processing strategy in which one proposes possible inputs and then determines whether or not these inputs may in fact be present in the input data. See also bottom-up processing.

Transducer

A device that converts energy from one form to another. In the case of sensory systems, a sensory system is a transducer in the sense that it converts energy fluctuations in the environment into a pattern of neural impulses.

Transient memory load

The momentary load on the primary memory system demanded by carrying out tasks such as mental arithmetic and understanding a sentence.

Tree structure

A graphical representational system that consists of a set of hierarchically related nodes in which each node is either the root of the tree and has no nodes above it, or is dominated by a single higher node. A node in a tree may dominate any number of nodes. A node that dominates no other nodes is called a leaf of the tree.

Trigrams

A stimulus item consisting of a sequence of three letters.

Tympanic membrane

The eardrum. The part of the ear that vibrates as a direct result of the pressure wave set up by the sound source. It is the first element of the auditory transduction system.

Typicality

Certain exemplars are more typical of a certain conceptual category than others. Thus, for example, a robin is a very typical bird whereas an ostrich is a relatively atypical bird. The measure of the degree to which a particular exemplar is a typical member of a category is called the typicality of that exemplar.

Vector

A directed distance in a multidimensional space. That is, a vector is a quantity that specifies both a direction and a distance from a point in space.

Waveform

An auditory waveform is a plot of the intensity of the pressure wave as a function of time.

Wavelength

The distance from one point in a waveform to the corresponding point in an adjacent cycle.

Weber fraction

In an increment threshold experiment, the Weber fraction is the ratio of the intensity of the increment ΔI to the intensity of the background against which the increment must be detected, I. See also increment threshold procedure.

Weber's law

Weber's law is said to hold whenever the Weber fraction is constant as a function of the intensity of the background, I. See also Weber fraction.

ILLUSTRATION CREDITS

Figure   Page

1.15   32   From J. E. Rose, J. F. Brugge, D. J. Anderson, & J. E. Hind.
1.16   33   Phase locked response to low frequency tones in single audi-
                tory nerve fibers of the squirrel monkey. *Journal of Neuro-
                physiology,* 1967, *30,* 769–793, Figures 1 and 7.
2.1   40   Reprinted by permission from *IEEE SPECTRUM,* vol. 2,
                no. 5, May 1965. Copyright © 1965, the Institute of Elec-
                trical and Electronics Engineers, Inc.
2.11   54   From "Pattern Recognition by Machine" by O. G. Selfridge
                and U. Neisser. Copyright © August 1960, *Scientific Ameri-
                can, Inc.* All rights reserved.
2.12   55   From G. Sperling, The information available in brief visual
                presentations. *Psychological Monographs,* 1960, *74,* 1–29.
                Copyright © 1960, the American Psychological Association.
                Reprinted by permission.
2.13   56   From D. E. Rumelhart, A multicomponent theory for the
2.24   70   perception of briefly exposed visual displays. *Journal of
                Mathematical Psychology,* 1970, *7,* 191–218. Copyright ©
                1970, Academic Press, Inc. Reprinted by permission.
2.14   57   C. W. Eriksen, & J. F. Collins. Some temporal characteristics
                of visual perception. *Journal of Experimental Psychology,*
                1967, *74,* 476–484. Copyright © 1967, the American Psy-
                chological Association. Reprinted by permission.
2.17   60   C. J. Darwin, M. T. Turvey, & R. G. Crowder. An auditory
                analogue of the Sperling partial report procedure: Evidence
                for brief auditory storage. *Cognitive Psychology,* 1972, *3,*
                255–267. Copyright © 1972, Academic Press, Inc. Reprinted
                by permission.
2.18   63   G. Sperling, A model for visual memory tasks. *Human Fac-
2.19   63   tors,* 1963, *5,* 19–31. Figures 3 and 4. Copyright © 1963,
                The Johns Hopkins University Press. Reprinted by permission.
2.20   64   R. G. Swensson. The elusive tradeoff: Speed versus accuracy
2.21   66   in visual discrimination tasks. *Perception and Psychophysics,*
2.22   67   1972, *12,* 16–32.
2.30   76   From M. I. Posner, S. J. Boies, W. H. Eichelman, & R. L.
                Taylor, Retention of visual and name codes of single letters.
                Journal of Experimental Psychology Monograph, 1969, *79,*
                No. 1, Part 2. Copyright © 1969, American Psychological
                Association. Reprinted by permission.

2.31	76	From O. G. Selfridge, Pattern recognition in modern computers. *Proceedings of the Western Joint Computer Conference.* Los Angeles, Calif., 1955. Page 92, Figure 3. Copyright © 1955. Institute of Electrical and Electronics Engineers, Inc. Reprinted by permission.
2.33*a*	78	Ambiguous figure from E. G. Boring, A new ambiguous figure. *American Journal of Psychology, 42,* 444–445. The unambiguous figures are based on those used by Leeper, 1935.
2.33*b*	78	Based on figure from E. Rubin, *Visuell wahrgenommene Figurer.* Copenhagen: Glydendalske, 1921.
2.33*c*	78	From L. S. Penrose, & R. Penrose, Impossible objects: A special type of illusions. *British Journal of Psychology,* 1958, *49,* 31.
2.38	89	From an unpublished paper by S. E. Palmer. A redrawn version of this figure also appears in Palmer (1975b).
2.39	90	From S. E. Palmer, The effects of contextual scenes on the identification of objects. *Memory and Cognition,* 1975, *3,* 519–526.
2.41	93	From R. K. Potter, G. A. Kopp, & H. C. Green, *Visible Speech,* Princeton, Van Nostrand, 1947. Page 314, Figure 13. Copyright © 1966, Bell Telephone Laboratories. Reprinted by permission.
2.42	94	From G. A. Miller, & S. Isard, Some perceptual consequences of linguistic rules. *Journal of Verbal Learning and Verbal Behavior,* 1963, *2,* 1–21. Copyright © 1963, Academic Press, Inc. Reprinted by permission.
2.43	96	From R. Shiffrin, D. Pisoni, & K. Castenada-Mendez, Is at-
2.44	97	tention shared between the ears? *Cognitive Psychology,* 1974,
2.45	98	*6,* 190–216. Figure 1. Copyright © 1974, Academic Press, Inc. Reprinted by permission.
3.2	108	From D. R. Reddy, L. D. Erman, R. D. Fennell, & R. B.
3.4	110	Neely, The HEARSAY speech understanding system: An example of the recognition process. *Proceedings of the Third International Joint Conference on Artificial Intelligence,* Stanford, Calif., 1973.
3.29	155	From J. D. Bransford, & M. K. Johnson, Considerations of some problems of comprehension. In W. G. Chase (Ed.), *Visual Information Processing.* Copyright © 1973, Academic Press, Inc. Reprinted by permission.

4.1   174   From S. Sternberg, Two operations in character recognition:
4.2   175   some evidence from reaction time measurements. *Perception*
4.3   176   *and Psychophysics,* 1967, *2,* 45–53.
4.4   178   From G. A. Miller, The magical number seven, plus or minus two: Some limits on our capacity for processing information. *Psychological Review,* 1956, *63,* 1–97. Copyright © 1956, American Psychological Association. Reprinted by permission.
4.5   179   From J. P. Cavanaugh, Relation between the immediate memory span and the memory search rate. *Psychological Review,* 1972, *79,* 525–530. Copyright © 1972, American Psychological Association. Reprinted by permission.
4.6   179   From L. R. Peterson, & M. J. Peterson Short-term retention of individual verbal items. *Journal of Experimental Psychology,* 1959, *58,* 193–198. Copyright © 1959, American Psychological Association. Reprinted by permission.
4.7   180   From A. W. Melton, Implications of short-term memory for a general theory of memory. *Journal of verbal learning and Verbal Behavior.* Copyright © 1963, Academic Press, Inc. Reprinted by permission.
4.8   183   From P. A. Siple, *Encoding in short-term memory: Implica-*
4.10   185   *tions from reaction time studies.* Unpublished doctoral disertation, University of California, San Diego.
4.11   186   From M. I. Posner, Coordination of Codes. In W. G. Chase
4.13   188   (Ed.), *Visual Information Processing,* Academic Press, Inc., 1973. Copyright © 1973, Academic Press, Inc. Reprinted by permission.
4.1   190   From L. R. Brooks, Spatial and verbal components of the
4.14   190   Act of recall. *Canadian Journal of Psychology,* 1968, *22,* 349–368.
4.16   192   From R. N. Shepard, & J. Metzler, Mental Rotation of three-
4.17   193   dimensional Objects, *Science,* Vol. 171, pp. 701–703. Copyright © 1971, the American Association for the Advancement of Science.
4.18   194   From L. A. Cooper & R. N. Shepard, Chronometric studies
4.19   195   of the rotation of mental images. In W. G. Chase (Ed.), *Visual Information Processing.* Copyright © 1973, Academic Press, Inc. Reprinted by permission.
4.20   196   From B. B. Murdock, The serial position effect in free recall. *Journal of Experimental Psychology,* 1962, *64,* 482–488.

Table	Page	
2.1	82	From E. Tulving, G. Mandler, & R. Baumal, Interaction of two sources of information in tachistoscopic word recognition. *Canadian Journal of Psychology,* 1964, *18,* 62–71.
2.2	86	From D. Graboi, *Physical shape, practice and meaning in visual search.* Unpublished doctoral dissertation, University of California, San Diego, 1974.
3.1	106	From D. R. Reddy, L. D. Erman, R. D. Fennell, & R. B. Neely, The HEARSAY speech understanding system: An example of the recognition process. *Proceedings of the Third International Joint Conference on Artificial Intelligence,* Stanford, Calif.
4.1	177	From G. A. Miller, The magical number seven, plus or minus two. Some limits on our information processing capacity. *Psychological Review,* 1956, *63,* 1–97. Copyright © 1956, American Psychological Association. Reprinted by permission.
4.2	190	From L. R. Brooks, Spatial and verbal components of the act of recall. *Canadian Journal of Psychology,* 1968, *22,* 349–368.

INDEX